IN SEARCH OF SAI DIVINE

By the same author

1985 Sai Baba and His Message –A Challenge to Behavioral Sciences

1985 The Sai Baba Movement

1985 Sai Baba on Human Values and Education

1991 Sri Sathya Sai Baba and the Future of Mankind

1992 *Sri Sathya Sai Baba: Leben Lehre und Werk* (German Language)

1993 Sri Sathya Sai Baba: His Life and Divine Role

1994 The Sai Trinity

1994 The Educational Theory of Sri Sathya Sai Baba

1996 Immortal Quotations of Bhagavan Sri Sathya Sai Baba

1996 In Search of Sai Divine

1996 Sri Sathya Sai Baba and the Press

1996 Sri Sathya Sai As Kalki Avatar

1997 Sri Sathya Sai Baba: *Understanding His Mystery and Experiencing His Love*

1997 World Peace and Sri Sathya Sai Avatar

1996 The Emerging Concept of Education in Human Values

1998 How to Receive Sathya Sai Baba's Grace

1999 Lord Krishna and His Present Avatar Sri Sathya SaI Baba

2015 The Triple Incarnations of Sai Baba.

IN SEARCH OF
SAI DIVINE

Exploring Sathya Sai Baba's mystery
and unique contributions as
the harbinger of the New Age

Satya Pal Ruhela

PARTRIDGE
A Penguin Random House Company

To order additional copies of this book, contact
Partridge India
000 800 10062 62
orders.india@partridgepublishing.com

www.partridgepublishing.com/india

Contents

Section - I
Sri Sathya Sai Baba: A Unique Incarnation

Section - II
Sri Sathya Sai Baba's Miracles

Section- III
Research Review of Writings of Devotees and Scholars from Various Fields on Sri Sathya Sai Baba

By the same author

1985   Sai Baba and His Message –A Challenge to Behavioral Sciences

1985   The Sai Baba Movement

1985   Sai Baba on Human Values and Education

1991   Sri Sathya Sai Baba and the Future of Mankind

1992   *Sri Sathya Sai Baba: Leben Lehre und Werk*: (German Language)

1993   Sri Sathya Sai Baba: His Life and Divine Role

1994   The Sai Trinity

1994   The Educational Theory of Sri Sathya Sai Baba:

1996   Immortal ⌐Quotations of Bhagavan Sri Sathya Sai Baba – A Spiritual Ready Reconer

1996   In Search of Sai Divine

1996   Sri Sathya Sai Baba and the Press

1996   Sri Sathya Sai As KalkI Avatar

1997   Sri Sathya Sai Baba: Understanding His Mystery and Experiencing His Love

1997   World Peace and Sri Sathya Sai Avatar

1996   The Emerging Concept of Education in Human Values

1998   How to Receive Ssthya Sai Baba's Grace.

1999   Lord Krishna and His Present Avatar Sri Sathya SaI Baba

2015   The Triple Incanations of Sai Baba.

Sri Sri Sathya Sai Baba's photo which He had gifted to S.P.Ruhela on 18 February,1999 after writing his blessings *With love* and signing *Baba*

DEDICATION

IN SEARCH OF SAI DIVINE

Dedicated to the evergreen memory of Sri Sathya Sai Baba, the unique incarnation of the modern age who by His supreme teachings of Love, Righteousness, Peace and Love, and miracles constantly laid stress on belief in God, singing God's names and His maxims of *'Love All and Serve All'* and *'Help Ever, Hurt Never'* and by humanitarian social service projects helped the modern distressed mankind and showed how to lead ideal life and be happy.

....

PRAYER TO BHAGAVAN SRI SATHYA SAI BABA

The One ever-present in the past, future and present God Sri Prasanthi Sai, the very soul of all living creatures, is righteousness incarnate and Dhanvantari's Embodiment. I pray to that very Lord Sathya, cast Your glance of kindness on me to ward off my sorrows hurdles and miseries. I take you refuge. I take you refuge. Kindly save me. Kindly save me.'

- Ancient Maharishi Vishwamitra's
prayer in *Vishwamitra-nadi:*
Discovered and informed by
(Late) Mr. M.R.Raghunathan, Chennai

....

SPIRIT MESSAGE

When you ask Me for blessings, ask Me for the biggest of all- the blessing of Me always being there with you..You will then never feel the pain of separation.. You will avoid all unnecessary travel, all the unnecessary rush to reach Me, all stress and pain. Do not limit Me to one place. I am present everywhere at all times. Know and realize that .There is no distance between us.

- Sri Sathya Sai Baba
(Divine Messages received and recorded by Mrs Seema M Dewan)

The portraits of Sri Shirdi Sai Baba and Sri Sathya Sai Baba inside
the prayer hall Prasanthi Nilayam *ashram* in Andhra Pradesh

(Courtesy: *www saireflections:.org*)

Sri Sathya Sai Baba writing for his famous *Vahin*i series of books

(Courtesy: *www saireflections:org*)

Preface

Rolland Robertson, editor of *'Sociology of Religion'* (Penguin, 1969), in his Introduction has observed that "one of the most intriguing intellectual phenomena in the mid-twentieth century is the widespread interest in religion at a time when there is also extensive agreement that religious belief, as traditionally undestrood, has declined in its intrinsic significance for most members of modern societies."

The importance of religion in generating and storing values and beliefs related to the meaning, purpose and significance of man's life, as was studied by classical sociologists like Emile Durkheim of France and Max Weber of Germany, is again being studied in modern times. Modern sociologists view the study of religion as part of general study of culture and knowledge. They are committed to a distinctive and wide-ranging perspective derived from within their own discipline, and to that extent they are able to ask questions which relate to all religions on a comparative basis or to distill out social features of one or a group of religious beliefs and the social processes by which and through which beliefs are maintained and expressed. Unlike the religious sociologist, the sociologist of religion seeks to illuminate the relationships between religion and science and moral and spiritual movements, and futurology.

I, the editor of this volume, am not a religious sociologist. I am also not a sociologist of religion of any considerable standing. I am a sociologist whose interests range from institutional change, education, culture, social science and knowledge to religion, folklore, social and spiritual movements and futurology.

The subject of this volume is the most surprising phenomenon – a unique Divine Human incarnation – Sri Sathya Sai Baba (1926-2011) whose declared mission was to "reconstruct the ancient highway to God."

The impact of His charismatic divine personality, ideal secular behavior, role functioning, and sublime and ever inspiring teachingsis still intact on His followers, and His diverse humanitarian social service works can be observed and studied and their meaning sought. Millions of his devotees all over the world believe him to be a unuique *Avatar* (Incarnation of God) or Divine

Being, who is more than holy man or saint. A number of his devotees and social and physical scientists have, during his life time till 2011, tried to closely observe, study and evaluate him, his role-functioning style, miracles and unique contributions to humanity. Their experiences provide basic data for behavioral scientists throughout the world to study seriously and to comment upon, and, second, they will help to enlighten further some of the millions of persons in both the east and the west

I, being a social science researcher and an humble and earnest Sai devotee for the last 40 years, have very laboriously collected their writings, studied them and reviewed them briefly, objectively, voluntarily-unsponsored or unsupported by anyone, but solely out of my love, desire and enthusiasm to pay this humble intellectual tribute to the great Universal Master and since He is the dweller of my heart, He has been the sole inner motivator since 1974.

This research review was originally published in 1996 by M.D. Publisher, New Delhi, under the same title and with ISBN:7533-021-X. It was appreciated by many readers –Sai devotees as well as non-devotees in India and abroad and even the Library of Sri Sathya Sai Institute of Higher Learning, Prasanthi Nilayam ordered for two copies of it soon after learning about its publication in 1996.

Since unfortunately that publishing house closed down after some year due to the illness of the publisher, this publication has been out of print and unavailable to the Sai devotees and intellectuals keenly interested in understanding this great incarnation and His contributions as the harbinger of the New Age of Humanity,

I have very enthusiastically and laboriously revised and updated it in the context of so many developments since the *Mahasamadhi* (passing away) of Sri Sathya Sai Baba on 24th April,2011. It is a very amazing, true, fortunate and blissful fact known to countless Sai devotees throughout the world that that even after shedding His mortal coil in 2011, Sri Sathya Sai Baba's spiritual mission and all the various spiritual and humanitarian social service activities have been continuing with great force and their impact is being felt in more thn 120 counties,

Not only this, the Ascended divine Spirit of Sri Sathya Sai Baba is still actively guiding, blessing, motivating and mysteriously and miraculously constantly rendering instant help, solace and *anand* (joy) to many of His devotees and others all over the world. Innumerable news items, His Spirit messages and many video recordings done by Sai devotees have been appearing on the internet and endless stream of the thrilling true testimonies of very fortunate beneficiaries of His divine grace continue being published in the *Sanathana Sasrathi* monthly journal of Sri Sathya Sai Sadhna Trust and new publications of Sai organization in over one hundred countries and billions of people have been benefitting from them.

In the very first personal interview granted to me in *Brindavan* over 40 years back - in June 1974- Sri Sathya Sai Baba had assured me *"I am l always with you."* Very true to His words He has miraculously saved my life five times and protected and miraculously helped me in my academic and professional and personal experiences of His boundless grace on me. In Chapter 34 (pages252-277) of my first book '*The Triple Incarnations of Sai* Baba published by Partridge Publishing Co. in June 2015. Billions of Sai devotees all over the world very well know that His miracles like suddenly breaking of the garland of flowers on His photo or sudden appearance of *Vibhuti* (holy ash), *amrit* (honey) etc. are the surest symptoms of His coming to bless the devotee/s. They are still happening at many places. Recently on the 10th September, 2015 in Prasanthi Nilayam just when the famous Sai devotee Prof. Anil Kumar started speaking on His glory to a group of devotees, the big garland of flowers on Sai Baba's photo suddenly broke; its video is on the internet and I have seen it with my eyes, Many others also might have seen that..Many such videos of His miracles happening even now can be found out and can be found out and seen on the internet by interested persons anywhere at any time.

Many miraculous' Sai Divine Inspiration' messages from His Spirit have been coming to a highly blessed Sai devotee Seema M.Dewan of South India since 2012 and they are often shown on the internet. They can freely be seen by anyone in the world if he/she searches the web site <adline103@yahoo.com>.

One of those rare most stunning messages is captioned '*The Return…*' whose following extracts need be considered calmly and seriously;

"The robes that I have left amidst you…I shall return to wear once again… You are to wait My return in the silence of surrender…Those that shall live the *dharmic* (righteous) *way* their simple devotion shall arrive when I come once again walk as the *Guru* (spiritual master) and teach the human mind to touch Supreme consciousness with the fountain of love that pours their hearts…I have only shed the clothes of My body…but that does not mean that My role has come to an end… It can never be known to any one…Even those that are close to My physical form know nothing of what I am doing .., and only I am aware of My *Sankalp* (Divine Will) … and I can make truth… No one else can never help me, only I can conduct what I do There is no one that can know or be aware of My next step.

I shall wear the golden and red robes... I shall continue to lead the mission of My previous body. I am not present in not one time...and place ... can enter what you call the past" and present for it...for I do not travel in the tunnels of time...I am the universal Self that can make time return to Me as I will... whenever I will...you are to know...recognize and follow the steps the present *Avatar* walked every single day...very single moment...I walked the steps of love... carried on My shoulders the weight of *Sanatana Dhama* Universal laws of truth).I poured on you My continuous state of *Atmic* bliss...It is your turn now to walk... It is your turn now to take the steps on which My footprint shall always remain...

Do not wait idly for My return... do not give up all that I have left with you in My this Mission and simply mourn and await My return... remember if you do that, you shall close the gifts I ave left with you and you shall also not be able to receive the gift *of Atmic Jnana* that I shall return to give to you....You have to live this moment...this moment with strength...You are not to wait for something that has yet to come...yet to happen.

Continue your livs immersed in My teaching and in the way of My life... continue to have faith that is the robes that I have to wear before you I am still with you ...always...My return to another body is inevitable...

Sreejeeth-Narayan has researched into most the Sai Baba's published discourses and discovered many hints given by Sai Baba and also his belief in the the *nadi* predictions and then he has come to this conclusion;: "...when Swami comes back He may not be bound by anything at all. There won't be anything any nee. Swami has already lived a lifetime of 85 years.. Now it could be second coming without any self imposed inhibitions, invoking a full manifestation of omnipotence. Given all the clues that have come, whoever can count against such a possibility?'

Whether others may believe in all these or not in all these, I do certainly believe in them. Most of the Sai devotees may recall that the first Sai Avatar –Sri Shirdi Sai Baba actually had come back to life in Shirdi after His death ("'I am going to *Allah* If I don't return in three days, bury Me here",. Saying these words He had actually died, and He did return in His body form after three days and then lived in the same Dwarkamai *masjid* wearing the same robes and continued His *avataric* mission till 1918. How can anyone of them deny this concrete precedent?

Many spiritual Seeker in the world might have heard of the great Mahavatar Babaji of the Himalyas (Nagraj Babaji)who is believed to be of more than 1400 years and have appeared again and again and is now teaching *Kriya-yoga* not only to Indians but Americans and many other nationals, and some highly blessed persons in India, Germany etc have met Him. A lot of thrilling information about Him Is available in books and the internet.

If the abovementioned predictions come true and Sri Sathya Sai Baba returns to Prasanthi Nilayam the next few years to complete His mission as the harbinger of the New Age of spirituality, it will be a great miracle and great fortune of the inhabitants and the modern super-industrial world would be thrilled. The scientists and all doubting Thomases will have to believe in the inexplicable spiritual mysteries, God and in the truth of the *nadis* by great ancient Indian sages. The news of it will be instantly flashed on TV and internet. Let us wait for some time!

The present work, which is my lifetime humble effort and unique contribution (as no one has yet done research review of writing on this great Incarnation) as a social scientist, spiritual researcher and writer, has been my missions and passion for which I have been toiling very hard for many *years,* sacrificing much and facing lots of hindrances with *Shraddha(devotion) and saburi* (patience) is now nearing publication by the divine grace of Sri Sathya Sai Baba. He has been my sole supporter, defender, motivator and sustainer although I was never in His *'in group'* or any office bearer of Sai Organization The celebrated British poet Milton wrote in one of his works *"They also serve who only stand and wait"*, and I have been just like that.

Very recently a new book '*Messages from the Universe - The Secrets of Destiny:* ***A medium's quest to find the secrets of destiny through the ancient Naadi Leaf Oracle from India. True story***, by the medium Craig Hamilton-Parker has been published (as informed by craig@psychics.co. In it Craig,who claims to be a medium, has also thrown light on this burning theme of Sri Sathya Sai Baba's return in very near future in two chapters. This book may be freely available from Amazon, However, I have not got and seen it, it seems to be interesting.

I am very happy to be able at my present advanced age of 80 years when I cannot even stand, walk, travel, legibly speak and talk and do any physical activity and even mediate or pray, still by His grace I am having mental poise, contentment and the necessary will power and energy to work on my computer daily to complete my hitherto unfinished spirituals mission in face of all trials and tribulations of my life. Work is worship for me and I am happy, with it.

I hope this work will be of interest and some utility to Sai devotees, social and physical scientists, spiritual seekers and others who wish to understand Sai Baba and His unique universal impact. It may give further stimulus to the devotion, discipline, and spiritual growth of Sai devotees.

Acknowledgements

I wish to acknowledge the help given to me and record my thanks and gratitude to:

- Sri Sathya Sai Baba
- Sri G S R C V Prasada Rao, Secretary, Sri Sathya Sai Central Trust for his goodwill and encouraging letter of 4th February,2015.
- Sri K.S.Rajan, Convenor, Sri Sathya Sadhna Trust, Prasanthi Nilayam.
- The Convenor, Sri Sathya Sai Sadhna Trust, Prasanthi Nilayam for giving his permissions dated 8 August and 12 August, 2014 for the images for this book.
- Mrs.Sonya Ki Tomlinson Warren, 'modern *gopi*', renowned spiritual artist, spiritualist, writer and ardent Sai devotee from U.S.A (wife of Prof. DavidTomlinson. of' 'Sri Sathya Sai Baba: *Kalki Avatar*,' and *'God is our best friend'* for this book and also for sending the PDF of her thrilling book '.*Sai Ruptures'* and her best wishes
- Sai Baba's elder brother(Late) Sri Sesham Raju whom I had met in February 1974 and learnt many things about the early life of Sai Baba..
- (Late)Prof. V.K.Gokak and Prof.S.Sampat - the first two Vice Chancellors of Sri Sathya Sai Institute of Higher Learning Prasanthi Nilayam for their generosity and motivation and encouragement to write books on the Sai phenomenon and human values.
- My esteemed friend(Late) Sri Adhya Prashad Tripathi, Professor and Head of the Department of Hindi, Sri Sathya Sai Institute of Higher Learning Prasanthi Nilayam for informing many new things and his thrilling experiences of Sri Sathya Sai Baba's grace.
- Sri Indulal Shah, the closest and the most eminent Sai devotee and the author of *'We Devotees'* and important articles 'Silent Spiritual Revolution' published in *Sanathana Sarathi* after Swami's *Mahasamadhi* in 2011 which have greatly influenced me,

- All the personalities from the fields of Religion, Philosophy, Psychology & Psychiatry and Education, Management, Physical Sciences and Medical Sciences whose invaluable writings on Sai Baba and His multidimensional contributions have been covered in this research review
- I wish also to appreciate the inspiring contributions of Sri Chakravati and Sri Ratnakar, Trustees, Prof.Anil Kumar, Sri G.L.An and, Editor, *Sanathana Sarathi*, and Sri Satyajit Saliban., Chief of *Vidhya Vahini* Innovative project of Sai Baba, which have greatly enlightened me and enriched my information on Sai Baba and His contributions to humanity although I have not met them personally and learnt sbot their contributions from *Sanathan Sarathi.* and internet all these years.
- I am grateful to my Sai devotee friends like Mr,Lucas Ralli of UK.,Ustad Tark Knapp. and Dr.Nikolay Nikow(Dr.Zen) of Germany, Prof. Duane Robinson and, Mr. Angira of USA and Prof. Brian Steel of Australia. Some others whose had good will for me but I do not remember their exact names now due to my old age.
- Mr.Pohar Baruah, Publishing Services Associate, Partridge India Publishing Co., Bloomington (USA) for his kind cooperation, efficiency and remarkable help due to which my ardent wish and dream to see this book published soon by the 90th Birth Anniversary of Sri Sathya SaI Baba is going to be fulfilled.
- I would be failing in my duty if I forget to acknowledge the various kinds of assistance given to me by my wife Mrs.Sushila Devi Ruhela, my sons Vinod Ruhela and Arvind Ruhela and my grand children Deepali Ruhela and Akshya Ruhela

2015
Dr.Satya Pal Ruhela
Retired Professor of Education (Sociology)
Head & Dean of Faculty of Education)
Jamia Milia Islamia (Central University).
New Delhi -10025
Residence;'*Sai Kripa*,
House No.126, Sector-37,
Faridabad-121003(India)
Email: spruhela@gmail.com

Sri Sathya Sai Baba being garlanded by His famous
she elephant Sai Gita in 1940s-1990s

(Courtesy *wwwsaireflections:org*)

Sai Kalki Avatar

Courtesy:
(Sonya Ki Tomlinson Warren, U.S.A.)

Sri Sathy Sai Baba materializing *Shivling*
from him mouh on Shivrari every year

(Courtesy:*www.saireflections.crg)*

Sri Sathya Sai Baba showing His miraculous
creation of *mangal sutra* for a Hindu bride.

(Courtesy: *www.sai reflections.org*)

Sri Sathya Sai Baba with Lord Krishna's
statue miraculously materialized by Him

(Courtesy: *www.sai reflections.org*)

an creates prototype of Hanuman statue in the Year 1990 during Foundation ceremony | 65 feet tall Hanuman statue standing on hilltop in Vidyagiri sta

Sri Sathya Sai Baba showing His miraculous creation of the prototype
of Lord Hanuman's statue in 1990 during the foundation ceremony; the
65 feet statue was constructed on the hill top in Vidhyagiri stadium

(Courtesy: *www.sai reflections.org*)

Sri Sathya Sai ultra modern Hospital, Prasanthi Nilayam in whch all treatments and operations are done free of cost for all patients

(Courtesy:*www.sai reflections.org*)

Commemorative stamp released by the Govt. of India on the occasion of Sri Sathya Sai Baba's 88th Birth day

Chapter - 1

SRI SATHYA SAI BABA:
A BIOGRAPHICAL SKETCH

Dr. S.P. Ruhela

The subject of this volume is Sri Sathya Sai Baba of the modern age who claimed to be the full incarnation of God. He possessed the miraculous characteristics, powers, and glory of a full avatar of God, the criteria for which have been laid down in the most sacred scriptures of the Hindus, and also by the leading spiritual masters of India like Swami Vivekananda, Sri Aurobindo, and Paramhansa Yogananda. The German sociologist Max Weber's classic analysis of a Prophet possessing charisma of a very high and benevolent order falls short of revealing the super-charisma of the Divine personality of Sri Sathya Sai Baba. His omnipresence and omnipotence have completely baffled physical as well as behavioral scientists, not to talk of the common man throughout the world.

His official biographer Professor N. Kasturi as well as thousands of those who have had the great fortune of going to Baba and receiving His Divine Grace personally, have testified that it is wrong to approach Sai Baba considering Him to be just a man or a saint of high order In fact, it has been the common experience of millions of Indians and foreigners who have had His seen him in person or in dreams and derived solace, cure, blessings or grace from Him, that He was in fact *Sarva Devta Swaroopam* or the combined incarnation of all gods and goddesses rolled into one.

It is indeed difficult, if not impossible, for any human being to cover, comprehend, analyze, understand, and then to write a profile of the life and personality of such a unique Divine Personality. Anybody who has attempted to do so is confronted with Baba's following declarations:

"My *Shakti*, My Power, My Mystery can never be understood, whoever may try, for howsoever long a period, by whatever means.

"Baba is beyond the keenest intellect, the sharpest brain.... So do not try to delve into Me; develop faith and veneration and derive joy through *Prem* (love). That is the utmost you can do; do that and benefit how can the limited know the depth of the unlimited? How can the ant delve into the mountain? It is beyond you to know how or why I create things in My hand."

I have tried to prepare this profile of Sai Baba by putting to the best possible use the various methods of scientific social survey and research learned by me as a student of sociology and social anthropology and also on the basis of my knowledge about Baba based on the study of all available books on Sri Sathya Sai Baba and His immediately preceding incarnation, Sri Sai Baba of Shirdi. I had first seen him in New Delhi in April 1973, just for two or three minutes, as one standing in the small crowd gathered outside the gate of the house where he was staying on his visit, In February 1974, I visited His ashram, Prasanthi Nilayam, located near Puttaparthi. I stayed there for four days and participated in the festival of *Shiva-Ratri* grandly celebrated there. I utilized this opportunity, granted by His Grace, to visit the village where He spent His childhood and went to the houses of His elder brother and elder sister. I had a brief talk with His elder brother Sri Seshma Raju and his wife, with whom Baba had lived and studied as a school student till He renounced His school education and the worldly life to play His predetermined role.

I met some people in the village, in the shops outside Baba's ashram, and also many devotees – Indians and foreigners. I heard from them a large number of stories about Baba's thrilling miracles, divine connections, transformations and moods. I did not have the good fortune of speaking to Baba till then. I stayed there for four days and tried to observe with an objective eye everything I could within that short period.

Birth of the Incarnation of Sai Baba

Sri Sathya Sai Baba was born on November 23,1926 in a very tiny, hilly, isolated village called Puttaparthi in the Anantapur district of Andhra Pradesh State of India. Not only His father Sri Pedda Venkappa Raju, but His grandfather Sri Ratnakaram Kondama Raju and one ancestor Sri Venkavadhoota also had been very pious, religious-minded people belonging to the Raju lineage of the Kshatriyas. It was a very ordinary lower middle class family, which was dependent on some farming. The family had rich musical, literary and dramatic traditions. Sai Baba's mother Eswaramma was also a very religious woman like her mother-in-law Lakshamma.

2

Months before Sri Sathya Narayan Raju's birth, a number of miracles started taking.

At the age of fourteen, Sri Sathya Narayan Raju disclosed to His parents and brother and the people around Him that He was in fact the incarnation of Sai Baba of Shirdi. While giving a discourse in 1968, Sai Baba disclosed for the first time that belonged to the clan of the ancient sage Bhardwaj Rishi who had secured the great boon from Lord Shiva that He (Lord Shiva) and His consort Shakti would be born thrice in the Kali Age – in the first birth as incarnation of Lord Shiva (Shirdi Sai Baba was that incarnation); in the second birth as the combined incarnation of Shiva and Shakti (Sri Sathya Sai Baba is that incarnation): He is also called *Ardhnariswar* (Half-man and half-woman God); and in the third birth as incarnation of Shakti (Shiva's consort). Sai Baba has prophesied that He will be called Prema Sai Baba.

On May 17, 1968, He declared:

"This is a human form, in which every Divine entity, every Divine Principle, that is to say, all the names and forms ascribed by men to God, are manifest.... You are fortunate that you have a chance to experience the bliss of the vision of the *Sarvadaivatwa- swarupam (the alli inclusive form of* all gods) now in this life itself."

Childhood

The first sixteen years of Baba's life *Bal Leela (*mysterious and joyous activities of childhood) predominated. The next sixteen years were spent mostly in *Mahimas* (Glorious activities) in order "to give *santosh* (contentment) to this generation. After the thirty-second year, Baba was increasingly active in the task of 'Updesa' or teaching erring humanity and directing the world along the path of *Sathya* (Truth), *Dharma* (Righteousness), *Shanti* (Peace), and *Prema* (Love)

In His childhood, Sathya Narayan Raju endeared Himself to all His relatives, villagers and teachers by His gentle and pleasing personality, extraordinary intelligence, great interest in dancing, singing, composing religious songs, cooking for the family, serving beggars, and insistence on vegetarianism. He would often amuse and surprise His schoolmates by materializing from nothing, fruits, sweets, toffees, lemon-drops, pencils, rubbers, *vibhuti* (holy ash) etc. He would take part in village dramas, scouting, and acts of social service.

On May 23,1940, He disclosed to His father and other members of the family, "I am Sai Baba. I belong to *Apastambha Sutra,* the school of Saga

Apastambha and am of the spiritual lineage of Bhardwaj Rishi. I am Sai Baba of Shirdi. I have come to ward off your troubles; keep your houses clean and pure."

On October 20, 1940, when He was just a child of fourteen studying in class VIII in the Government High School, Urvakonda where His elder brother Sri Seshama Raju was working as a teacher, He returned to His brother's house soon after His going to school in the morning. Standing on the outer doorsteps, He cast aside his books and called out, "I am no longer your Sathya. I am Sai." His sister-in-law came out from the kitchen and peeped out; she was almost blinded by the splendor of the halo around Sathya's head. She closed her eyes and shrieked. Baba addressed her, "I am going, I don't belong to you. Illusion has gone. My devotees are calling me. I have my work. I cannot stay any longer."

Soon His brother came running. Baba said to him, "Give up all your efforts to cure Me. I am Sai. I do not consider Myself related to you." He moved into the garden of a neighbor, Sri Anjaneyulu and sat on a rock in the midst of the trees. People came into the garden from all directions bringing flowers and fruits. He taught them His first *bhajan* there:

"*Manas bhaj tr Guru charanam, duster bhavsagar tarnam.*"
(O Man, Mediate in thy mind on the Feet of the *Guru*,

They alone can take you across the difficult ocean of worldly life.

After three days, His mother and father arrived and pleaded with Him to come home. He retorted, "Who belongs to whom? It is all illusion – untrue." Ultimately, the parents were able to persuade Him to return to their village Puttaparthi, on His condition that He would live outside the family home, and henceforth they would abstain from ridiculing Him or disturbing His task of meeting devotees.

In His village, Sai Baba stayed in the house of a Brahmin neighbor Subamma for a number of years during adolescence. She looked after Him and His innumerable devotees pouring into her house from all directions of India, comfortably in the spirit of highest devotion and service through her hospitality.

In 1949, the idea to build a separate *ashram* for Baba and His devotees occurred to some devotees and Baba blessed it. The construction started on several acres of land, about a mile from Puttaparthi. Baba Himself designed,

4

supervised and helped the construction work of the Worship Hall and other buildings in the *ashram,* which was inaugurated on November 23, 1950, on the twenty-third birthday of Baba. It was named *'Prasanthi Nilayam'* (Abode of Peace). Since then, it has been the main centre of Baba's activities.

Sai Baba's Mission

"I have come to reconstruct the ancient highway to God. My task is the spiritual regeneration of humanity through truth and love. My main tasks are fostering the Vedas and fostering devotees. This Sai has come in order to achieve the supreme task of uniting as one family the entire mankind, through the bond of brotherhood, of affirming and illumining the *Atmic* Reality of each being in order to reveal the Divine which is the Basis on which the entire Cosmos rests."

In these electrifying words, Sai Baba declared His mission. In the fulfillment of these great declarations, Baba had, since the age of fourteen, been engaged in a surprising number of tasks for the welfare and spiritual regeneration of humanity. He operates at two levels. As a human being made of flesh and blood, He meets an ever-increasing number of people from all parts of the world, and does innumerable things for their cure, well-being, and moral uplift. "My life is My message" —with this declaration He exhorted all to be exemplary men and women.

More than this, He operated at the level of a mysterious Divine Spirit – as an omnipresent and omnipotent God in this Kali Age, always engaged in showering His mysterious and miraculous graces innumerable devotees as well as even those did not follow Him and who out of their ignorance and folly speak ill of Him. As one who knows the past, present and future life of each one of the human beings in this world, was ever busy in dispensing divine justice to people for their actions and in helping them to feel contented materially as well as spiritually.

He had also the great and unique task of administering to the world of souls—departed souls as well as the souls waiting to be reborn in human and other forms. How He able to accomplish all these surprisingly diverse, difficult and miraculous things with utmost poise and efficiency was greatest of all His miracles. The simple answer given by Him is: "There is no mesmerism, miracle, or magic in what I do! Mine is genuine divine Power. I am *Sarvadaivatwa-swarupam* (all forms of gods and goddesses rolled into one). I am Indweller of every heart. Let us try to have a bird's eye view of Baba's a activities. He gave His holy *darshan* (glimpse) to thousands of people who went to His ashram or to the places visited by Him. He grant private interviews to those who had earned great merit in their past and craved for it in their present lives, as also to those who were suffering excessively due to some serious problem, disease, or calamity. He not only advised and consoled them but even materializes medicinal holy *vibhuti* (ash) and other mysterious things like *Japmala* (prayer garland) rings, lockets, amulets, crosses.

Spirit used to shower fantastic range of grace on His devotees and even non-believers, depending on their past *karmas* as well as His mere wish. He materialized many things miraculously, in His right hand, or out of it, on or near His photos in devotees' houses hundreds or thousands of miles away in the different parts of the world. These have included lockets, rings, necklaces, or chains of gold, silver. *panchdhatu* (five metals rolled into one)rings and diamond etc., carrying the embossed or enameled pictures of Shirdi Sai Baba, Sri Sathya Sai Baba, Lord Krishna, Lord Shiva etc., statues of various gods and *goddesses* of the Hindus, and crosses for the *Christians*, fine fragrant *vibhuti*, *kumkum* of various colors, *amrita, Gangajal* (holy water of the Gangese), honey, fruits, dry fruits, sweets, toffees, watches, small statues of gods and goddesses, medicines, religious scriptures like the Gita, photographs, Dollar coins, Sai Baba stamps, Indian currency notes signed by Him with ball pen, His handwritten and signed Divine Message or chits carrying His instructions and numerous other objects. Diverse kinds of His miracles and grace have been received by many people through out the world and some of them been written about in many books in which devotees have very faithfully recorded their actual experiences. The purpose of these miracles was to inform the devotees that He had come to their houses and left these "visiting cards," and to encourage and help the devotees in their journey on the path to spirituality.

Always true to the words or assurances given to His devotees, Baba some times visited their houses in the form of either Sai Baba in flesh and blood, or in the form of any other person, form or even snake. Sai devotees all over the world have had many such thrilling experiences of receiving Sai Baba in many forms. There may be many reasons for these mysterious appearances of Sai Baba, By appearing in these various forms, Sai Baba was empirically demonstrating the great spiritual reality forgotten by the modern man that God in fact resides in every living creature and so all persons, animals and birds etc. should be treated with compassion and respect.

Of the one hundred and eight names of Baba chanted by every Sai devotee before starting the *Sai Bhajan*, one is *apad bandhawa* (the brother who rushes to help a person at the moment of crisis). There are countless incidents reported which empirically prove that this description of our Lord is indeed correct.

Sai Baba once disclosed to an American devotee that He never slept even for a second, as all the time He is ready to rush forward to help devotees in distress. Out of His genuine love, He again and again relieves His devotees by taking on Himself their ailments. He cured incurable ailments —even cancer and mental disorders by giving personally or sending *Vibhuti* miraculously on the photos and statues of Baba and other gods and goddesses in their shrines to be used by the sick person as medicine, or just by making His *sankalpa* (determination) in His Mind to cure the particular patient.[6]

Baba's official biographer, Professor N. Kasturi has written in *Sathyam Shivam Sundaram* (Volume II, page 255) about another wonderful dimension of Baba's divine works:

"It will be a thrilling chapter, if one could collect and compile the events of the last days of the devotees of Baba, who have merged in Him. They die in silent serenity, in prayerful surrender, or in the midst of the Bhajan they share, or during the recitation of Pranava (OM), they get *Amritha* from nowhere and sip it as they die; they see Baba before them with their departing sigh and leave, after prostrating to Him; they have *Vibhuti* emanating from their heads, in token of His blessing! O, it is, amazingly sweet and heartening – the way in which Baba showers His Grace, when His devotees bid farewell, to the bodies wherein they dwell."

Devotees belonging to all religions visited Him with great faith in Him and were benefited. Baba had declared that all religions, all names of God used by men, and all people irrespective of their sex, nationality, religion, caste, class or culture, affiliations are His, and that He had not come to this world to start any new religious cult, or favor any particular religion, community, nation, or His own home, village or state.

Sai Baba's social works are many. He embarked upon the most crucial task of the educational reconstruction and moral regeneration of India. He has established a Post-Graduate Girl's College at Anantapur (some miles from Prasanthi Nilayam). He has started Girls' colleges at Jaipur and Bhopal. A boys' college has been started by Him in His Brindavan ashram. Sri Sathya Sai University has three campuses now a number of Sai schools and colleges are in india and in some forting countries in which value based education is provided and no fees are charged. Sai Baba had started a unique super-specially hospital "Sri Sathya Sai Institute of Higher Medicine" at Prasanthi Nilayam in 1991 and a similar hospital in Whitefield, Bangalore. Medical treatment and care in these modern and most sophisticated hospitals is free for all

Baba had been organizing annual Summer Course on spirituality and Indian culture since 1972 for the benefit of college students and foreigners. Baba delivered His divine discourses in such courses, which were full of deep spiritual knowledge communicated in a very lively, simple, and heart-captivating manner.

Baba started *Bal Vikas* classes at thousands of places in India and abroad where children are taught the essentials of good conduct, spirituality, and Indian culture.

Many colorful festivals are organized in His ashram, most important of which are Guru Poornima, Baba's Birthday, Dussehra, Diwali, Onam, New Year's Day, Ram Navami, and Shiva Ratri festivals. Numerous spiritual programs are often held by Sai devotees from various Indian states and foreign countries, the details and beautiful photos of which are regularly published in the *Sanathana Sarathi* monthly journal of his ashram show that Sai Baba patronized and encouraged people of all nations, races, cultures their spiritual practices with equanimity and utmost love, attention and encouragement. On a number of occasions even Chinese and Russian devotees have presented very impressive cultural programs before Sai Baba and thousands of people. This is unique and rare in the whole world that cultures are appreciated in public. He often distributed food to countless devotees, poor people and beggars. He gave thousands of divine discourses, granted personal interviews to many devotees, distributed vibhuti to them by His own hand and allowed them to do *Padanamaskaram* (saluting Him by touching His divine Feet).

He laid great emphasis on social service activities He revived throughout India the ancient Indian institution of itinerant singing God's glory in the early morning, *Nagar sankirtan* and *Sai bhajans* have become popular all over the world wherever His followers live. Thursday is the special day for Sai worship. *Sai bhajan* sessions can be attended by anybody. Baba formed strict rules for conducting of Sai bhajans and for dealing with Sai devotees. His devotees and *ashram* have been rendering many kinds of social services to unprivileged people in many countries.

Baba has rightly made this self-assessment of His role as the great incarnation of God: "No avatar has done this before – going to the masses, counseling them, uplifting them, directing them along the path of Truth, Duty, Peace and Love."

Sai Baba's Charisma

Sai Baba's personality was truly charismatic. He ias an ideal example of a cultured person. He liked peaceful, clean and pious places. He was very gentle and graceful in speech and in behavior. His simplicity impressed everyone. He ate the food of the poorest of this land, without any milk, curd, butter or *ghee* and has no taste for sweets.

He was not seen wearing any ornament, wrist watch, shoes, head-dress, or clothes other than His long *chola* (shirt) and *dhoti* (loin cloth). What distinguished Him from other God men and great saints of the modern world was that while they accept money, flowers, and worldly things from all or most of their followers, and some even charge fantastic fees for granting interviews and teaching Yoga or foretelling the future, Baba was always giving rather than receiving. At the most, devotees and visitors could be allowed to offer incense, broken unripe coconuts and flowers at the big statue of Lord Ganesha installed just in front of the main entrance of Prasanthi Nilayam ashram. Rarely did Baba accept flowers or garlands from devotees, but instantly, He lovingly gave them to other devotees.

Baba biographer Prof. N. Kasturi had written that Baba was "the most tireless worker at the Prasanthi Nilayam, designing, arranging and supervising every little act that conduces to the proper functioning of its various world-wide activities." It is said that nothing is done there or in other places where organizations function in His Name, without His express permission and blessings.

One of the Baba's greatest features was that He did not insist on observing any die-hard rituals. One could worship Him by uttering the name of any God anywhere, at any time, and preferably in the shrine or a little corner of one's own house rather than in any temple. None had to change his religion in order to believe in or worship Sai Baba. No costly *prashad* (offering of food or sweets), *bhandaras* (mass feasting), gifts to Brahmins, priests or any intermediaries was required according to Him. There are no rules debarring women, lower castes and tribes or foreigners from entering His *ashram* whose gates are open for all people.

As a matter of fact, Baba had repeatedly told His followers:

"You must have noticed that I do not speak about Sai in My discourses, nor do I sing of Sai during the *bhajans* with which I usually conclude My discourses.... I do not want the impression to gain round that I desire this name and this form to be publicized. I have not come to set afoot a new cult. I do not want people to be misled on this point. I affirm that this Sai form is the form of all the various names that man uses for the adoration of the Divine. So, I am teaching that no distinctions should be made between the name – Rama, Krishna, *Ishwara*, Sai – for they are all my names." Epilogue

The concept of equality of men does not work in spiritual matters, as Baba has stated: "The cry of equality now being used as slogan is a vain and meaningless cry; for how can a man, inheriting a multiplicity of impulses, skills, qualities, tendencies, attitudes, and even disease from his ancestors and from his own history be all of the same type?"

The improvement of the world is a slow process. Already there are millions of Sai devotees all over the world, who have started introspecting and improving their personal, family and community lives, according to the humanistic or universal religious and spiritual teachings of Baba. Their number is growing bigger and bigger every day. The foundation of the New Age or the Sai era of peace, duty, truth and love has already been laid.

Sai Baba did not perform miracles and did all sorts of humanitarian activities just to show off. They were genuine and out of his kind-hearted, witty, and loving Divine personality. They were meant to make devotees feel joyful, forget their miseries, and encourage or motivate them to tread on the path of spirituality. Baba did not want these miracles to be publicized by devotees. Of course, a number of those people who have yet not had the joy of witnessing these miracles sometimes become jealous and raise doubts or criticisms out of ignorance.

The expenditure of the *ashrams* and Sai University, Colleges, Summer Courses, Hospitals, water schemes etc. is met out of the collections of voluntary donations of rich people to the Central Sri Sathya Sai Trust. Wealthy people who have become followers of Baba are ever prepared to donate or sacrifice all or a part of their wealth at the slightest prompting of Sai Baba in their conscience. The common man is not asked to make donations to Baba or His Trust. If anybody wants to donate, there is no need for that person to contribute through anybody else, or approach Baba; he can deposit money in the Central Sri Sathya Sai Trust account with any branch of Canara Bank, and obtain a receipt from the bank in case he wishes to show it to Income Tax authorities. No entry fee for visiting His ashrams or fee for granting interview, gifts or charities are taken by Him or anybody else in His name.

Groups of volunteers from different states regularly come to do *seva* (voluntary service) in the ashram and in Baba's hospitals and educational institutes and in the adjoining village of Puttaparthi. They also handle the crowds and the canteen, water, cleanliness, traffic, security and book sale and all other services during the festivals in the ashrams or elsewhere.

Is Baba really God? To this often-raised doubt, Baba had given this most befitting reply: "You have not heard Me fully. I say I am God; I say also that you are God. The only is that I know that you and I are God and you do not know it....Do not worry about My Advent, worry about your own future. Even if all the fourteen worlds unite against Me, the work for which I have come will not suffer a bit; even if earth and heaven combine. My truth will remain unshaken."

Baba used to sing this song composed by Him in Telugu when He was young:

> "That *Nand Bala* (Krishna) has come down today as *Ananda Bala* to identify His kith and kin,
>
> That Rama Chandra has come down today as *Aaram Chandra* (Abode of Happiness) to identify His servants,
>
> That (*Eswara*, God) has come down today as Bal Sesha to play with the group of His playmates.
>
> That Maha Vishnu has come down as MahiVishnu (Vishnu or Master of earth) to assume and employ His weapons.
>
> *Paramatma* (God) is the manipulator of thisof puppets, He stands on the arena of life making the puppets dance as He pleases.
>
> It is for you only to see and enjoy the play, describe it a little, derive pleasure, but you can never fully comprehend it"

He gave this vision of optimism to the entire world which should enthuse all those deeply worried about the future of the mankind through out the world: "Take if from Me. The entire world will become one. There will be only one caste, one religion, and one God. What is needed is such unity. Today, there are several differences between individuals on the basis of caste, creed, religion, language, nation, etc. Such differences should disappear and unity should prevail. The Veda has emphasized this unity in the declaration *"Ekam Sath Viprah Bhudha Vadanthi"* (Truth is one, the wise say it in different ways). That is the real world we are visualizing."

Sri Sathya Baba (Divine Discourse in Education Conference 20th July 2008).

His devotees all over the world recite the *Sai Gayatri mantra* and sing *bhajans* and render selfless *seva* (social service) in many ways and lead their lives according to His valuable secular teachings in order to receive His divine grace.

Chapter - 2

SRI SATHYA SAI BABA: HIS IDENTITY AND ROLE

Section 1
Sai Baba on Himself

I

"Lord Krishna had clearly declared his divine identity in Gita: *"I am the divine being who is the father of this world as also its mother, sustainer and ultimate cause. I am the purifier and the one thing to be known. I am also the holy word 'OM', and the revealed knowledge embodied in the Vedas".*

Bhagavad Gita, IX (29)

"Whenever *ashanti* (disharmony) overwhelms the world, the Lord will incarnate in human form to establish the modes of earning *Prashanthi* (peace) and to reeducate the human community in the paths of peace."

At the present time, strife and discord have robbed peace and unity from the family, the school, the community, the society, villages, the cities and the state. The arrival of the Lord is also anxiously awaited by saints and sages. *Sadhus* (pious people) prayed and I have come. My main tasks are fostering of the Vedas and fostering of the devotees. your virtue, your self-control, your detachment, your faith, your steadfastness, these are the signs by which people read of my glory.

You can lay claim to be My devotee only when you have placed yourself in My hands fully and completely with no trace of ego. You can enjoy the bliss through the experience the Avatar (incarnation) confers. The Avatar behaves in a human way so that mankind can feel kinship, but rises into his superhuman heights so that mankind can aspire to reach the heights and through that aspiration can actually reach Him. Realizing the Lord within you as the motivator is the task for which He comes in human form. Avatars like Rama and Krishnahad to kill one or more individuals who could be identified as enemies of the *dharmic* (righteous) way of life and thus restored the practice of virtue. But now there is no one fully good. And so, who deserves the protection of God? All are tainted by wickedness, and so who will survive, if the *Avatar* decides to uproot? Therefore, I have come to correct the buddhi (intelligence) by various means. I have to counsel, help, command, condemn and stand by as a friend and well-wisher to all, so that they may give up evil propensities and recognizing the straight path, tread it and reach the goal, I have to reveal to the people the worth of the Vedas, the *Shastras* (scriptures) and other Spiritual texts, which lay down the norms. If you accept Me and say yes, I too respond and say yes, yes, yes. If you deny and say no, I also echo no. Come, examine, experience, have faith. That is the method of utilizing Me.

I do not mention about Sai Baba in any of My discourses, though I bear the name as Avatar of Sai Baba. I do not appreciate in the least the distinction between the various appearances of God - Sai, Rama, Krishna etc. I do not proclaim that this is more important or that the other is less important. Continue your worship of your chosen God along the lines already familiar to you. Then you will find that you are coming nearer and nearer to Me, for all names are Mine and all forms are Mine. There is no need to change your chosen God and adopt a new one when you have seen Me and heard Me.

Every step in the career of the *Av*atar is pre-determined. Rama came to feed the roots of *Satya* or Truth and *Dharma* or Righteousness. Krishna came to foster *Shanti* (Peace)and *Prema* (Love). Now all these four are in danger of being dried up. That is why the present Avatar has come. The Dharma, that has fled to forests, has to be led back into the villages and towns. The unrighteousness, that is ruining the villages and towns, has to be driven into the jungle.

I have come to give you the key of the treasure of *Ananda* (bliss) and to tell you how to tap that spring, for you have forgotten the way to blessedness. If you waste this chance of saving yourselves, it is just your fate. You have come to get from Me tinsel and trash, the petty little cures and promotions, worldly joy and comforts. Very few of you desire to get from Me the thing I have come to give you, namely, liberation itself. Even among these few those who stick to the path of *Sadhna* of spiritual practice and succeed, are a handful.

Your worldly intelligence cannot fathom the ways of God. He cannot be recognized by mere cleverness or intelligence. You may benefit from God, but you cannot explain Him. Your explanations are merely guesses, attempts to cloak your ignorance in pompous expressions, Bring something into your daily practice as evidence of your having known that secret of the higher life from Me. Show that you have greater brotherliness; speak with more sweetness and self- control. Bear defeat as well as victory with calm resignation.

I am always aware of the future, the past as well as the present of every one of you. So I am not so moved by mercy. Since I know the past, the background, the reaction is different. It is your consequence of evil deliberately done in the previous birth and so I allow your suffering to continue, often modified by some little compensation. I do not cause either joy or grief; you are the designer of both these chains that bind you. I am *Anandaswarupa.*, take *Ananda* (Bliss) from Me; dwell on that *Ananda* or bliss and be full of *Shanti* or Peace.

My acts are the foundations on which I am building my work- the task for which I have come. All the miraculous acts which you observe are to be interpreted so. The foundation for a dam requires righteous materials; without these it will not last and hold back the waters. When the Lord is incarnated, He has to be used in various ways by man for his uplift.

The Lord has no intention to publicize Himself. I do not need publicity, nor does any other *Avatar* of the Lord. What are you daring to publicize — Me? What do you know about Me? You speak one thing about Me today and another tomorrow. Your faith has not become unshakable. You praise Me when things go well and blame Me when things go wrong. When you start publicity you descend to the level of all those who compete in collecting plenty by decrying others and extolling themselves. Where money is calculated, garnered or exhibited to demonstrate one's achievements, I will not be present. I come only where sincerity, faith and surrender are valued; only inferior minds will revel in publicity and self-aggrandizement. These have no relevance in the case of Avatars; they need no advertisement.

The establishment of *dharma* (righteousness) - that is My aim. The teachings of dharma; the spread of dharma—that is My object. These miracles, as you call them, are just a few means towards that end. Some of you remark mat Rama Krishna Parmhansa has said that the *siddhis* or yogic powers are obstructions in the path of the *Sadhana*. Yes, *Siddhis* may lead the *Sadhka* or the spiritual aspirant astray. Without being involved in them he has to keep straight on or his ego will bring him down to the evil- the temptation of demonstrating his *yogic* powers. This is a correct advice which every aspirant should heed. But mistake lies in equating Me with the *Sadhaka* like the one whom Rama Krishna wanted to help, guide and warn. These *Siddhis* or yogic powers are just in the nature of the Avatar. The creation of peace with intent to protect and give joy, is spontaneous and lasting. Creation, preservation and dissolution can be accomplished only by the Almighty. No one else can. Cynics carp without knowledge

They who learn the *Shastras* or scriptures or they who cultivate direct experience can understand Me. Your innate laziness prevents you from the spiritual exercise necessary to discover the nature of God. This laziness should go, it has to be driven out of man's nature, in whatever shape it appears. That is My mission. My task is not merely to cure and console and remove individual misery, but it is something far more important. The removal of misery and distress is incidental to My mission. My main task is the re-establishment of Vedas and Shastras and revealing the knowledge about them to all people. This task will succeed. It will not be limited. It will not be slowed down. When the Lord decides and wills, His Divine will cannot be hindered.

You must have heard people say that Mine is all magic, but the manifestation of Divine power must not be interpreted in terms of magic. Magicians play their tricks for earning their maintenance, worldly fame and wealth. They are based on falsehood and they thrive on deceit. But this body can never stoop to such low level. This body has come through the Lord's resolve to come. That resolve is intended to uphold the *Sathya* or Truth. Divine resolve is always true resolve. Remember, there is nothing that Divine power cannot accomplish. It can transmute earth into sky and sky into earth. To doubt this is to prove that you are too weak to grasp great things and grandeur of the universe.

I have come to instruct all in the essence of the Vedas; to shower on all this precious gift, to protect *Sanatana Dharma*—the ancient wisdom and preserve it. My mission is to spread happiness and so I am always ready to come among you, not once but twice or thrice, as often as you want Me.

Many of you probably think that since people from all parts of India, even foreign countries outside India, come to Puttaparthi, they must be pouring their contributions into the coffers of the Nilayam. But let Me declare the truth. I do not take anything from any one except their love and devotion. This has been My consistent practice for the last many years. People, who come here, are giving Me just the wealth of faith, devotion and love. That is all.

Many of you come to Me with problems of help and mental worry of some sort or the other. They are mere baits by which you have been brought here, but the main purpose is that you may have the grace and strengthen your faith in the Divine. Problems and worries are really to be welcomed as they teach you the lesson of humility and reverence. Running after external things produces all this discontent. That type of desire has no end. Once you become a slave to the senses, they will not leave hold until your death. It is an unquenchable thirst. But I call you to Me and even grant worldly boons, so that you may turn God ward. No Avatar has done like this before: going among the masses, counseling them, guiding them, consoling them, uplift them, directing them along the path of *Sathya, Dharma, Shanti* and *Prema.*

My activities and movements will never be altered whoever may pass whatever opinion on Me. I shall not modify my plans for *Dharamsthapna* — the establishment of righteousness, My discourses, or My movements. I have stuck to this determination for many years and I am engaged in the task for which I have come, that is, to inculcate faith in the path of Prashanti. I shall not stop, nor retract a step. Not even the biggest scientist can understand Me by means of his laboratory knowledge. I am always full of bliss, whatever may happen. Nothing can come in the way of My smile. That is why I am able to impart joy to you and make your burden lighter.

I never exult when I am extolled, nor shrink when I am reviled. Few have realized My purpose and significance, but I am not worried when things that are not in Me are attributed to Me. Why should I worry? When things that are in Me are mentioned, why should I exult? For Me it is always yes, yes, yes. If you give up and surrender to the Lord, He will guard and guide you. The Lord has come just for this very task. He is declaring that He will do so and that is the very task that brought Him here.

I know the agitations of your heart and His aspirations, but you do not know My heart. I react to the pain that you undergo and to the joy that you feel, for I am in your heart. I am the dweller in the temple of every heart. Do not lose contact and company, for it is only when the lump of coal is in contact with the live amber that it can also become live amber. Cultivate nearness with Me in the heart and you will be rewarded. Then you too will acquire a fraction of the supreme love. This is a great change. Be confident that you will all be liberated. Know that you are saved. Many hesitate to believe that things will improve; that life will be happy for all and full of joy, and that the *Golden Age* will recur. Let Me assure you that this Dharmaswarupa—this Divine body-has not come in vain. It will succeed in warding the crisis that has come upon humanity."

II
Who is Sai?

"God is inscrutable. He cannot be realized in the outer objective world. He is in the very heart of every being. Gemstones have to be sought in deep underground; they do not float in mid-air. Seek God in the depths of yourself, not in the tantalizing kaleidoscopic Nature. The body is granted to you for this high purpose; but you are now misusing it, like the person who cooked his daily food in the gem studded gold vase that came into his hands as an heirloom.

For this Sai has come in order to achieve the supreme task of uniting as one family the entire mankind, through the bond of brotherhood, of affirming and illuminating the Atmic Reality of each being in order to reveal the Divine which is to basis on which the entire cosmos rests, and of instructing all to recognize the common divine heritage that binds man to man, so that man can rid himself of the animal, and rise into the Divinity which is his goal.

I am the embodiment of Love; Love is My instrument. There is no creature without love; the lowest loves itself at least. And its self is God. So, there are no atheists, though some might dislike Him or refuse Him, as malarial patients dislike bitter pills or diabetic patients refuse to have anything to do with sweets. Those who preen themselves as atheists will one day, when their illness is gone, relish God and revere him.

I had to tell you -so much about My truth, for, I desire that you should contemplate on this and derive joy there from, so that you may be inspired to observe the disciplines laid down' and progress towards the goal of self-realization, the realization of the Sai that shines in your hearts."

- Sathya Sai Baba's discourse on 19 June, 1974

III

I am the servant of every one. You can call Me by any name. I will respond, for all names are mine. Even if I am discarded by you, I shall be behind you. Denying the sun does not make him disappear. Do not try to measure Me. You will only fail. Try rather to discover your own measure but God is infinite and trying to know God means becoming God, in attempting to know Me you become merged in Me. The finite merges in the Infinite. My task is the spiritual regeneration of humanity through Truth and Love. I have come to show you both Dharma Marga and Brahma Marga. If you approach one step nearer to Me, I shall advance three steps towards you. Effort and Endeavour are duties of man. Success or failure depends on the Lord's grace. Engage yourself on your allotted task every day with consciousness of the living presence of the Lord always by your side. Engage *yourself* in *(recitation of God's Name)* which is the best *Sadhana (meditation)*. That is the highest *Japam* (chanting). the most profitable *Thapas* (penance).Fill the name with love. Saturate it with devotion that is the easiest path for all of you."

- Sri Sathya Sai Baba

IV

'The purose of the present Avatar is difernt from that of Rama and Krshna because The forces of good and bad ere present in every being and the process of transformation has to be effected in a context very different from the previous *Yugas*. In the *Kali Yuga* the process of tranfrmatiomn has to be individualized. EvEry one has to correct himself.. "Child. You have to sve yourself, I am present within you as a witness.' This is the Lords's message."

- Sri Sathya Sai Baba

VII

"This Sai has come in order to ahieve the supreme task of uniting the entire mankind as one family through he bond of brotherhood, of affirming and shining the atmic reality of each beng in order to reveakl the divine, which is the basis on which the entire cosmos rests, and of instructing all to recognize the common divine heritage that binds man to man, so that man can rid himself of animal and rised into the divine, which is hids goal."

- Sri Sathya Sai Baba

VIII

"You may not be able to see it, but it is clear before My eyes. As days pass, even those who are now unable to recognize the Truth of Sai will have to approach with tears of repentance and experience Me. Soon this will be worldwide.

Sai has been firmly restraining this development. When once it is allowed to manifest, the whole world will be transformed into an abode of peace (Prasanthi Nilayam). So come forward, all of you determined to practice in daily living the ideals laid before you. In the coming years you may not get the chance you have now."

- Sri Sathya Sai Baba Birthday Discourse, 1983

IX

"I have come to light the lamp of love in your hearts, to see that it shines day by day with added luster. I have not come to speak on behalf of any exclusive religion. I have not come on any mission of publicity for any sect or creed or cause, nor have I come to collect followers for any doctrine. I have no plan to attract disciples or devotees into my fold or any fold. I have come to tell you of this unitary 'faith, this spiritual principle, this path of love, this virtue of love, this duty of love, this obligation of love."

X

On His 34th Birthday on 23 November,1964, Baba had emphatically revealed to mankind:

"I am the Sri Nath, Lokanath and Ananthnath, the same God who saved Gajendra (Elephant in the mythological Story), the saintly boy Dhruva, poor Kuchcla (Lord Krishna's classmate Sudama), and helpless Prahlad, son of demon King Hiranyakashyapu

- Sri Sathya Sai Baba on His 34th Birthday on 23 November, 1964

Section 2
Prophecies About the Advent of Sri Sathya Sai Avatar

Many thrilling prophecies have been made by ancient religious scriptures, and by famous spiritualists and prophecy-makers of the world, about the coming of the great incarnation of the Lord in the form of Sri Sathya Sai Baba in this century.

Let us briefly examine them:

- Swami Maheswaranand (1990) has mentioned that the ancient Hindu scriptures like ***Jaimini Mahabharata*** written by Sage Jaimini and ***Bhrigu Sanhita*** written by Sage Bhrigu had prophesied about the Avatar of Sri Sathya Sai Baba thousands of years ago.

- In *Bhrigu Sanhita* it had been mentioned that the Avatar bearing the name of Sathya (Truth) would reside at a place named 'Prasanthi Nilayam' (Abode of Peace). To the wonderment of many who have consulted *Bhrigu Sanhita,* the sacred book even contains prophecies as to when they are destined to go to meet and have the blessings, including certain materialized gifts and cures, from Sri Sathya Sai.
- According to Ra Ganpathi (1985):The ancient document **Agastya nadi** written by Sage Agastya had prophesied thus:

"The Avatar Sathya Sai will be medical master of lightening efficiency: He will found many educational institutions, produce literature on righteous conduct, preach throughout His life on spirituality. He will leave home at a young age and launch upon the establishment of dharma as His life's mission. In the previous life he was Sai Baba of Shirdi."

The *Brahma nadi* contained this prophecy:

"The Avatar creating an illusion as though He is a human being a denizen of Parlhi (Puttapathi village), Sathya Sai Narayan, the reincarnation of Shakti-Shiva, (the incarnation of Shirdi Baba, peace in person in the peaceful precincts (the word used in the *nadi* is *Santalaya* (i.e. Abode of Peace) of Parthi on the bank of the river Chitravati, will be a reincarnation of Sri Krishna, Sri Linga, Sri Rudra Kali, Sri Shakti, Sri Vishnu, an embodiment of Truth in the garb of a human being."

The amous *Suka-nadi* astrologer (Late) Gunjur Narayan Shastry of Sri Lakshminarasimha Jhotishyalaya, Bangalore had the *Suka-nadi* which had had made this prophecy about Sri Sathya Sai Baba (39)

"He will be *Avatar.*

He will establish eternal happiness in the world through love, bliss, light (knowledge); the temple He would live in would be a repository of penance: He will delight in the service of humanity. He will be an Avatar.".

- Shakuntala Balu (1983) could gather these highlights of these **Suka-nadi** prophecies about Sri Sathya Sai Baba:

He will be a great incarnation of God - of Vishnu and Shirdi Sai, having all powers of God. He will be born for protecting and propagating Dharma (righteousness) and he will have a mission to fulfill. He will have healing powers and the power to cure himself by sprinkling of water. He will use his healing powers not only for the people of this world but also for the beings of the other world and on a higher plane of *Devatas* (celestial gods and goddesses). At times he will take on the illness of others. He will have power to lengthen life.

When the *Kali yuga* influence grows even more intense, people will see his true might and will acknowledge that he is the supreme power. Then mankind will bow to him as a great Emperor and he will be revered as Mahapurusha (Superman) in the world."

According to *Suka-nadi,* it was saint Kabir who returned to earth as Shirdi Sai Baba, who in turn came as Sathya Sai Baba and who will also return to earth in another form.

Sri Sathya Sai Baba will perform great miracles

He will always retain a youthful look, age notwithstanding.

He will be a *Brahmachari* (bachelor).

He will establish an *ashram.* There will be *many Bahu-Chakra vahanas* (vehicles having many wheels) in his ashram.

He will establish educational institutions and hospitals.

He will have equal attitude towards men and women. His glory will spread and many people will come near him. But all will not be able to get his grace due to their past sins.

He will be *Premswaroopa* (Embodiment of Divine Love), Anandswaroopa (Embodiment of Divine Bliss) and Gyanswaroopa (Embodiment of Knowledge).

At the *Pralaya kaal* (the end of one cycle of the world) He will show that He alone can control the fury of nature.

He will show himself in many places simultaneously, though he will actually be at one place. There will be many divine acts and manifestations done by him.

He will have the power to die whenever he wishes to give up His body (*Ichchamarana prapti*).

He will also plant a tree in Brindavan (Whitefield, a suburb of Bangalore) and that place will become a *Siddhi Kshetra* (a field of energy) and Ithe tree will be worshipped as *Kalpa-Vriksha* (wish-fulfilling tree).

The original *Suka nadi* contains greater details about the day, time, family tree, etc, of Sri Sathya Sai Baba *Avatar.*

- A 17th century Arabic book of the Sliia Muslims entitled ***Bihar-ul-Anwar,*** compiled by Mohamed Jaqir Bin Mohd Taqi-Al Majlis-Al-Isfahani, is said to have highlighted the prophecies of Prophet

Mohamed about the great Master of the Universe, Hazrat Mehdi, who would come to the earth.. Zeba Bashiruddin of Sri Sathya Sai Institute of Higher Learning, who is an ardent devotee of Sri Sathya Sai Baba, has authored a revealing article "Hazrat Mehdi and Baba: Truth of a Prophecy" which has been published in *Sanathana Sarathi* (Nov. 1991). In it she has shown that all the prophecies about Hazrat Mehdi apply perfectly to Sri Sathya Sai Baba.

According to that source:

❖ "Muslims all over the world believe in the advent of a great leader and a guide.

They all know him as Mehdi (Master). The Prophet, Hazrat Mohammad, has indicated that Hazrat Mehdi will appear for the welfare of Muslims in the last decades of the fourteenth century Hijri (this century has just ended). Il will be a time of trouble and materialism. The Quranic values and their practice will be ignored, and men's hearts will turn to the worship of the world and its glamour, "the other Gods" of Quranic language. I lie prophecy goes on to postulate that Hazrat Mehdi will restore the Truth and "Islam" will be the religion of the entire world.

The Prophecy

The signs regarding the time and the person of Hazrat Mehdi, more than 150 in number, were related by the Holy Prophet to Hazrat Ali, the fourth Khalif and repository of Sufi secrets. These signs became a guarded treasure of the Imams, descendants of Hazrat Ali, and formed a part of the Shia tradition of Ihe Prophetic sayings. In the 17th century ad the well known scholar, Md. Baqir Bin Md. Taqi-Al Majlisi-Al Isfahani (1627-98) collected them in his voluminous book, *Bihar-ul-Anwar*, written in Arabic. The two Persian translations that contained the Prophetic sayings about Hazrat Mahdi are Khas-ul-Anwar and Bihar-ul-Anwar (Part Dwazdhum).

A few of these selected sayings of the Prophet of Islam are listed here. It is left to the reader to recognize who the great Master is as seen by the Holy Prophet in a vision, and described by him fourteen hundred years ago.

The Master, commonly known as Hazrat Mehdi, will be seen by those who will search for him. (page 240) (All subsequent references in this article are to the Persian translation of *Bihar-ul-*Anwar. Imam Mohammad Baqir suggests that" only those who know the real meaning of 'I' will believe in **"Hazrat Mehdi"**. The holy Prophet called him as "Abu Abdullah",

(Father of the seekers of God). Much has been said about the name Father of Humanity in Bihar-ul-Anwar. He is also addressed as *Saheb-e-Asr* (Master of Time), *Walli-Allah* (Friend of God), *Khalifat-ullah* (God's Vice regent), "for surely he will follow the code of Moses, Joseph, Jesus and Mohammad" (p. 330).

The Insignia of Hazrat Mehdi

Other signs as stated in Mohamed-Baqir's work are: Many Mohammedans will not know about His advent for a long time. That holy spirit will wear two garments, one inner and the other outer (p. 239). The Robe, Orange in color, will be of such a shape that the contours of His back will be seen clearly (p. 292, 777). His dress, Orange in color, will spread Light among the people (p. 245). His dress will be of Light (p. 229).

His hair, thick and dark, will reach His shoulders (p. 25). His eyebrows are joined in the centre (p.242). His other features are: Broad and clear forehead (p.263): Straight nose with a dip in the beginning: a mole on the cheek, reminding of Hazrat Mosa; bright as a star; teeth with a parting in the two front ones (p.243); Black eyes (p.777); Average height, compared with the Jewish height (p.239). The color of the face-is described variously as shining like a gold-bronze coin; so bright that it is impossible to recognize the real color (p. 263-93). The general impression: full of compassion, dignified, exalted (p.239).

Attributes and Qualities of Hazrat Mehdi

His attitude to everyone will be brotherly, as if He knows them well (p.314).

He will love all Prophets and Saints; and whatever He wants will he done. 1 le will overcome all opposition (p. 242).

His devotees will find protection (p.342). People will find Him heavenly bliss personified (p. 341).

I le will he a shelter for-the helpless and I he rejected (235).

He will distribute A'b-e-Tulmi Kmisr (spirituality) to people in the morning and evening (p. 343). (The reference is to Baba's daily *darshans*).

Divine light will be manifested from Him (p. 252).

He will not bring a new religion (p. 6). (Baba has stressed often that He is not preaching a new religion).

All knowledge and essence of all religions will bloom in His heart like a new garden (p. 238).lie will fill the earth with peace; lie will be a friend and an adviser (p. 287). He will show the Straight Path (p. 352).

The World Scenario

The world situation is summed up in a number of striking images, describing aptly the situation at present. The majority of mankind will be like animals, devoid of discrimination (p. 349). Evil bad habits will be common order of the day. There will be earthquakes and men will die without any reason. They will consider His advent as a sport and a rumor but it will be the Truth. (909 Hazrat Imam Gazali).

Hazrat Mehdi will free people from slavery, remove the lies from their minds, (p. 287), destroy Satans and cure insanity (p. 329).

Around the place where He will live signs of prosperity will be visible in heaven and on earth (p. 294).

Men will crowd like clouds where I le will live and fall like rains(p. 389).

He will not live in Mecca (p. 240); 11 is reign will begin from the east and His banner will go round the world (p. 306).

Not only mankind but Angels will be with Him (p. 274).

He will have the collective wisdom of all Prophets (p. 115).

The Prophet of Islam then, turning to the invisible crowds to come in the future, addressed: "O, ye Muslims know this that He whose birth is hidden from you is your Master. He is MEHDI". (p. 292).

According to Zeba Bashiruddin these words undoubtedly revealed the Truth that Sai Baba is none other than Hazarat Mehdi. It requires faith to accept Truth and indeed Allah shows a straight path to those whom He wants for He is all-knowing and wise."

- Sri Sathya Sai Baba (1975) had overwhelmed the Christian world by declaring that it was He who had sent Christ to the world, and that his incarnation has been prophesied by Christ and was well recorded in the Bible over 1,900 years ago. The relevant extract of that startling revelation made by Baba on the Christmas Day of 1975 is as under:

"...There is one point that I cannot but bring to your special notice today. At the time when Jesus was merging in the supreme principle of divinity, he communicated some news to his followers which has been interpreted in a variety of ways by commentators and those who relish the piling of writings on writings and meaning upon meaning, until it all swells up into a huge GOD. All the articles which were in heaven followed him upon white horses, clothes in white linen, white and clean. And out of his mouth goeth a sharp sword, that with it he should smite the nations; and he shall rule them with a rod of iron; and he treadeth the winepress the fierceness and wrath of Almighty God. And he has on his vesture and on his thigh a name written "KING OF KINGS AND LORD OF LORDS" (Revelation 10-11-16).

Victor Kanu, eminent African Sai devotee,-the former High Commissioner of Sierra Leone to U.K. and President of the. Sathya Sai (UK) Society for Education in Human Values, and Editor of Sai World Gazette, aptly interpreted and explained the foregoing Revelation in the Bible in these words:

"The white horse symbolizes the white cars which Sai Baba uses. He is known to change the color of any vehicle given to him to white. "Faithful and True" are literally Sai Baba's name, Sathya means truth. Sai Baba has the eyes of Shiva which is like "A flame of fire". And even his visible eyes look fiery.

"On his head were many frowns" symbolizes Sai Baba's extraordinary hair, each hair presenting a crown and the sum total of them looking like a crown on his head. No one knew the meaning of Baba's name until he disclosed it himself.

"A vesture dipped in blood" Ills the description of Sai Baba's red lobe, "out of his mouth goeth; i sharp sword" symbolizes his words of wisdom which cut down and clear the forests of ignorance and shed light on life.

"The Word of God" is Truth (*Sathya*). Sathya Sai Baba is the word of (lod-Truth made flesh and becoming the Mother and Father of the universe, Sai (true Mother) and Baba (Father).

All the students and Sai volunteers and others around Sai Baba are always "clothed in fine linen", while and clean. Visitors to l'ullaparlhi arc encouraged to do the same.

Sri Sathya Sai Baba was born with two marks- one on his chest (vesture) and the other on his thigh. The marks resemble an eagle. According to the theory of Avatars, a mark of this kind on the chest is a unique feature of an Avatar. To have two such marks distinguishes a *Purna Avatar (*Full Incarnation), as we have in Sai Baba, from the rest".[5]

The world famous French prophecy-maker of the 16th century. **Michael de Nostradamu**s, in his widely publicized predictions about the course of future events throughout the world, had indicated the coming of a very great world leader in our times. It has been of interest to a number of researchers to try to unravel the meanings of his predictions. Noorbergergen (1991),[6] Sanjay Kant (1990),[7] Ashok Kumar Sharma (1991)[8] and Narayan Datt Srimali (1975)[9] have highlighted the following predictions of Nostradamus about the emergence of a very great Leader or Emperor of mankind in our times

He would be born in the east, not in Europe.

He would be born in Asia in a peninsula surrounded by three seas, in a land of five rivers.

His name would start with the sound S

He would treat Thursday as his special day.

The whole world would first love him and then be greatly afraid of him.

His popularity will touch the sky and he will be venerated as a great Victorious Emperor of the world.

These predictions seem to fit Sri Sathya Sai Baba immensely. All those who are fully aware of His divine aspects, His worldwide activities and His extraordinary influence on the hearts of peoples of all nations, religions and races, feel convinced that Nostradamus had prophesied about Baba only. Bearing testimony to this fact is Sanjay Kant's book.

India's great spiritual master Sri Aurobindo had declared on 24th November 1926 that God Himself had been born just on that day, and he suspended all activities of his Aurobindo Ashram at Pondicherry on that day to observe the advent of God in solitude.

Section 3;
Sathya Sai Baba as Reincaration of Shirdi Sai Baba

Sri Sathya Sai Baba had disclosed to his parents on 23 May 1940, as a fourteen year-old boy, that he was Sai Baba of Shirdi born again.

- Two devotees of Shirdi Sai Baba from His lifetime, **Shirdi Ma** and **M.S. Dixit** were reportedly convinced of Shirdi Sai Baba's prophecy that He would come again after eight years. They recognized Sri Sathya Sai Baba as the same Shirdi Sai Baba who has come again. According to Ra Ganapati (1985):

Dixit had requested Shirdi Baba, "Please give me the joy of serving as your gateman." This request which he was not blessed with at Shirdi was granted to him at Swami's White Field Ashram 'Brindavan'. Dixit was appointed there to open and close the outer gates whenever Swami's car used to go through.

- Before passing away in 1918, Sri Shirdi Sai Baba had confided in **Abdul**, his trusted devotee and companion in Dwarka Mai Mosque at Shirdi, that He would come again assuming the name of 'Sathya' eight years after his death. This was disclosed by Sri Sathya Sai Baba on 28 September 1990, while describing His previous life as Shirdi Sai Baba *Avatar.*

Here is an extract from His discourse:

"Towards the end, Abdul Baba came to Shirdi Sai Baba. Baba told him: "I shall appear again and give you *darshan.*" "When will that I asked Abdul. Baba (old him, "It will be after eight years."... When he asked in what form (he next advent would take place, Shirdi Baba told Abdul Baba alone "I will give *darshan* in the name of Sathya for upholding Truth.

"The two bodies are different, but the Divinity is one. The first advent was for revealing Divinity. The Second Advent is to awaken the Divinity (in human beings). The next advent is for propagating Divinity. The three Sais are: Shirdi Sai, Sathya Sai and Prema Sai Baba."

It was on 6 July 1963 that Baba first disclosed this:

I am Shiva-Shakti, born in the *gotra* (lineage) of Bhardwaja, according to a boon received by that sage from Shiva and Shakti, Shiva himself was born in the *gotra* of that sage as Sai Baba of Shirdi: Shiva and Shakti have incarnated as Myself in his gotra now: Shakti alone will incarnate as the third Sai (Prema Sai Baba) in the same *gotra* in Mysore state (now Karnataka State)".

This complete story as told by Baba is reproduced by Sandweiss (1975)'" in his book.

All the above-mentioned references prove beyond doubt that Sri Sathya Sai Baba is the unique incarnation of God come in His full effulgence for the uplift of humanity. Many Sai devotees believe that he is the Kalki Avatar11 about whom prophecy had been made in the *Bhagavath* and *Kalki Purana* and other scriptures

The folloiwing books and web sites providea lot of information on Sathy Sai Baba as the incarnation of Shirdi Sai Baba:

- Kakde R.C, and Veerbhadra, *Shirdi to Puttaparthi* (1899)
- Rao, Ghandikota, Subba, SrI Sathya Sai Avatar of Love(1993)
- Shirdin Sai Baba and Shirdi Sai Baba(2013) (Latest publication oif Sri Sathya Sai Books & Publications Trust, Prasanthi Nilayam)
- Arjun D. Bharwani'web site: *Shirdi and Sathya Sai are One and Same*
- Shardai devi's websioe *From Shirdi Sai to Satha Sai*
- Saidham, Nottingham, UK
- saidarar.usa

References

1. Maheswaranaiid, Swami, *Sai Avatar*. Panajim. Goa: Shanti Bhai S. Tailor, 1988.(In Hindi)
2. Ganapati, Ra, *BABA: Satya Sai* (Vol. I).Madras: Sai Raj Publications, 1985.
3. Balu, Shakuntula, *Living Divinity*. SB Publications, 1983.
4. Basahiruddin, Zeba, 'Hazrat Mehdi and Baba: Truth of a Prophecy', *Sanathana Sarathi*, November, 1991.
5. Kanu, Victor, *Sai Baba: God Incarnate*, London: Sawbridge Enterprises.
6. Noorbergen, Rene (Ed.), *Nostradamus Predicts the End of the World*. New York: Windsor Publishing Corporation, 1981.
7. Kant, Sanjay, *God Descends on Earth*: As Prophesied by Nostradamus and Edgar Cayce. Panjim, Goa: New Flash Publication, 1990.
8. Sharma, A.K., *Nostradamus Ki Bhavishvaniya*. Delhi: Diamond Pocket Books.1993. (In Hindi).
9. Srimali, N., Amar Bhavishyavanian. New Delhi: Mayur Paperbacks, 1976. **10 Sandweiss,** 10.Sandwess,S, *Sai Baba: Holy Man and Psychiatrist*. San Diego, California: Birthday Publishing Co., 1975.

Commorative postal stamp of Rs.5 released by the Govt of India on the occasion of Sri Sathya Sai Baba's 88th Birthday

Chapter - 3

SRI SATHYA SAI BABA'S TEACHINGS

1. Love is God. Live in Love.
2. Work is worship. Duty is God.
3. Devotion must be tested in the crucible of discipline. It must be directed along the lines of duty.
4. Education without character, science without humanity, and commerce without morality are useless and dangerous.
5. There four Fs that you will have to fix before your attention: Follow the Master, Face the devil, Fight to the end, and Finish at the goal. Follow the Master means observe dharma. Face the devil means overcome the temptations that beset you when you try to earn wealth or wherewithal to live in comfort. Fight to the end means struggle ceaselessly; wage war against the six enemies that are led by *Kama* or lust. And finally, Finish at the goal, means, do not stop until the goal of *Moksha* or Liberation from ignorance and delusion ceases.
6. Everybody is saying, "I want peace." Peace is like a letter in an envelope. The I of "I want peace" is the front part of the envelope and "want" is the back. The "Peace" itself is the letter inside. Throw away the envelope, with its "I" and "want"; keep the precious letter of peace.
7. The fundamental cause for the rise in prices of commodities is the decline in the price of man. Man must realize that he is priceless; he should not regard himself as a cheap nut or bolt, that he has no higher purpose in life. He should know that he is the imperishable, unconquerable *Atma* (soul) and the body is only a vehicle for the *Atma*.
8. Man has to worship God in the form of man. God appears before him as a blind beggar, an idiot, a leper, a child, an old man, a criminal, or a mad man. You must see even behind these veils, the Divine Embodiment of Love, Power and Wisdom, the Sai, and worship Him through seva or service.

9. The strength of *dharma* alone is the true strength. Truth and not the strength of the weapons is the real intrinsic strength.

10. Religions are different but the goal is the same; even as the cows may be different in color but the milk is the same; ornaments may be different in shape but the gold is the same.

11. Remove this ego boundary, - Sri Sathya Sai Baba then only can you recognize the vastness of yourself

12. My task is the spiritual regeneration of humanity through truth and love. I have come to show you how to live usefully and die profitably! If you approach one step nearer to Me, I shall advance three steps towards you. (52)

13. You will not be wrong if you characterize Me as the personification of love.

14. My mission is to grant you courage and joy, to drive away weakness and fear.

15. Even those who swear that they did not find any trace of God in the depths of space, or who aver that God is dead, or that even if alive, He has outlived His use for man, that he has ever been a handicap and a costly nuisance for man, they too have to admit that there is something inscrutable beyond the reach of reason, something which pervades the world and reveals itself in Love, Renunciation, and Service. That something is God.

16. Many of you plead for a message from Me. Well, My life is My message. You will be adhering to My message if you so live that your lives become the evidences of dispassion, courage and confidence, revealing eagerness to serve those who are in distress.

17. Start early, drive slowly, reach safely.

18. This human form (of Sai) is one in which every divine entity, every divine principle, that is to say, all the names and forms ascribed by man to God, are manifest. Do not allow doubt to distract you. If you only install in the altar of your heart steady faith in My Divinity, you can win a vision of My Reality.

19. As far as I am concerned, there is only one rope that binds Me: love. That love will make you quiet and happy. it will comfort you, it will inspire you to merge with Me.

20. Every time the hand is lifted, lift it for Him. If you lift the hand to help, to serve, to console, to encourage another man, you are lifting it for God. Because in every man there is God, use all your talents for serving others; that is the best way of serving yourself.

21. I do not accept from you flowers that fade, fruits that rot, coins that have no currency beyond the boundary; give Me the Lotus that blooms in your *Manasarovara*(lake), in the pure pellucid waters of your inner consciousness; give Me the fruit of your holiness and steady discipline.

22. No nation can be built strong and stable, except on the spiritual culture of its women.

23. An educational system that keeps children away from God – the only refuge, the only kinsman, the only guide and guard – is a system where the blind are engaged in blinding those who love for light.

24. Fear is the biggest cause of illness. Transfer your faith from pill to Providence; put your trust in Madhava (God), not in medicines; resort to prayers, *sadhana, dhyanam* and not to injections. They are the vitamins you need. No tablet is as efficacious as Rama-Nam. Accept the sadhna way to peace and happiness and health.

25. Man must be both bright and light like the lamp that floats on the Ganga at Hardwar. If the weight of the worldly desire is added, the lamp will sink and the light will go out.

26. Walk this earth, with your head held high, your spirits soaring, your heart open to Love. Believe in yourself and in the God within you. Then all will go well. Wherever you walk, I am there. Whomsoever you contact, I am in that Person. I am in each. From each, I will respond. You cannot see Me in one place, and Miss Me in another! For, I fill all space. You cannot escape Me, or do anything in secret.

27. Life as a worker is most valuable and fundamental. Work, worship and wisdom are three stages on the God-ward path.

28. Seek the light always: be full of confidence and zest. Do not yield to despair; it can never produce results.

29. Engage always in good deeds, beneficial activities, speak the truth, do not inflict pain by word or deed or even thought. That is the way to gain *Shanti*; that is the highest gain you can earn in this life.

30. Drop the delusion that you have become old or diseased, or that you have become weak and debilitated. But remember, elation is Heaven, despondence is Hell. Have always some work to do and do it so well that you get joy.

31. Splendors, prosperity, wisdom, non-attachment, creation, preservation and destruction – these seven are the unfailing characteristic of avatars. Wherever these are found, you can identify Godhead.

32. The cry of equality now being used as a slogan is a vain and meaningless cry; for how can man, inheriting a multiplicity of impulses, skills, qualities, tendencies, attitudes, and even diseases from his ancestors and from his own history be all of the same stamp? Those who promote inequality are those who most loudly proclaim this modern doctrine of equality.

33. The Lord is ever behind you; turn your back from the world. He is face to face with you.

34. Be fair, be true, be strong in your convictions. Then you have My blessings in all that you undertake.

35. *Seva* in all its form, all the world over, is primarily sadhna. It is spiritual discipline of mental clean up.

36. Don't analyze and allot blame. Sympathize and shower love.

37. Endurance with joyful resignation of the ups and downs of life is the real road to peace.

38. Purify your vision, sweeten your speech, sanctify your deeds – that way lays liberation.

39. I declare that I am in everyone, in every being. So do not hate anyone, or cavil at any one. Spread Prema always, everywhere. That is the best way of revering Me.

40. Turn the key to the right, it is unlocked. Turn to God and righteousness, the lock opens, the chain falls away. Turn to the left, you become bound; the bolt falls in; the chain holds fast. It is just a question of the point of view – Outlook or In look? Out-query or In-query?

41. Remember, you have to come to Me, if not in this birth, at least within ten more births. Strive to acquire Grace; Grace is the reward for *sadhana*; the highest *sadhan*a is to follow the instructions of the Master.

42. Practice – that is the real thing in spiritual matters. Scholarship is a burden; it is very often a handicap. So long as God is believed to be far away, in temples and holy places, man will feel religion a burden and a hurdle. But, plant Him in your heart and you feel light, burden-less, and even strong.

43. Live in the *consuming* conviction that you are the Atma. That is the hard core of the *Sanathana (ancient)* teaching.

44. Patience is all the strength the man needs.

45. It is easy to conquer anger through love, attachment through reasoning, falsehood through truth, bad through good, and greed through charity.

46. The end of wisdom is freedom, the end of culture is perfection, the end of knowledge is love, and the end of education is character.

47. Many of you have seen in railway compartments the notice "fewer luggages make travel more comfortable." In that sense, our life is a long journey. This long journey, because we are accumulating a lot of luggage in the form of many desires, becomes somewhat troublesome. When we can diminish this luggage consisting of desires, then to some extent our journey of life is going to be less troublesome.

48. There are many bulbs with different voltages and different colors. But in all these bulbs there is only one current. Even though we may see many forms, many names, various things in this world, many races, many creeds and many castes in this world, we must know that God is present in all of them, the inner being is in reality only one.

49. Indians must all be united and, through unity, try to safeguard the higher values of Indian culture. India has been a leader and a sacred country which has given spiritual leadership to the entire world for centuries. All the great cultures which have been accepted in other countries originated at some time or other and in some form or other in this sacred land.

50. Money comes and goes, but morality comes and grows.

51. The name of the Lord must dance on your tongues for ever. The Lord's name is like an effulgent lamp.... Your mouth is the main entrance to the house of the body. When you have a lantern at the main gate, the light can be seen without and within, so the sacred flame of the Holy name sheds light inward and outward.

52. Above all, do every act as an offering to the Lord, without being elated by success or dejected by defeat; this gives the poise and equanimity for sailing through the waters of the ocean of life.

53. Remember, Sai does not live in structures of stone or brick and mortar. He lives in soft hearts, warm with sympathy and fragrant with universal love.

54. Consider all your acts as worship. Duty isGod; work is worship. Whatever happens, accept it gladly as His handiwork, a sign of His compassion.

55. God weighs the love that prompts you to save, the compassion that urges you to alleviate pain. Sathya Sai organizations must take up *seva* as *sadhna*, must see Me as *Sarvantaryami* (All-knowing), and do *seva* as *puja*.

56. There is only one caste – the caste of humanity. There is only one language – the language of love. There is only one God – He is omnipresent.

57. You should never underestimate your powers; engage yourselves in action commensurate with that power. For the rest, talk of destiny to your heart's content. It is wrong to desist from the appropriate *Karma*, placing reliance

on destiny. If you do so, even destiny will slip out of your hands. Whoever he be, he must engage himself in *Karma* (action),

58. The Lord will reward by His grace the work that is done sincerely and gladly, not work that is done through fear of superior officers. If your heart is pure, then your work will be pure.

59. Whenever I appear in a dream, it is to communicate something to the individual; it is not a mere dream, as is generally known. It is a real appearance.

60. This Love is My distinctive mark, not the creation of material objects or of health and happiness, by sheer exercise of will. You might consider what you call miracles as the most direct sign of Divinity, but the Love that welcomes you all, that blesses all, that makes Me turn to the presence of the seekers, the suffering and the distressed in distant lands or wherever they are, that is the real sign. It is that which declares that I am Sai Baba.

61. Love lives by giving and forgetting, Self lives by getting and forgetting.

62. Remember, with each act of love and service, you are nearing the Divine presence; with each act of hate and grab, you are moving farther and father away.

63. Cleanse the mind of all the animal and primitive impulses which have shaped it from birth to birth.

64. Calling the Lord's name is essentially beneficial. Only you do not really believe that it can cure you or save you. That is the tragedy.

65. Such is the fate of man: he has always ignored God and pursued the paltry joys of pride and greed.34

66. Why make a sad world sadder by one's desperate counsel, lamentations and suffering? Adopt worship to assuage your own grief, overcome your own sorrow and plunge into the cool waves of the sea of the Grace of God.

67. Devotion is not a uniform to be worn or certain days when you gather for worship and then be laid aside when the service is over. It must mean the promotion of an attitude that is ever present. It is the sustenance of the heart, just as food is sustenance for the body.

68. All the changes are unreal; reality alone is changeless, stable, and permanent.

69. Joy and peace do not exist in external objects; they are in you, in yourself.

70. Culture must be directed towards the reform of character.

71. Wherever my followers sing of Me, there I will install Myself. The Lord is always there and everywhere, whether you sing of Him or not. The singing

only makes Him manifest, as the radio receiver catches the tune from the ether when it is switched on the correct wave length.

72. For the contented man, life is an endless festival.

73. The proof of the rain is in the wetness of the ground, the proof of devotion is in the peace the aspirant has attained.

74. Truth can never die, untruth can never live.

75. It is quite easy to practice 'oneness' while working in an organization. This can be achieved by concentrating one's attention on his work one is doing. One should regard work as Divine. If one regards work as Divine, that work will be transformed into worship. Thus, if one considers his work as an offering to God, he will also be able to attain excellence is work and the results will be favorable. One should identify on oneself with one's own work and should get merged in it.

Sai Baba's Three Commandments

Practice three things: *Ahimsa, Sathyam, Brahmacharya.*

- Remember three things: Death, Pains of *Samsara*(worldly life)and God.
- Remove three things: Egoism, Desire, and Attachment.
- Cultivate three things: Humility, Fearlessness and Patience.
- Eradicate three things: Lust, Anger and greed.
- Love three things: Liberation, The Wise, Selfless and Service.
- Admire three things: Generosity, Courage, and Nobility.
- Hate three things: Lust, Anger and Pride.
- Revere three things: Guru, Renunciation, and Discrimination.
- Control three things: Tongue, Temper, and Tossing of Mind.

Sri Sathya Sai Sadhna Trust, Prasanthiu Nilaram has since ist January,2009been publishing an e newsletter *'Sai Spiritual Showers* 'for free distribution for those who are unaware of Sri Sathya Sai Baba's Spiritual treasure. Spiritual seekers throughout the world may like to be enriched by this unique and immensely beneficial online service.

Chapter - 4

SRI SATYA SAI BABA'S MESSAGE FOR THE 21ST CENTURY – S.P. Ruhela

Sri Sathya Sai Baba, the *Purnavatar* (Integral Incarnation of God) of the age, whom all his devotes lovingly address as 'Swami', has covered the entire gamut of morality religion and spirituality in his countless discourses, messages, teachings and pieces of advice to individual devotees all through the year since he launched his career as Avatar (Incarnation) at the age of 14 in 1940. In the numerous worldwide deliberations of his latest and the most favorite program of 'Sai Educare' lots of things are being mentioned as his significant messages by speakers bubbling with enthusiasm and devotion.

Swami's messages or teachings have by now assumed the shape of a very vast ocean. So it is really difficult as what to select and what to omit out of this vast ocean of his messages when one is asked to make their judicious assessment and clearly state as to what are his salient, radiant or distinctive messages. Based on my over three decades long involvement with the study, research and writing on the Sai movement, I have judiciously come to the conclusion that the following points can be identified as the salient or most distinctive and truly representative messages of our Swami for the new millennium, and they deserve serious attention of and consideration by all Sai devotees and other enlightened inhabitants of the word.

1. The distinction between the worldly life and spiritual life should be done away with, and one should be believe that "All life is spiritual."
2. Love all and serve all. This is the only remedy to eliminate all sorts of hatred, conflicts, tensions, exploitation, wars; suspicion etc. throughout the World Man must try to become superman. Sri Aurobindo had also greatly emphasized this point that man has for a very long period of his existence on his planet been merely 'Animal man'; for some recent centuries he has been claiming to have become 'Man', but this claim is dubious and

unacceptable in view of the widespread *anomie* (norm-less-ness) prevailing in the world. It is high time that man should now actually and seriously strive to become 'Superman' – the sooner he does so, the better it will be for the mankind and the world. Swami seems to be hammering this idea constantly that the functional sort of spirituality for the New Millennium and particularly for the 21ˢᵗ century per se must essentially consist of a genuine commitment to the five foremost universal values – Truth, Righteousness, Peace, Love and Non-violence.

The New Millennium can ill-afford to put up with dishonesty, hypocrisy, jealousies, conflicts, religious and cultural fundamentalism, tendencies of separatism and alienation, violation of norms, laws and rules, crimes exploitation and all kinds of disjunctive social processes which are detrimental to the unity, integration, progress, dignity and moral and spiritual elevation of man. It is necessary for all people in the world to thoroughly understand and intrinsically believe in this fact that sense of security, trust, understanding, unity and purity, commitment to virtues, ideals. Time-tested good traditions, customs and noble precedents also are prerequisites for the future survival of mankind and its progress and advancement in the real sense of these terms. The world has already become a 'global village' and the people of all the nations have became one another's neighbors over-riding the geographical distances and their political territories due to radio, T.V., computer, internet and tremendous and frequent explosions of knowledge and the global urge for peace emerging from the hearts of peace people of the world.

3. Swami has shown us the way, set ideal models of social services and social engineering. Like a teacher educator, he has given model lesson to us to emulate his strategies. His examples, strategies, models, concepts and behavioral attributes as innovator, leader, planner and executor of socio cultural and spiritual projects for the bettering the socio-economic, cultural, moral and spiritual lot of the 21ˢᵗ century mankind should be studied closely, understood, properly assessed and then duly followed by all those social planners, social engineers, cultural and spiritual leaders, innovators and political leaders who have the earnest urge in their hearts to improve the battered and burnished lot of the vast majority of the human beings who are living in conditions worse than those of animals.

The following five major thrusts of Swami must be recalled in this connection:

(i)   He stressed that free medical care to all people who are ill should be made available to them. He has established an excellent Super-Specially Hospital at his Prasanthi Nilayam town in which totally free treatment is given to patients irrespective of their social-cultural backgrounds. Similar Sai Super-Specialty hospital is also functioning at Whitefield.

We know that there are countless very rich people in many countries who are rolling in wealth and squandering on all sorts of super luxuries and debasing vices. They are wasting millions of dollars on their immoral and meaningless pursuits, and many of them just do not know how and where to spend their money on good causes. If their conscience can some how be raised by informing them about the unique models of social service presented by Sri Sathya Sai Baba in South India, surely some of them (if not many) will be most happy to give funds for establishing similar free hospitals for the poor people in their own countries and also in other poor countries. Not only rich people have given and still giving large donations in the forms of funds, machines and costly medicines to Swami's hospitals, many Sai devotees regularly render their voluntary seva (service)in Swami's hospitals with love and dedication.. This exemplary model service can be emulated by those people who cannot afford to donate funds or equipments.

(ii)   Swami holds that free education should be given to all students. In his schools and colleges, this ideal has been put into practice. Only some annual charges for boarding and some other items are taken there.

(iii)   Swami wants that Education in Human Values must be given to all students – not only children in schools but even to adolescents and adult students in colleges and universities. A massive program of education in human values, now renamed as "Sai Educare" is being carried out by dedicated Sai devotees in a number of countries now.

(iv)   Swami greatly stresses on doing social service in villages, slums and poor localities. He has taught us all that service to man is service to God.

(v) Swami has provided drinking water to thousands of villages in Andhra Pradesh by mobilizing contribution from rich people in India and abroad.

4. Swami greatly emphasizes the sanctity and unity of the human family the basic social unit and the first and the foremost agency of socialization of children. The family must be of caring, sharing, loving happy..

5. Swami teaches that one must pay the highest respect to others and offer due courtesy towards all females.

6. Majority of the people Inhabiting our planet are old, and so the future of the world is really in the hands of the youth, who ought to be given due guidance, proper encouragement and opportunities to develop themselves fully and contribute to the nation's unity, progress and advancement and work for global harmony and peace. They should be saved from the currents sadist fads, vices, fashions and all other variants of the sensate culture.

7. Swami does not like ritualism and exploitation of the people in the name of irrational rituals conducted by priestly class. He wants that all diehard, outdated and harmful rituals, customs and practices should be discarded and people all over the world should be educated and sensitized to understand and appreciate the finer attributes and teachings of all religions and schools of spirituality and the emerging concept of Universal Religion for the New Age of the Humanity.

8. The concept of 'Global village' and its synonym 'Sai family' must be put into properly understood and practice actual behavior. All narrow, artificial and dysfunctional differences and conflicting tendencies must be quickly done away with. In the present age of sophisticated satellites, computers, super-industrialization, globalization and the widespread impatience or yearning for the early dawn of the New Age, there is no room for favoritism, discriminations, trade union tactics, corruption, bossism, dictatorship, exploitations and all those things which seek to create frustration, agony to the human mind and to degrade human dignity and deny other' legitimate rights.

9. All sorts of bad habits or vices like drinking, gambling, sexual immorality, economic corruption, exploitation, hypocrisy, destruction of precious natural resources, indecent public behavior, polluting the environment etc. should become be curbed and human beings should be taught to lead healthy, moral and socially accountable lives.

10. Swami's foremost and constant emphasis during the last six decades has been that people must truly become godly, firm believers in the *Karma* theory, *Karma Yogis*, real servants of society and saviors of the ecological balance, and faithful adherents of the ideals of their religion and culture and have patriotism for their country of their birth.

11. Swami has been laying emphasis on believing in God, recitation of God's name, *bhajan*-singing, lovingly rendering selfless service to the helpless and needy people and trying to transform human beings into ideal moral and spiritual personalities. One's liberation can be achieved only by his or her genuine love, sincerity, transparency in character and behavior and adherence to the high values of ethical and spiritual life and doing selfless service to others.

12. Swami once said "We cry when we are born, we cry when die, in between we cry so many times, but do we cry when injustice is done to anyone in society?" This, I think, is the most important message of Swami in the context of today's world. The whole edifice of peace in the world and the very possibility of the dawn of the New Age or New Era in the near future rest on this very premise. Social reform and political cleansing is the crying need of every nation today,

13. The last most significant point discovered by me in the countless messages of our Swami is the message of Optimism. Unlike most of the religious preachers and spiritual gurus who project themselves as the Prophets of Doom, mostly talking of sin, misery, despondency, hell, divine retribution, guilt and the like, Sri Sathya Sai Baba holds before us the vision of optimism. All can and have to enter the *Golden Age* or the, he exhorts us, by following his basic teachings and advice as highlighted above. He exhorts all his devotees and his organizational functionaries to face the challenges of the of the 21st century with firm faith in God as well as in one's own self, and to work with determination, enlightenment, sense of commitment, purity and unity,

Thus not only Sai devotees but all enlightened and objective followers of other spiritual gurus and all earnest inquisitive spiritual seekers who are really concerned about the moral and spiritual elevation of man in the New Millennium can clearly understand and appreciate the distinctive attributes of the Sai utopia of spiritual regeneration of mankind which is possible to attain by following the moral, social service and spiritual leads given your Swami.

Difficulties are bound to be there and they are already there. Intra-organizational cleansing and inter faith collaborations are urgently called for. Mutual jealousies, bossism suspicion towards others and the tendency of considering oneself to be better or holier thant others are found to be there in organizations Let us not be oblivious of the fact that there are so many saints, God men and God women and other Gurus in the world who are also presently engaged in the important task of reforming and elevating the mankind. We all need to respect them as we do our Swami and know how to seek mutual collaboration with them and work for the same noble task.

Chapter - 5

SRI SATHYA SAI BABA'S CONTRIBUTIONS TO MANKIND

On the passing away of the 85 year old Sri Sathya Sai Baba on 24th April, 2011 glowing tributes were paid to Him by many distinguished devotees and personalities all over recalling His teachings and countless selfless humanitarian services. His contributions as *Avatar* are so many and so astounding that it is impossible for anyone to describe them fully. Even then, I as one who has been very fortunatefor being under His divine grace for 39 years i.e., half of my age so far, I wish to recall them very briefly as a devotee and as an objective social scientist who has been observing His mission's activities with a great deal of curiosity.

I would like to mention the following most significant contributions ofthis great spiritual personality whom the great German sociologist Max Weber would have called *'Prop*het', most people call him 'Universal Teacher', and whom billion of His devotees belonging to all races, religions, cultures, and social strata in over 160 nations have been venerating as *Avatar* (Incarnation of God).

1. In all his discourses, writings, interviews granted to countless people and conversations Sri Sathya Sai Baba invariably highlighted the existence and importance of God. He saved people from falling into the trap of the non-believers who have been advocating such misleading theories –' There is no God', 'God is dead', 'In the modern age of great scientific and technological advancements there is no need of God'. He made all people who came in His contact to realize the importance of Vitamin G i.e..taking the name of God to get relief in one's illness and tide over their worldly difficulties. He exhorted all:

   • Make God the foundation of your life, Carry on the normal duties.

Duty is God. Work is worship. Spiritualize all your actions and treat whatever happens to you as actions for your good. Learn to experience perennial bliss in union with God. Never forget God."

- "God permeates the entire universe. God is present in every human being, nay in every living being. The entire creation is the manifestation of Divinity. It is not enough to simply have a human body. As God is present everywhere, in every being, practicing human values are considered to be so sacred and important. Hence, you must cultivate the human values of truth (*Sathya*), righteousness (*Dharma*), peace (*Santhi*), love (*Prema*) and non-violence (*ahimsa*). Never tell a lie under any circumstances. If you adhere to truth, righteousness will follow. Where truth and righteousness go together, there peace will be. Where there is peace, there will be love too. There can be no place for violence when there is love. First and foremost, one has to develop love. 'Love is God, God is Love. Truth is God, God is Truth.' Truth and Love are verily the embodiments of Divinity. (Divine Discourse, 25 December, 2009)."

2. Sathya Sai Baba spread the *Vedantic* philosophy, and succeeded in making the world realize the great importance of the *Vedas, Gita,* and Indian scriptures and the scriptures of their respective religions. 3 He stressed upon the greatest universal values of *Sathya* (Truth), *Dharma* (righteousness*), Shanti* (Peace) and *Prema* (Love) and madethem the basis of all his spiritual and social welfare activities and mega projects for the welfare and uplift of mankind.

3. His greatest contribution was that He convinced millions of people that by only Love and Service one can lead peaceful happy and prosperous worldly life and achieve God realization. *"Love All, Serve All"* and *"Help ever, Hurt Never"* were His two most important messes to the present turbulent, selfish, competitive, heartless mankind whose very survival is threatened. He always advised all to observe ceiling on desires and not to waste, time, money and resources and lead a simple and honest life. He advised all to struggle hard for one's rightful claims remembering God. His words "You cry when you are born and you cry when you die and in between you cry so many times in your life, but do you ever cry when injustice is being done to a helpless creature?"

4. He started the institution of *Seva dal* (Sai Volunteers). He strongly motivated His devotees to render selfless humanitarian service by declaring that wherever they would be doing so, he would be resent be present in his spirit form silently watching, protecting and helping them, This great assurance has always been experienced as true by all Sai devotees who have been rendering services as *Sevadal* for over six decades. Many of them, including the present author, have had personal thrilling experiences how Baba protected them miraculously in the dead of night from likely accidents such as snake bite, sudden illness, disastrous situations, To receive the divine grace of Sai Baba is the basic reason behind the countless devotees rendering *Seva* in innumerable throughout the world. In an illuminating comprehensive article published in *Sananthana Sarathi* some years back were listed as many as 80 ways in which selfless service may be rendered by people in the world.

About 1000 or even more Sai devotee men and women come to Prasanthi Nilayam and many more to other Sai *ashram*s, Sai institutions like hospitals and their sites to serve as *Sevadals* at their own expense. They render all kinds of services li *'Narayan Seva'* (feeding the hungry), medical camps, serving in villages, slum areas, maintaining order, during festivals, educating children, giving blood donations, giving skill training to women of weaker sections of society, planning and running many kinds od services in villages like conducting cattle camps for the rural live stock, providing drinking water and sanitation facilities etc. The Sathya Sai Village integrated Programme (SSSVIP). SSSVIP gives the Seva Dal members the rare opportunity of serving the rural poor through systematic and integrated approach in the areas of Agricare, Educare, Medicare, Sociocare and Spiritual care.

5. Sri Sathya Sai Baba delivered thousands of discourses, wrote as many spiritual books and composed and sang many very enchanting *bhajans*. They are now available on the web site *'Radio Sai' and* anyone can benefit from them any time. The valuable spiritual treasure of His spiritual teachings are available in the issues of the unique free e newsletter 'SAI SPIRITUAL SHOWERS' published by Sri Sathya Sai Sadhna Trust since 1st January, 2009, Sri Sathya Sai Books and Publications Trust(web site *ssbpt,org*) has been bringing out many enlightening books in English and in some Indian languages in the last six decades, Besides them, as many as 41 e books on spiritual

themes have been brought out by them which may be had from Amazon and Smashwords, or writing to the *ssbpt,org* web site.. The Audio-visual wing of Sri Sathya Sai Sadhana Trust has brought ou for sale a number of CDs of Sai *Bhajans* and VCDs of *bhajans,* dances, dramas and festive celebrations which can be had by ordering to their e mail address *bpt.org*. The images of Sri Sathya Sai Baba may be purchased online from the website *'saireflections,org* by' anyone throughout the world. All these materials are the unique invaluable everlasting spiritual contributions of Sai Baba Trusts to the world in order to globally spread spirituality in the present *Kali Yuga* (Age of Kali 7). As the harbinger of the New Age of mankind Sri Sathya sai Baba had started worldwide spiritual movement or revolution any decades back He had launched it by publicly declaring as under:

"A revolution more powerful and pervasive than any man has undergone so far neither political, economic, scientific and technological, but deeper and more basic is now. It is the a Spiritual revolution. It sharpens the inner vision of man so that he can see his *atamic* reality. Its impact will surely develop and enrich all communities and transform mankind into a stream of *sadhn*a flowing smoothly to the limitless sea of humanity. The Revolution of love is both means and end. It will awaken the springs of love all over the world in the field of Education, Morality, Law, Politics, Commerce and Science. It will inspire man to loving service, revealing the Brotherhood of and the Fatherhood of God."

Prof. N. Kasturi, His biographer, secretary, closest devotee and founding editor of *Sanathana Sarathi* had in his book *'Loving God'* (1982) wrote: 'So long as human beings have spiritual hunger and faith in the divinity of God, Prophets and incarnations of God, such a unique spiritual and moral variant of social movement is bound to grow and enlighten mankind.'

In 1990s I had prepared an analytical sociological research paper on Sri Sathya Sai Spiritual Movement. I then gave a seminar on this theme in the Department of Sociology, Faculty of Humanities and Social Sciences, Indian Institute of Technology, That research paper was later on published in my books *'Sri Sathya Sai Spiritual Movement'* (1984) and *'Sri Sathya Sai Spiritual Revolution* (200::ISBN:-1-7341-193-570). I had analyzed this spiritual movement in this paradigm:

(i)   Genesis of the movement

(ii)   Its Ideology

(iii)   Its social base

(iv)   Its organization and leadership

(v)   The career of the movement

(vi)   The significance of the movement t

(vii) Social control

(viii) Impact

(ix)   The future

In that paper I had in 1994 observed:

'The impact of tie movement is visible now from many other things. This has led to the emergence of Sai community based on the ideals of the family of mankind, recognizing no barriers of sex, community, caste, country, class or profession. The movement has given a great impetus to the growth of a global interest and participation in cultural and spiritual renaissance taking place in India under the leadership of Sri Sathya Sai Baba. This movement has opened up great vistas of social reform giving perfectly equal status to women in religious and social matters, by derecognizing social stratifications, promoting dowry-less, interclass and inter-community marriages and cutting the roots of superstitions diehard rituals and bigotry.'

After Sri Sathya Sai Baba's taking *Maha Samadhi* in 2011 great Sai devotees Indu Lal Shah and Sarla Shah in their masterpiece article 'Sarvam, Sathyam Jagat', published in *Sanathana Sarathi* have written thus:

'SILENT SPIRITUAL REVOLUTION

'We have known revolutions in politics, social and economic fields and even revolutions in art and culture but not a spiritual revolution, signifying complete transformation or overhaul of an existing order in a given society. We, living in this era are most blessed to witness the Spiritual Revolution whichistaking place for the first time in the history of mankind..

"Revolution" is the most apt word for the phenomenal self-employment and professional opportunities to the inhabitants......No title or prize on the earth can glorify Bhagavan's contribution to humanity. Therefore, the people have given Him the title recognizing Him as *Avatar*, the redeemer of mankind right from His school days.',

The authors have reminded all Sai devotees and active Instrumentschosen by Swami (organizers of all Sathya Sai institutions, Sathya Sai Seva Organizations in India and abroad, office bearers of alladministrative units and trustees to keep in mind while carrying out His mission..

"…….Swami has left His physical body only. But He is still there as a Supreme Divine Spirit watching everything from His *Maha Samadhi* and constantly witnessing every act or omission committed by us or every word spoken by us or thought encouraged by us, or any plot or design structured by us,'

2. Sri Sathya Sai Baba launched a number of important social service projects for the manity, most important and widely known all over the Sai world are the following. Information about them is available to the public throughout the world from their web sites of Wikipedia –the free encyclopedia, Sri Sathya Sai Central Trust. Sri Sathya Sai Sadhana Trust, Sri Sathya Sai International Trust, and the websites of these projects and from *Sanathana Sarathi* - monthly journal of Sri Sathya Sai Sadhana Trust, and reports on these projects.

Important sources of information; Web sites:

Sri Sai Central Trust –Wikipedia, the free encyclopedia *httpl/en.wikipdia.org/ wiki/Sri Sathya Sai Central Trust.*

Sri Sathya Sai Central Trust
www,srisathyasai.org.in

Sri Sathya Sai Sadhanana Trust Publications Division
www,sssbpt.org

Sanathana Sarathi
www.sanathanasarathi.org
editor@sssbpt.org
Bhagavan's photos on line
www.saireflections.orgonline
Bal Vikas Wing of Sri Sathya Sai Organization, India
httpl/sssbalkvikas.org
Sri Sathya Sai Eswaramma Women's Welfare Trust
www.ewwt.org.in
Sri Sathya Sai Iinstition of Higher Learning; For Employment opportunitiesd

registrar@sssihl.edu.in
sssihl.edu.in
Radio Sai Global Harmony
ww.radio.sai.org
www.:// srisathyasai.org/Annnouncement/ress relwase
Press Release on 23 May 2013- Sri Sathya Sai Central Trust PressRelease
23May2012.htm
Sathya Sai Disaster Services
sathyasai humanitarian relief.org
www.sathysaihumanirarian.
News and activities of Sri Sathya Sai Organization of Australia and PNG;
Report of disaster services by Australian devotees
http;//saiauistralia.org.au/.au/.allinks.html

Full report on Haiti Earthquake Relief by Sai devotees is available on Haiti Earthquake Relief Website. Sathya Sai International Organization volunteers were the first NGOs to reach HAITI \after the serious earthquake there on 12 January,2010.

- Service Wing, Sri Sathya Sai Seva, Organization, Delhi-NCR
- Uttarakhnd Disaster Status Report from Sri Sathya Sai *Seva* (13 July, 2013)

http://htttp://media//.,radiosai.or/journal/vol Uttarakhand-Disaster -Sri Sathya-Sai-Seva-
Status Report from Sri Sathya Sai Sava
Relief to the Poor —Sri Sathya Sai Central Trust(January 2001, Bhuj (Gujrat) earthquake
www.srisathyasaI.org,in/Pages./Projects/Reliefpoor

Sai System of Education

Sri Sathya Sai developed his unique system of education in the modern world which is a healthy amalgamation of the ancient Indian Vedic *Ashram* type system of education and the best of the educational practices of the modern age of democracy, science, technology, fast expanding frontiers of knowledge focused on the demands of the future of mankind and the survival of our planet.

In my research article' The Educational Theory of Sri Sathya Sai Baba'published in *University News* and my book *"Sai System of Education and the World Crisis"*(1996) I had analyzed this system and found it to be based on following eleven philosophical postulates of Sri Sathya Sai Baba:

1. Belief in the existence of One God who is mniporesent, Omnipotrnt sand omniscient,
2. Equality and unity of all people of the world on the basis of the principle of oneness of *Atma*.
3. Brotherhood of man abd Fatherhood of God.
4. Universal values of truth, righteousness, peace and love.
5. Spiritual elevation is the supreme goal of human life,6. Fusion of the modern knowledge of science and technology with the spiritual knowledge and moral and cultural traditions of of India which us the Guru of the world.
6. Secularization, Liberalization and Humanization
7. Unity of all religions and faiths; there us only oie religion – the Religion of love.
8. Free the human soul and mind from all kinds of irrational, diehard hackneyed, dysfunctional customs, rituals, systems, practices and bondages,
9. Man should follow the *Atma Dharma* not merely his *Swadharma*and *Paradharma*; he should behave morally, lovingly and conscientiously in the spirit of universal humanism and altruism.
10. Modern time is the most important among the past, present and future times.

Sri Sathya Sai Baba's educational theory is the combination of the philosophies of Idealism, Pragmatism, Reconstructionism and futurism. Idealism is the base and the prominent constituent of it. His educational philosophy being so dynamic, functional and potent, all his educational projects are firmly based on it and do ty are being very much appreciated worldwide. It may be recalled that on 20-22 July.,2008 Sri *'Sathya Sai World Education Conference'* was held at Prasanthi Nilayam in which as many as 99 educational experts from all over the world participated and they highly endorsed the Sai System of Education. The proceedings and the report of that very important educational conference in the first decade of the 21ˢᵗ century are available online.

❖ SRI SATHYA SAI EDUCATION PROJECTS:

1. **Education in Human Values** (EHV)

Sri Sathya Sai Baba laid utmost stress on Education in Human Values right from the beginning of His mission. The most important values emphasized by Him are Truth, Righteousness, Peace and Love. All values are covered in these four. He said that the three most important things in life are: (1) Love for God,(2) Fear of sin, and (3) Morality in society, All education –informal as well as formal should be develop them.

2. *Bal Vikas* (Informal Education)

He started this very important and fundamental informal system of education for devotees' children and adolescents to be carried out voluntarily with love and devotion by enlightened selfless devotees *"Bal Vikas Gurus'* in their houses They should teach *slokas, mantras,* prayers, hymns, religious songs, stories, lives of great saints and other ideal personalities, motherland, culture, religion and goood things ofc life lay the foundation of good character in boys and girls. This movement has spread in all those countries live. *Bal Vikas* places high ideals before parents and transform their lives as well. It is being appreciated in all countries. Informal weekend classes in human values known as *Bal Vikas* or Sai Spiritual Education (SSE) are being conducted in in 15,300 centers in India and in 81 foreign countries. education. The current global enrolment in this programme is said to be about half a million.

SSE or *Bal Vikas* is the brainchild of universal teacher, Bhagavan Baba, whose vision of education goes beyond more eradication of illiteracy or acquisition of degrees. Defining noble character as the desired end of education, Baba stresses education must equip the learner for life and not merely for a earning a living. For the past 42 years, he has been filling the vacuum in the education system not just in India but also around the world through a well-designed strategy, with SSE as the delivery medium. The Sai education module celebrates universal spirituality, promoting love and respect for all faiths by focusing on their universal values. The five human values of Truth,

Right Conduct, Peace, Love, and Nonviolence are elicited through lessons based on the interactive teaching techniques such as stories, songs, prayers, or quotations, silent sitting, and games or group activities. Conducted for children 5-13 years, the 9-year program is divided into three groups, each with 3 sub-levels. Upon graduation, young adults enter the society as mature and balanced agents of positive change.

Pointing to the program's lasting success, its National Joint Coordinator Mrs. Vidya Srinivasan, says "Even years after graduating, wherever our students go, they stand out in a crowd due to their radiant personality and the way they conduct themselves. In many places, a SSE diploma is seen as an edge by employers, for it tells them something positive about the person's moral fibre."

Formal Education:

(i). Sri Sathya Sai Institute of Higher Learning (SSSIHL) This 'Deemed University has four campuses:
   - Post Graduate College. Prasanthi Nilayam (A.P.)
   - Sri Sathya Sai College for Women, Anantapur((A.P.)
(3) Sri Sathya Sai College, Whitefield, Bangalore /Bangaluru.(Karnataka)(4) Sri Sathya Sai College, Madanhalli (Karnataka)
Thre are two more Sai colleges in other states not affiliated with SSSIHL
   (1) Sri Sathya Sai Collge, Whitefield, Bangalore /Bangaluru.(Karnataka)
   (2) Eshwaramma College for Women, Jaipur (Rajasthan)
   - Sri Sai Mirpuri _Music College, Prasanthi Nilayam

Institutes of Sathya Sai Education were established to manage and oversee standards in the Sathya Sai Schools, to train teachers in Education in Human Values (EHV) and to form professional links (or partnerships) with government or private schools for EHV. They have the task of developing EHV programmes appropriate to their local culture, to create awareness and guide government schools to establish such programmes. The question arises as to what extent the Sathya Sai Schools and Institutes have succeeded in their avowed aims and objectives

- Sri Sathya Sai Institute of Education, Mumbai
Srii Sathya Sai Institute of Education, Australia

Schools;

There are 99 full time Sri Sathya Sai Schools in India and 41 Sathya Sai Schools globally follow this model of learning.

<u>Non-Formal Education:</u> Recent Innovative Project:
<u>Vidhya Vahini Project</u>

On His 85th birthday, Sai Baba inaugurated Sri Sathya Sai Vidya Vahini Project of education using web-based tools to enhance the learning for children in rural and slum. This brings together modern cutting-edge technology, value based learning, secular curriculum and teacher training under one umbrella. A partnership between the Sri Sathya Sai Central Trust, Tata Consultancy Services and school boards across the country, *Vidya Vahin*i allies several different strategies to meet the educational needs millions of Indian children deprived of this basic right.

It is programmed to achieve aspect of cognitive thinking, motivation and empowered action by utilizing technology to driver a synthesis of value-based education and curriculum. Methods of teaching include the articulation and expression of values in core subjects (cognitive thinking), the conscious involvement of teachers in exemplifying the value (motivation), and the all-inclusive participation of students in service-based project (empowered action). <u>Web Sites:</u>

<u>http://sri</u> sathyasaividhyavahini.org
<u>http://sri</u> sathyasaividhyavahini.org
<u>http://www,youtube.com/watch*\3FV%3D9Ha4gosjRR\fU</u>
Vidhys Vahini Project Service Wing, Sri Sathya Sai Seva, Organization, Delhi-NCR

Sri Sathya Sai Vidhya Vahini -An overview – Satyajit Saliban- YouTube
<u>http://wwwtoutube.com/watch%3fV%3DfQyUw6O0-1i</u>http://www.
<u>thgeprasanthireporterr.org/2012/08/sri_sathyasaividhtyavahini-soraig-high/</u>
<u>sri</u> -sathya-sai-vidhya-vahini-
<u>http://sri</u> sathyasaividhyavahini.org
<u>http://sri</u> sathyasaividhyavahini.org
<u>http://www.youtube.com/watch*\3FV%3D9Ha4gosjRR\fU</u>
Sri Sathya Sai Vidhya Vahini -An overview – Satyajit Saliban- YouTube
<u>http://wwwtoutube.com/watch%3fV%3DfQyUw6O0-1i</u>

http://www.thgeprasanthirepoorterr.org/2012/08/ssat\ahyasaividhtyavahini-
soraig-high/sri -sathya-sai-vidhya-vahini-soaring-hig/h.org
http://sri sathyasaividhyavahini.org
http://sri sathyasaividhyavahini.org
http://www.youtube.com/watch*\3FV%3D9Ha4gosjRR\fUSri Sathya Sai
Vidhya Vahini -An overview – Satyajit Saliban-
ouTubehttp://wwwtoutube.com/watch%3fV%3DfQyUw6O-1i
http://www.theprasanthirepoorterr.org/2012/08/srisathyasaividhtyavahini-
soraig-high/sri -sathya-sai-vidhya-vahini-soaring-hig/h.org SERVICES
-

4. Sri Sathya Sai General Hospital. Whitefield. It provides these services-
Out Patient Department, Admissions (Inpatients), Deliveries,,DBG/
Gneiss Surgeries). It does four kinds of surgical Processes – General Surgeries,
ENT Operations, Opthmology. Surgeries, Orthopedic Surgeries and Urology
Surgeries, Minor Surgeries, and Dental Surgeries

5. Sri Sathya Sai Mobile Hospital Project
This yet another of Sai Baba's loving and innovative initiatives to holistic
healthcare to poor villag SSS Mobile Hospital

6. Sai Mobile Hospital is a unique and free rural outreach holistic health
service launched on March 30th 2006 by Bhagavan Baba. A unit of the SSS
Medical Trust, it operates from the 1st to 12th of every month at 12 base villages
to each of which are attached another 6 villages. In practice however, patients
are drawn from nearly 400 villages.
The hospital-on-wheels is managed almost entirely on voluntary basis. Five
hundred doctors from the state of Andhra Pradesh belonging to 12 specialties
serve in rotation. This diagnostic bus comes equipped with an ultra sonogram,
x-ray plant with automatic processor and a laboratory which can perform most
of the pathological and bio-chemical investigations.
Given the program's outreach, its larger agenda is based on a triangular
approach of Curative thrust, Preventive focus and Spiritual base.
The curative thrust owes its strength to the presence of specialists belonging
to Radiology Medicine, Surgery, Orthopedics, ENT, Dentistry, Ophthalmology,
Gynecology & Pediatrics on any given day. They work under a common roof

integrating their efforts to solve many an intricate problem. Six hundred to seven hundred patients are seen every day at each of the nodal points.

The curative work is further strengthened by * pharmacy which ensures that parents with chronic ailments like epilepsy, diabetes, hypertension, heart disease and asthma are provided with continuous and uninterrupted supply of medicines (one month's worth till the next visit).

Patients requiring follow-up treatment like surgical intervention are referred to Baba's Super Specialty hospitals and their problems are monitored till the logical solutions are arrived.

On the diagnostic front, for the few tests that cannot be undertaken on the bus, the team has an innovative system in place. Samples are collected and delivered to the SSS Super Specialty Hospital for testing and reporting.

The preventive work consists of health education based on five major themes: cleanliness, nutrition, healthy air and water, harmful effects of smoking and alcoholism, proper physical exercise and mind relaxation.

Education on these subjects is offered through audiovisual presentations, demonstrative sessions, interactive meets and photo exhibition. It is further reinforced by regular screening through the local cable television.

The spiritual base of the service involves educating and motivating the villagers on the importance of positive thinking, human values and age-old practices like prayer and meditation all of which foster positive health.

With this holistic strategy, ninety percent of community's health problems are solved because the approach is professional, proactive and integrated and takes care of common ailments, chronic ailments, preventive ailments, asymptomatic diseases and endemic diseases. Only problems requiring major surgical intervention are referred to the base hospitals.

The impact of the service is tremendous. On the curative front it has given a sense of great security to people living in hundreds of villages around Puttaparthi. It is a boon for patients with chronic ailments who can never dream of buying medicines on a continuous basis. The preventive services have created a huge wave of awareness on major health issues, thereby translating into positive lifestyle changes. The spiritual component of the service has strengthened the community bonds, reviving the practice of human values as a way of life for achieving health and happiness.

ers at their doors in Andhra Pradesh and Maharastra states,

7. **Sai Sanjeevani Project**: It being conducted free of cost by a group of eminent Sai devotee doctors at Whitefieks. Recently details about it have been available on the Internet on the **N.ANANTHRAMARAMESH'nananthram esh@yahoo.co.in [saibabanews]** saibabanews@yahoogroups.com <u>via</u> returns. groups.yahoo.com

> Dr. Narayana Murthy, an Anesthetist, who has made it his life's mission to serve in Swami's institutions, has done so for over 20 years in the Sathya Sai General Hospital, Whitefield, Bangalore. A man who believes his greatest achievement was to be an "instrument in Sai's hands" was moved by the work being done at Sai Sanjeevani and has graciously given us his thoughts.

> We were happy to host eminent doctors, Dr. Vinit Shah (Pediatric Cardiologist, London), Dr. V. M Kurian (Senior Cardiovascular Surgeon, Madras Medical Mission, Chennai) and Dr. Krishna Prasad (MD Emergency Medicine, Aurora Health Care, Wisconsin). Dr. Kurian & Dr. Krishna Prasad have been dear friends of Dr. Krishna Manohar (Chief Surgeon, Sai Sanjeevani) for 40 years. They were happy and proud to see their best friend here. A Special thanks to Dr. Ramani (Managing Director and Trustee of Sankara Eye), Shri. Vimal Golchha (Director, Corporate Affairs Hira Power and Steels Ltd), Shri. Jitendra Barlota (General Secretary Chhattisgarh Chamber of Commerce and Industry) and Shri. Abhas Joshi (playback singer and AMUL STAR Voice of India) for visiting us this month.

> Do continue to stay in touch. We sincerely value it.

> -- Your Sai Sanjeevani Team

Our Work   **Out-Patient Services**

Surgeries

683 surgeries have been conducted in Sai SanjeLevani so far. Of these, **458** were pediatric cardiac surgeries. **46** pediatric cardiac surgeries were conducted in December, 2014

Accrding to their own publlished report on the Interner, seen accessed by us on 13 Januar,2015, the details of their recent contruibtioon is under:

273 outpatient registrations were recorded during the month - **103** new pediatric cases, **32** adult cardiac consultations and **138** revisit pediatric cases.

Out of a total of **241** ECHOs performed this month, **103** are new pediatric cases as shown in the table below. Also **64** pre-operative and post-operative inpatient screenings, **42** revisit and **32** medical follow up ECHOs were performed.

Surgeries - December 2014

Our Work   **Out-Patient Services**

Surgeries

683 surgeries have been conducted in Sai Sanjeevani so far. Of these, **458** were pediatric cardiac surgeries. **46** pediatric cardiac surgeries were conducted in December, 2014

273 outpatient registrations were recorded during the month - **103** new pediatric cases, **32** adult cardiac consultations and **138** revisit pediatric cases.
Out of a total of **241** ECHOs performed this month, **103** are new pediatric cases as shown in the table below. Also **64** pre-operative and post-operative inpatient screenings, **42** revisit and **32** medical follow up ECHOs were performed.

---

8. Healthcare in Africa:

Disease prevention has been a major focus of the Sai Organization in all its medical work. Sai Organization in Africa, Indonesia, Laos and India have distributed mosquito nets impregnated with insecticide in malaria endemic areas. Over 85,000 nets have been distributed in Kenya alone, reducing the incidence of malaria by more than 50 percent. Also, mass immunization, environmental hygiene and education in healthy living through lifestyle changes are an integral part of such preventive health programmes.

Africa carries up to 90% of the global malaria burden, one of the biggest health concerns in the recent years. Over a million children die from the disease every year in sub-Saharan Africa, while 34,000 of them are from Kenya which has over 8.2 million malaria cases each year. In 2005, the Sathya Sai Organization in Africa collaborated with the government of Kenya to distribute the insecticide-treated nets free of charge to the most vulnerable communities. They distributed the 'Sai nets' directly to the users, cutting out middlemen, emphasized on the spread of preventive awareness, and held periodic follow-ups and checks.

A join study done by the Kenya Health Department and University of Nairobi revealed that the number of malaria incidence had dropped by over 50% in areas where Sai Nets were distributed. Since the success of the first project, the Malaria Control Programme of Kenya has requested the volunteers to undertake many such distribution projects in all major malaria-endemic regions of the country.

❖ WATER PROJECTSs:

Rayalaseema region in which Puttaparthi is located is drought-prone area. Scarcity of water was not the only problem; there was excess of fluoride in water which caused diseases and deformations in those who drank it. Looking at the magnitude of the problem, successive governments could not devise any scheme to solve it even after five decades of Independence; God is the refuge of those who have no other refuge. Seeing the sad plight of refugeless millions, Bhagavan took up Anantapur Water Project in March 1995 and completed it in a record period of 18 months, bring relief to a population of 9.5 million. The then Prime Minister of India P.V. Narasimha Rao inaugurated the first phase of the project in a grand function at Prasanthi NIlayam on 18th November 1995. Citing the example of this project in their Ninth Five Year Plan document, the Government of India started. "...Sri Sathya Sai Trust has set an unparalleled example of private initiative in implementing a project on their own, without any State's budgetary support, a massive water supply project, with an expenditure of Rs. 3,000 million to benefit 731 scarcity and fluoride/salinity-affected villages and a few towns in Anantapur district of Andhra Pradesh in a time frame of about 18 months". On 23rd November 1999, the Government of India released a postage stamp and a postal cover in recognition of the pioneering service rendered by Bhagavan Sri Sathya Sai Baba by providing safe drinking water to the rural masses.

Bhagavan's subsequent water project provided water to 320 villages of Medak and Mahaboobnagar district, and 220villages of East and West Godavari districts of Andhra Pradesh. These water projects benefited a total population of 18 million people of nearly 1,500 villages. Chennai Water Supply Project which provided water to the residents of this metropolitan city and fulfilled their long-felt need was another great need of water.

Sri Sathya Sai
Drinking Water Supply Projects

to Intl Sai Org

Sathya Sai Baba's project, begun in 1994, which brought water to more than 700 villages in the the Indian state of Andhra Pradesh (where Prashanthi Nilayam is located). This project was directed by the Sri Sathya Sai Central Trust and carried out by Larsen & Toubro Limited, with the collaboration of the Government of Andhra Pradesh. The project cost over U.S. $63 million, which was donated to the Sri Sathya Sai Central Trust without any kind of solicitation.

For the moment, here are some statistics on the project.

Project highlights

No. of villages covered	750
Population covered	900,000
Design population	1,250,000
Project cost	US$63 million

Construction highlights

Main trunk lines	750 Km
Branch lines	1550 Km
Overhead service reservoirs (40,000-300,000 liter capacity)	268
Ground-level service reservoirs (20,000-60,000 liter capacity)	125
Ground-level balancing reservoirs (100,000-1,000,000 liter capacity)	21
Booster stations	40
Summer storage tanks (60 acres)	4
Summer storage tanks (32 acres)	3
Infiltration wells	13
Bore wells	250

Chapter - 6 (i)

Lord of Miracles

Dr. S. Bhagvantham

I have a background of science. How I reconcile this with what Bhagavan Shri Sathya Sai Baba does is a question which has troubled me much. I will relate a few things, which I hope will furnish some kind of an answer to it. It is only my personal experience. It does not mean that every rational person, or every other agnostic will go through the same process.

It is a phenomenon with Baba that each person who goes to His ashram does not go through the same process as other i.e., some take one year or two years to reconcile themselves to the situation that in Baba there is something different from ordinary persons. For some it happens in two minutes. I have seen confirmed atheists come there be chance, spend ten or fifteen minutes, and come out completely changed. The main point I want to say is, do not think that my experience, and my my way of thinking, is identical with anyone else. I have seen miracles performed by Baba, perhaps in thousands, my long association with Him has brought me to a position where I do not attach much importance to the miracles. But for a new person who goes to Him, it is different. Nine out of ten, they are attracted by some and then begin to ask, how does this happen? They start thinking, "I cannot do it, Baba is doing it, so Baba is different from me." Then they conclude, "Others cannot do it, so Baba is different from others." Going a little further "Nobody can do it. Baba is doing it, therefore, Baba is different from anybody else."

I will narrate one or two miracles which had some significance in my own evolution, but I want to say that I have reached a stage where I have come to regard that the performance of miracles is not the best side of Baba. There is something very much deeper and very much more significant which we must know.

Let me return to the fact that I am a scientist, and have a rational way of thinking, This incident which I will narrate to you relates to several years ago, when I was very proud o be a scientist. It was just by chance tha I came in contact with Baba. Somebody told me that he is a Divine person. I must caution here scientists, who think that Science means learning a discipline such as physics or chemistry, and anything else are not worth heeding. This shows a closed mind which is very contrary of what science teaches. Science teaches that you should not have prejudice, that you should not come to a judgement before you apply your own mind to decide something. Unfortunately, many people who are half-learned come to a judgment either by using some logic, or by using somebody else's experience, without knowing and going through the matter themselves. This is very unscientific.

In March/April 1972, when Bhagavan was in Delhi, there was no place to move for about a couple of miles around the place where He was staying. This is new. Fifteen years ago it was not like that. There were only about a hundred people one evening with Him and He said, "Shall we go for a walk?" and we walked down into Chitravati river adjoining His ashram.

We sat down on the sand. He started provoking me saying that all scientists are atheists, and all scientists want everything demonstrated before they can believe it. They ask, "Is there God?" They want to see God, they cannot see God, they say there is no God. This is what we call conjunction. Unless they see something, they do not believe it. And you also like that. Don't you believe in God? Don't you believe in Divinity? Don't you believe in our tradition and our scriptures?"

I told him, "Baba, one does not even have to learn anything to become an atheist. There are many people who are ignorant, who are not learned and who do not believe in God. There are many who are learned, and the more learned you get, the more unbelieving you become. Many people believe in God. I come from a family of good tradition. My father and grandfather were all Sanskritists; they believed in God, yet on account of modern trends, I have learnt science to earn my living. Although I cannot say that I am a very religious man, yet you should not conclude that I do not believe in God."

I narrated the story of a distinguished American scientist, Oppenheimer, who discovered the first Atom bomb. I told him that when the first nuclear explosion occurred, Oppenheimer was asked what he thought of the nuclear explosion and it is on record that Oppenheimer quoted a verse from the Bhagvad Gita. He said that the brilliance was such that it could only be described in the language used by Arjuna when he had the manifestation of the Lord. Arjuna described it by saying that the brightness is as if there were one thousand suns shining in the sky.

I said, "If an American can quote an Indian text at the height of his scientific attainment, why do you think I, an Indian of a traditional family, do not respect Indian traditions and text?"

I narrate this to show that the conversation has been set by me, the place where we sat was decided by me, and the idea of *Bhagvad Gita* was brought into conversation by me. Then He said: "Oh I see. So you believe in Bhagvad Gita, and you, a scientist, respect *Bhagvad Gita*, read *Bhagvad Gita*."

Again, the rational in me asserted itself, and I said, "Of course I respect, of course I read it, but I will read only when I want to."

There were a hundred people sitting there and He lifted a handful of sand with both hands and asked me to stretch out my hand and He put the sand into my hands and under my very eyes it turned into a small text of the *Bhagvad Gita*. You can see by the sequence of events that I chose the place. I say because it could not have happened that someone planted the *Bhagvad Gita* in the sands. I brought the conversation about the *Bhagvad Gita*.

The rational in me said if it is a printed text, it must be printed in some press. I immediately asked Baba, "Baba, you said that it is a printed text of *Bhagvad Gita*. Where has it been printed?"

I said this in the hope that I would be creating a small problem for Him. The man who was greatly disturbed was myself and the one who was completely undisturbed and was enjoying the conversation was Baba. He smiled and said, "Yes, it has been printed in the Sai Press." He further remarked "Well, Bhagavantam, I would like to know what science has got to say about it. In fact, it cannot say anything about what has happened."

People used to think that Baba favors some persons in authority, and I think among these hundred people there must have been four or five who thought that this gentleman is the Director of the Institute, he has got position, and therefore, Baba is favouring Him, with this gift of *Bhagvad Gita*. Some young man asked Bhagavan, "Can I also have a *Bhagvad Gita*." Bhagavan answered, "Yes, You can pay four annas and buy it in Bangalore."

But I cannot forget his calling on a very ordinary looking person who did not have even a shirt to wear. He was sitting in the group. He called him by name and that poor man was most surprised to be called by name. He told him: "Oh man, you are very poor, you have come here, you have been seen sitting under the tree in my ashram for the past four days. You are a devotee of

Harnath Baba and Kusum Kumari. You have been going around begging for money as you want to build a temple for Harnath Baba in your village." All this was true. "You have come here to ask me for a donation to build the temple." He gave long lecture to him. He said "This is very wrong. God is in every one of us. God is in you. Why do you go in search of God? Temples should not be built. Particularly, you should not ask for temples to be built. Do not do this. Go back home and I will give you an image of Harnath Baba. Put it in your own *puja* room and worship him, but do not build a temple. God does not live in temples unless he lives in your own heart." He gave him a long lecture, as He would give to any devotee. But I was still thinking of the *Bhagvad Gita*. He must have brought it here and given it to me, I thought.

To teach me a lesson what He did was this. This individual was wearing a badge on which there were Harnath Baba and Kusum Kumari, because he was collecting money for building a temple. Bhagavan lifted again some sand, and that became a silver image of Harnath Baba and Kusum Kumari, and first He gave it to me. He said, "I have done it for my friend and you have a look at it." I had a look at the badge. It was an identical replica of the badge which he was wearing. I even found that on Kusum Kumari the badge contained a round red tilak (mark), a symbol of womanhood and there was a red *tilak* on the face of the silver image produced.

He knew that I would examine every detail to see whether He had produced a replica or had brought Kusum Kumari's image from somewhere. He knew that. So, I satisfied myself that in every detail it was a complete reproduction of the badge which the poor man was wearing. He looked at me, smiled and asked, "Are you satisfied? Has science got to say anything about it?"

Then He took it from me and He gave it to the poor man.

This again demonstrates that in the presence of divinity, position and authority do not count, poverty and riches do not count. It is only devotion and the grace of God that counts. And if He chooses, He will certainly give this grace to a man of position as well as to a man who does not count at all. He told him, "Do not beg for money. Begging is not good. Do not search for God. God is in your home. Go back, put it in your puja room and worship it," and so on. This was one of several occasions when He said to me, "What has science to say about this?"

This went on year after year. One day we were sitting on the shores of Cape Comerin (Kanya Kumari). On the sea shore there were about twenty people around Him. He was playing with the water in the sea. He was asking some people how we address the ocean. One young man said that the ocean is called 'Ratnakara'. Then He commented "If it is called *Ratnakara,* it must contain *ratnas* or diamonds, and the ocean should give us diamonds." I said, "Yes Baba, if you wish. You can get diamonds." The people present wanted to see how He was going to get diamonds "from the ocean." "Oh, yes," He said, in His *leela,* in a childish way, and took a hand full of water from the ocean, and the water became a beautiful little diamond necklace in His hands. He showed it to me and said, "What shall we do with it?"

Even then I could see that the production of the necklace itself was pretty difficult. When He asked what should be done with it, I noticed that the necklace was a small one, and as He has a big head I thought I should ask him to wear it. Then He said "Oh, I see, I should wear it." Then he held the necklace tight in His hand. It became a bigger necklace and He put it around His head and looked at me and said, "Well I have worn it."

I can relate several such incidents at the end of which He was generous enough to recognize that I have this conflict in me of trying to reconcile two opposing points of view. This went on for three years, and at the end of the three years, at a public meeting in Madras, where there were more than 10,000 people present, I was forced to admit that as a man of science I tried to find a rational and logical explanation for all that I had seen, but I had failed. There are many things which science cannot explain, things which are beyond science. Bhagavan Sathya Sai Baba is not subject to the ordinary laws of science. He is beyond science and what He does cannot be explained by normal means. Thereafter He stopped performing miracles for me.

Science, which has tremendous amount of logic, and is very useful has its limitations. It deals with things which relate to your five senses of perception, but there are many things which do not come under the purview of the normal senses of perception, such as emotion or intuition. If a man comes and says, "I feel that the grace of God has saved me from a catastrophe," a scientist can only throw up his hands in despair and say, "I do not understand."

Another interesting facet of Baba is his ability to be present at different places at the same time. Physical presence is something which I cannot really describe. I can explain history, but divinity cannot be explained. The few who have had personal experience of being in the presence of Bhagavan Sri Sathya Sai Baba know that there can never be a substitute for experiencing divinity directly with Bhagavan Baba. I say this because I have had a chance of talking to a number of people, and they are so immensely happy. Some of the young people come out and say that they have never seen anyone including their own mother and father or their families, expressing so much affection and in such a way. This cannot be expressed. It can only be experienced. These days all our leaders – political, social and religious go on the platform and preach so many things which they themselves do not practise.

The other extraordinary quality which Baba possesses is his enormous patience in dealing with the problems of people. On an average He sees at least two hundred people per day. I have verified that the two hundredth man is as happy as the first man and hundred and ninety-nine people, and has specially spent a little more time with him. This is not humanly possible. This can only be a quality of divinity. On festival days there are more than 50,000 people and quite a few are aged and sick. Yet, Baba never suffers by seeing pain or delights in seeing success. He is tranquil and steady; nothing affects Him. You can see Him smiling at the end of a hard day's work. He preaches *Karma* Yoga. He preaches Action. He preaches that you should work hard and do your duty, as work is worship and duty is God.

IN THE ALTAR OF YOUR HEART

Prof. N. Kasturi

"Who am I?" asked Sri Sathya Sai Baba once in a letter and answered, "I am yours," "What is mine?" He continued, and answered, "You." "Where do I reside?" was the next question, and His reply was, "In the altar of your heart." "Where do I cast my glance?" "All round." "What is my task?" was the last of the questions and the answer He gave was, "To help the devotees to live happily and guide them along the path of liberation till they attain the Goal." Those who have known Baba's overwhelming love, His enthusiasm for curing and consoling, and His efforts to induce all who come into contact with Him to rebuild themselves on stronger foundations of discipline and morality will certainly recognize these answers as the best summary of what Baba is to them.

At the age of fourteen he walked out of school and home, declaring, "My work is urgent; it can't wait. My devotees are calling me." This was in 1940. Ever since, lakhs of persons have won His grace but each of them has felt that Baba had a special attachment to him. "I am yours," He says. "Demand grace from Me as of right; there is no need to fawn or flatter." He spends His time wherever He is instructing, inspiring, correcting, encouraging spiritual aspirants, alleviating mental and physical pain, comforting distracted minds, or repairing and healing damaged or broken individuals and families. "This is the task for which I have come. Make full use of Me while you have the chance," He exhorts.

He leaves His body and rushes to the side of those who call on Him for guidance or relief. Listen to Charles Penn of Pacific Palisades, California, who has been receiving regular lessons on *sadhana*. "On the morning of September 20, 1965, He said, "Before starting on Brahmamarga and commencing your *sadhana* – disrobe. Cast the clothings of jealousy, hate, anger, pride, greed, desire aside. But you shall not be cold; for you still have one garment on – the garment of Love." He allows nothing to stand in the way of His journeys to assuage the afflicted. On many an occasion, He has let His body 'fall' and, with the *sukshma sharira* (subtle body) or some other appropriate body, enacted the role of saviour at the scene of the probable calamity.

He identifies Himself so fully with all that the declaration "I am yours" is profoundly true. Like the Sai Baba of Shirdi, who He announces Himself to be, Baba takes upon Himself the illness of those whom He wants to protect. On June 29, 1963, He had an 'attack' of cerebral thrombosis which incapacitated the left half of the body. He was 'unconscious' for three days, four "heart attacks" occurred during the week. The learned specialist who examined Him pronounced it as tubercular meningitis, which He could scarcely survive.

July 6 was sacred Guru Purnima, when about four thousand devotees from all parts of India assembled to have His *darshan,* and Baba insisted that He be carried down the winding stairs into the prayer hall. Leaning on two men, with a third lifting the left foot for the platform step, the left hand limp by His side, His face wrapped in a handkerchief which curbed the grand halo of hair, blinding one eye, His muscles switching with palsy, his right palm always shaking, Baba was placed on the silver chair and propped with pillows. When He flopped to one side even the bravest wept. The lolling tongue could not shape what He wanted to say. I interpreted it and announced to the gathering what He was trying to communicate. "I never fall ill, do not fear, do not grieve."

He signaled for the microphone to be held before Him; but His futile attempts to speak only intensified the atmosphere of grief. Baba wanted water, and when this was brought in a silver tumbler, He put His palsied right hand in it and sprinkled the water on the limp left arm and on the left leg. The left arm could now be bent. He stroked the left leg with both hands and set up, casting pillows aside. He could see now with both eyes and speak in that melodious voice of His. Starting His speech with the usual *"Premaswarupulara"*, He continued for over an hour. His first sentence was, "Since the Lord is the refuge of the forlorn, I had to take on Myself this illness and the heart attacks, for the sufferer would not have survived them." He had doffed the disease as quickly as He had donned it. The answer, "I reside in the altar of you heart," does not mean simply that He is the *Ishtadeva* (one's chosen God) of many. No, Baba means that He is the *Antaryamin,* the innermost motivator of all beings. When once asked whether the *Siddhi* which makes Him aware of the inner working of other minds could be learned by *sadhana,* Baba replied, "This is no *siddhi* or power. I do not get into your mind and emerge with the knowledge of what goes on inside it. I am there all the time. You can do nothing without My being aware of it."

Of course, it is difficult to realize how He, who has assumed this human form, can also be the resident of every heart. Baba warns us against glib explanations of the mystery. He wishes that we should study the *shastras* carefully, so that we can unravel it. "If you know yourself you can know Me too; for your truth is the truth of the universe as well as My truth." Perhaps the Vedic dictum, *Brahmavid Brahmaiva Bhavati* (He who has known Brahman becomes Brahman himself) may afford a clue. One thing is certain: the glimpses of glory that we get when we are with Baba, watching His activities, the flashes of illumination we experience when we listen to His Comments, these remind us of the description that Sri Krishna gives of Himself in the *Bhagavad Gita* and of nothing less.

Baba has said that His glance "falls all round." He sees everywhere. How else can we be explaining the showers of vibhuti that fall from His pictures in the shrines of devotees in a hundred different towns and villages all over world? How else can we explain the long flash of blinding light that emerged from His picture when a former Chairman of the Shirdi *Samsthan* had hesitated, underneath that picture, to have vibhuti brought from Sathya Sai Baba put on his tongue? He is in every picture of His.

As a correspondent wrote in *The illustrated Weekly* (October 3, 1965), Baba appears twice in a week at a house in Manjeri, Kerala, and stayed for hours, talking, resting, singing, consoling, teaching, and granting boons, when all the while He was also at Venkatagiri and Whitefield. He dismisses this phenomenon with the explanation, "It may appear strange to you, but to Me it is My very nature. It is just My way. When I want a thing, I wave My hand. When I want to get a thing done, I just will it. When I want to go to a place, I just go." Unless you know the way the universal and the infinite behaves, you cannot understand Him.

Now about the answer to the last question of the series. "My work is to help the devotees to live happily." The devotees have sufficient education to know that happiness is not won by the pursuit of sensory pleasures. It is a treasure of the inner consciousness won by *sadhana,* by the contemplation of the source of all the happiness, the Lord. *Baba* grants this superior vision and promotes self control and self knowledge by timely warnings and advice.

"My work is to guide them along the path of liberation, till they attain the goal." Twenty-five years ago, He announced that this was the mission on which

He had come again. He names it *Dharmasthapana* (establishment of norms for social and individual progress), Sadhuposhana (fostering the good and spiritually minded), *Dinapalana* (protection of the humble and the detached), and *Vedodharana* (revival of the study and practice of scriptural discipline). His over-whelming pity and affection towards the human community which has strayed into the wilderness shines through every word that He utters, every letter He writes, every deed He does.

Even a hundred cynics cannot escape this influence towards a more meaningful progressive life filled with love and service to one's fellow men. Baba's supremely eloquent discourses carry right into the hearts of lakhs of fascinated followers the message of the basic unity of all life, indeed of all creation. "Faulty vision alone makes us see the one as many; Man fell when he saw the one as 'many'; he will rise when his vision is corrected. *Tat* (that and *Twam* (you) are the same; *Sarva*m *Brahmanayam* (all *Brahman*); *Naiha Nanasti Kinchana* (there is no 'many' here; there is only one)." Such is the ancient lesson that Baba teaches us today.

Baba recognizes the pundits of India who have learnt this ancient wisdom in the traditional manner, as useful instruments for human uplift. They have been neglected for too long; they have become dispirited by poverty and lack of reverence. Their number too is fast declining. So Baba has given them fresh significance, a new purpose in life – to instruct the men and women of our land and of the world in "the science of contented living" and "the steps for the acquisition of an unruffled mind," as a preliminary to the realization of the self.

I have been, since 1948, a witness of the ever-widening horizon of Baba's glory. Since 1958, I have spent all my waking hours in His august presence. I have heard His thrilling discourses at Trivendrum and Badrinath and at scores of places. I have been enraptured by their wisdom, their universal outlook, their sweetness and lucidity. I have seen eminent scholars of the land awestruck at the profundity of His interpretations and the appropriateness of His explanations of rituals and rules. I have experienced firsthand many a miracle which stuns science. My wonder, my joy, my faith – these are growing every day with more proofs of His powers, wisdom and grace. Each day I am aware of a miracle grander that I have known, a pronouncement from his lips profounder than I have heard so far, an alchemy which transforms someone's character. That is the good fortune that I invite you to share with me.

Chapter - 6 (iii)

SOME THRILLING MIRACLES OF SRI SATHYA SAI BABA

About the *mahima* (glory) of Sri Sathya Sai Baba's two predominant interrelated characteristics –love and miracles, it has been very aptly mentioned in the '*Prem Mahima* Diary 2013' distributed by Prasanthi Nilayam throughout the world for their enlightenment and daily use.

'For a while, through his miracles, He squeezed eternity into the instant; captured the cosmos in a corpuscle; bridged the heaven and the earth; and unified man with God. Man's questions are answered, quest fulfilled and path discovered Now, we understand the almighty a little better: the greatness of his power, the goodness of His love, and also the guarantee of His grace that can correct our actions, control our destiny, and consummate our lives, through miraculous interventions. "Miracles are My Visiting Cards": He wills it happens. And everything that ever happens is always by His will. Miracles are His visiting cards, dropped to let us know that His will is done. No miracles are coincidences: all are Saincidences! He willed and the rain stopped. Cancers were cancelled and accidents averted! His formidable will was strong as a diamond, *Varjra Sankalpa*. Even the dreary political desert sands made way to waters that flowed to quench the thirst of the poor populace of Rayalaseema and Chennai. Laws of nature or rules of society, nothing can limit the power of God's will. His *Mahima* is not bound by time and space, either! He could remind a foreign devote how he was saved in his childhood, decades before He Himself took birth. And we are not even talking about the random playful acts of grace, which devotees enjoyed in His physical presence, such as materializations of the holy-ash, sweets, trinkets and souvenirs. Nor are we touching upon remote manifestations of His grace in the form of ceaseless flow of honey or *vibhuti* out of His pictures in devotees's homes. But then, one wonders if there is any distinction between His *Prema* and His *Mahima* for the two are united in Him. Love is His power.'But let us ask, what invokes the response from His *Mahima* to act in our favour in the hour of need? A chant? A prayer? Or a ritual? "Transformation of Man is My Biggest Miracle. Through I can, I will not change the mind of anyone. Mind is the man. If mind is different, man is different", said Baba once. Ther seems to be a gentleman agreement between God and man. God doesn't like to interfere with the free will of man. It said in the Git, "*Uddhareth athma athmaanaam, Athmaanam avasaadayeth*". Man is responsible for his own rise or downfall. God could at best be as a friend, guide and philosopher to Arjuna, the. In the worst case, He became the slyer of the demons who stubbornly refused to change their ways. Of course, Baba assured that, in this age, God wouldn't like to punish any one because each has mix of good and bad. If the bad were to be punished, no one would be left alive. He rather would correct and transform them into good human beings through love. Transformation of man had been the essence of Sri Sathya Sai Baba's mission over the decades. Individually and collectively, He interacted with, instructed and inspired millions to transform themselves into worthy human beings. 'Animals to man and man to god' was the double loop refinement that He advocated. He enunciated the human values and established organization to foster man with god. Miracles with Message: "*Aham sathya bodhakah*", He declared: 'I am a teacher of Truth'. He never let go of an opportunity to drive home spiritual truths to those around Him, be it a small spiritual truths to those around Him, be it a small talk or a public discourse. Miracles too were a medium for Him to convey message of morality to humanity. No wonder, then, devotees eagerly share and listen to the miraculous experiences, so that they can pick up the underlying mortal lessons for their own benefit. The lesson could be compassion to animals which was conveyed when a miraculous *vibhuthi* layer engulfed the cat that was being beaten up by a girl in Assam. Or it could be a more profound lesson of faith, conveyed through materializations of Rama's ring or Jesus' cross. He, through His miracles powers always reinforced the well-established traditions and beliefs of all regions and religions, and never encouraged any eccentricities. The positive impact of His *Mahima* is readily seen in the righteous life styles of His devotees across the globe, who voluntarily serve the society i pro-establishment ways using modern means. of Love: Sai's *Mahima* stupendous through it was, never overwhelmed, alarmed or disturbed anyone who experienced it. People loved to experience more of it, all the time. Not out of curiosity, but to relish His sweet and tender love that came packaged in the miracles. The miracles showed how gentle, caring and protective He is of each of us. "Why fear, when I am here?!" The miracles gave us courage to carry on in adversities and confidence to take on challenges. They comforted the suffering souls, and cajoled the straying sprits into path of goodness. They were all miracles of love. God's love for man responding to man's love for God! But then, one wonders if there is any distinction between His *Prema* and His *Mahima* for the two are united in Him. Love is His power.'

In this chapter some of his most thrilling miracles are being presented since presumably most of the Sai devotees may not be knowing about them - their purpose and implications. II In this chapter some of his most thrilling miracles are being presented since presumably most of the Sai devotees may not be knowing about them-their purpose and implications.

Baba's miracles revealed by physical scientist Dr.R.N.Shukla

❖ Once, a few decades ago, several internationally acclaimed Indian scientists, associated with ISRO (Indian Space Research Organization), wished to meet Sri Sathya Sai Baba after a conference at Bangalore. I had the good fortune to accompany them to Puttaparthi. Next day in the morning, a special meeting was arranged for the five of us, scientists, in Baba's sitting room. Baba spoke to us elaborating on ancient space-science and research in the culture of India, Bharatiya Samskruti. He mentioned about the contributions made by Maharshi Vishwamitra, Rishi Bhardwaja and others. He also spoke about the Guru Gurukul traditions of ancient India, citing the famous Rishi-Gurukuls of Sandipani, Mahamuni Agastya and others, along with the specialty discipline of each. As we were leaving, Baba blessed the scientists by gifting each of them the... astrally procured and materialized diamond pearl rings, emerald pendants and so on. Everybody got overwhelmed by Baba's gifts and the depth of his discourse on ancient scientific developments.

Dr. V. G. Bhide, one of the scientists, was blessed with an emerald ring. All of a sudden he approached Baba, with his emerald ring in his palm and prayed thus, "Baba you have blessed me by this ring, created astrally, for which I am very happy and convinced. But Baba, for my curiosity, can you kindly make this ring disappear now?" Baba just gave a broad smile and said, "Dr. Bhide, I have personally done nothing at all! But as your meeting with me is over now, we must disperse!" We all came out of the hall somewhat unhappily.

But suddenly I got a thought and I turned to Dr. Bhide and asked him to open his palm containing the emerald ring. There was no trace of the ring! It had vanished! This was a practical lesson taught to us scientists not to suspect and question those realized beings that have taken human form and descended amongst us purely to shower their lghrce and love on all mankind.

❖ In July 1991, I had a chance to go to Bangalore.

My wife was anxious for Baba's blessing. I was also invited to deliver some lectures at the University in Prasanthi Nilayam. We decided to go by the Kurla express from Mumbai, get down at Dharmavaram from where Prasanthi Nilayam is about 80 kms away. But both of us slept through and missed getting down at Dharmavaram. We woke up only when the train reached Bangalore. We were a bit perturbed at this. However, to our great happiness, our co-passengers in the train told us that Baba was at Bangalore and we could see him the next day morning at Whitefield. What a blessing!

Next day, we had Baba's Darshan and Pada-sparshan. The *Vibhuti* he gave us had the cheerful fragrance of the night queen flowers (*Ratirani*). But this was during the day! Both of us were totally awestruck by this experience.

❖ I was then requested to give a talk before devotees, in the College Auditorium, along with two others. Baba told each of us tg talk on particular topic for 40 minutes. Baba said.," Dr. Shukla, you talk on Cosmic Energy, Dr. Philips on terrestrial Chemistry and Dr. Chu on the Baba biography, a book written by Dr. Chu. General discussions will follow in the end". I insisted on being permitted to study and reached Baba's Aura which he allowed after some initialreluctance. Aura is the human Bio-energy picture of normal electromagnetic current voltage measurement done through social meters. Presently, Aura detection is done by PIP Camera (Poly Phase Contrast Photography).

Using an accurate multimeter, I read 5 volts and 8 ampere as voltage and electric current readings, as Baba's Aura. This was recorded thrice and the readings were the same. Baba then laughed and asked me whether I was satisfied with the readings, and asked me to take the readings again. I took another set of readings. The multimeter hands initially refused to move, but suddenly clicked the record infinity voltage and amperes reading! Baba could increase his own internal energy and convent his human bio-energy into small tiny nano-gold particles that emerged out of his skin as Shining lustrous golden Aura as measured later by our PIP Camera. This recording was done not just by us but also by the Japanese. German and Dutch scientists present in our group. We all ere so startled! But Baba told us jokingly that we should merge in Baba, and become B.A.B.A – double graduates of Baba Spiritual University – Being, Awareness, Bliss, Atma! (Courtesy DIVINE GRACE: SRI SATHYA SAI BABA, Special Publication, IndiaToday,2012)

❖ Once this writer, just on the eve of his departure from Puttaparthi in a hurry to catch a plane that very morning in Bangalore, was called by Swami to his modest living-cum resting room in the upstairs of Prashanthi Bhajan Mandir. Without being told that I was studying *THAITTIREEYA UPANISHAD* during myweek end spare time in Delhi (where I was then a resident representative of a UN agency) Baba, in his infinite grace expounded for nearly one full hour the essence of this famous Upanishad. When I began to write it all down, Baba remarked thatthere was no need to take notes; he assured me that whenever the need arose, I would automatically recall his teachings! While Baba's teaching was proceeding, Kasturiji came up to request Baba for Swami's article for the monthly Sanatana Sarathi, the issue of which was just then going to the printer. Swami, with a wave of his hand, produced the article and gave it to Kasturiji in my direct presence! When Swami concluded his Upanishadic teaching, he materialized a king-sized hot laddu (a type of Indian sweet) as his prasadam to be distributed to members of my family. Furthermore, Swami assured me that I would definitely catch the plane as it was flying late that day. I reached Bangalore airport with all anxiety but to my pleasant astonishment I was the last passenger on the long delayed flight! I recall another individual teaching session with Baba also in the Prasanthi Mandir upstairs room. Baba explained to me for almost an hour the five most significant Brahamasutras – analytical aphorisms on the supreme Reality. As the saying goes, Brahma Vidhyaa Vidhyaanaam – the Brahmic knowledge is the came of all learning. The teaching by Swami was marked as usual by profundity and simplicity, using parables, and filled with good-hearted humor on the other side.

Apart from these exclusive individual teaching sessions, I had the greatest good fortune of listening in the interview room to Baba's teachings on the *Bhagvat Gita*. Thus I was initiated by Baba himself into the Vedantic lore of the holy scriptural texts called *Prathama Trayee* viz *Bhagvat Gitas, Brahma Sutras* and Upanishads! Hail to Bhagvan Sai, he *Gyanbodhka* Guru. When he performed the Upanayanam of my eldest son in the early 1960s and also of my youngest son in the early 1980s, he not only materialized turmeric anointed *Yagnopaveetham* (holy threads) but also patiently taught the *Vatus* (the young boys) the meaning and significance of *Gayatri Mantra* recitation, the *Sandhyavandana* (daily prayers) ritual, and the importance of celibate living. Salutations to the world teacher Sri Sathya Sai Baba, *Sayinam Vande Jagatguram* (World Teacher, Universal Master) *Sankalpa* refers to the powers of *Siddha Purana* with acquired – and therefore delectable Yogic powers, whereas *Sankalpa Siddha* signifies the state "mere Willing is Fulfilling"! Swami's undeletable miraculous powers are the most natural and spontaneous manifestations of his love and grace to the devotees. See and enjoy Swami's Miracles. That it is not possible to fully understand Swami is aptly expressed by Baba himself when he stated: "In order to understand me, you will have to stand under me for so long that your legs are likely to collapse!" Then, what about experiencing him? To this Swami replied that experience is something like experimentation, with yesterday's experience being different from today's and one's experience being very different from other's. Experimentation a mental act and the Lord cannot be reached, understood or experienced by the mind, *APRAAPYAANASA SAH* as the THAITTIREEYA UPANISHAD states. If one cannot fully understand or experience, what then, Swami? He says, Enjoy – be in joy and end(your mind) in joy! Just as in the Upanishad saying *AANANDHO BRAHMANOVIDHVAAN* – The knower lives in Brahmianc Bliss alone.

3. R.D..Awle, an ardent Sai devotee in his write up *"Miracles of Sri Sathya Sai Baba; POTENT EVIDENCE'* (2001) has publicized many thrilling miracles of Sri Sathya SaI Baba. Some of them are reproduced here with profound courtesy du to him.

❖ Apparations

Over the years, many people have reported that Sai Baba has appeared beforethem in various places around the globe in a living form – yet he has 'physically' left India only once.

One example is Connie Shaw, the American author and lecturer, who states in her book *'Wake Up Laughing'* that Baba had appeared in her homein Colorado over fifty times! At one point he appeared in the middle of the night, waking her from sleep with a tap on the shoulder, to request that she take over the presidency of a local Sai Center. Since the center was mainly comprised of Indians and she felt it would be inappropriate for a Westerner to lead them, she refused his request. The next night he came again, and again she refused. When he appeared for the third consecutive night she finally relented and agreed to lead the center. When she reluctantly told the president of the center about the apparitions, he confessed that on the same three nights Baba had appeared in his home as well, requesting that he resign so Connie could take his place! Another example is James Sinclair, an American businessman who had never heard of Sai Baba, and who saw, on two occasions, an orange-robed man with an afro appearing and disappearing in his house in the USA. Inquiring at a spiritual book store if any living Master fit the description, he was shown a photo of Sai Baba, whom he instantly recognized as the man in his home. When Sinclair finally made it to Baba's *ashram*, the first thing Baba said to him was, "I came to you twice!"

❖ Miracles at Sri Ranga Patna (Pattanumm) orphanage in India

The Sri Ranga Patna orphanage, founded in 1984, is located on the Banglore - Mysore road* some15 km. north of the city of Mysore, India. A man named Halgappa has been selflessly serving the fifty orphaned children that reside in the supported only by donations and dedicated staff, this orphanage cares for these children. A small temple or shrine is part of the photographs of Sai Baba materialize *vibhuti* in this temple. The temple available for all to see, whioch hold and experience the continuous *amritha* orb honey(nectar). *Amritha* is being continuously manifested from those lockets of Sathya Sai Baba and Shirdi Sai Baba, and which were blessed by Baba years ago(immediately after which they began manifesting *Amritha*).

Testimonies on the internet The testimonies of some foreign visitors are avaible:

In an orphanage in South India, there is an ongoing miracle.. On a thumb-nail sized silver lockets of porcelain, one bearing the likeness Sri Sathya Sai Baba and the second depicting Shirdi Sai Baba. Given to the manager Halgappa by Sri Sathya Sai Baba over many years ago, they have been miraculously materializing *amrita* ((honey) I decided to viit the place and see for myself. The manager of the orphanage Halgappa scooped one of them with a spoon and put it in the palm of my right hand. It was * piece of porcelain with Baba's facepainted on it – there was no mechanism to hide. I watched like a hawk as a few drops of a amulet into my palm – but this meant nothing, it had just been trickling the amritha. It continued to trickle from the amulet over a few minutes, he repeated this procedure four times,– and the amrit was still trickling. What I saw that day was a miracle. (I tasted the nectar: it's definitely not of this world. Many, including Dr.Gersten have seen it and reported it on the internet. This miracle is still continuously going on for the last over 20 years. Any one can go there and observe it there with his on eyea and taste the miraculous honey there. A detailed descriptionof this miracle with its actual photographs and accounts of visitors is evadible on the internetin these files:File:://1:Sathya Sai Miracles –Miracle at Sri Ranga Patne orphanage IN Mysore, I...*http://groups.yahoo.com/group/saibabanews/message/2*

Miracle I had witnessed at Baba's *ashram* in 1996.in the middle of his Christmas discourse, Baba waved his hand and materialized a small gold-covered book – bringing a gasp of amazement from the crowd of 50,000, me among them! (I was seated very close toBaba – and was certain it was a genuine miracle). That night at around 9 o'clockI heard that Baba had announced earlier that angels would be flying above the ashram that evening.

❖ Baba Takes Lord Venkateshwara's Place

I was recently a partial witness to an incident which provides another powerful due to Baba's identity. One of the most famous shrines in India is the hilltoptemple to Lord Venkateshwara (a form of Vishnu), in Tirupathi, Tamil Nadu. Venkateshwarais considered by many Hindus to be the Supreme Lord, and the idolin this temple is known all over India for the powerful blessings it bestows. As with many of the subsects in Hindsuism, there is an understandable quality of exclusivityin the devotees of that shrine, especially among the priests who perform the worship; for generations their families hav been single-mindedly devoted to Venkateshwara alone. One day in late November, 1998, the priests were performing a special pada puja (foot worship) ceremony to the Venkateshwara idol, when suddenly the idol's feet were transformed before their eyes into the feet ofa living man. Looking up, they beheld, in place of the Venkateshwara idol, theliving form of Sathya Sai Baba. "If you want full darshan", he told them, "come to whitefield enxt week!" Baba then disappeared, elaving Venkateshwara in his place. I was in Sai Baba's Whitefield Ashra on December 6th, 1998, the day the priests from Tirupathi, dozens of them, arrivedt o receive the full darshan of the living God who had appeared before them in their shrine. (Courtesy: R.D.Awle)

❖ *Baba and Ramana Maharshi*

And speaking of *Jnanis,* at the moment of the death of Ramana Maharshi (one of the greatest Self-Realized Masters of the last century), and extraordinary eventoccurred in Baba's ashram, giving us a clue both to Baba's identity and his relationship with Ramana. A Sai devotee named Vaadu reported what happened:

"...the night when Ramana Maharshi passed away in Tiruvannamalai (April 14, 1950) I was with Swamiji [Sai Baba]. Krishna [another young devotee] and my self were both there. That evening, around 9:00, we continued whatever it was wewere doing (I think we were doing a puja) when suddenly Swamiji looked up at us. There was a peculiar way of looking he has which means that he wants to goto his room. The moment Krishna and I went through the door into the room and closed it, Swami fell down. I was ready for it. Krsihna and I both held hands, and Swami was lying across them. Then [He] rose up into the air, from our arms. Hewas a stiff as a board. He started murmuring – something about 'Maharshi hasreached my lotus feet.' And then the sole of his right foot split open, and nearlytwo kilograms of beautiful, well-scented vibhuti poured out from the sole of his foot. I collected the vibhuti while [He] was still levitating in the air. Then [He] came down and returned to [His] senses and asked what (He) hadsaid. I said, "Swamiji, this is what you said: 'Ramana Maharshi has passed away'.And this is what came out of your feet." He said: "Put it into packets and give it out as *prasadam*."

A day or two after this incident, we learnedfrom the newspapers that(Ramana) Maharshi had died. It had been at the time that Swami said Maharshi hadreached (His) feet." So, at the time of his death, Ramana Maharshi merge din Baba's feet! Is it not therefore clear that Sai Baba is a full embodiment of the Divine Self, the supreme

4. The following miracle has been reported from UK on thre Internet after Swami's *mahasamadhi* in 2011:

❖ Sri Satha Sai Baba – *Namaskar* Miracle in UK

There has been huge mention across the world of Baba's "Namaskar"(Salutaion)1 actions in Sai Kulwant Hall a few days before being admitted into hospital (in March 2011). As many of you already know, Baba never ever has done this and it is thought to be his way of bidding farewell to all his beloved devotees and ensured it was caught on camera. Please see images on this websites. However, one devotee in London, UK has been extremely lucky to experience Baba in his own home. There are photos and statues of different Gods covered in vibhuti of different colors. I personally go to his home every week for bhajans and the house has a feeling of warmth and positive vibrations. The family is very kind in opening up their home every week for devotees to pray and join in the *bhajans* with them. Yesterday, there was a birthday in the family and Baba was sure not to miss out on giving his blessing. The devotee I mention had printed an image of Baba's "farewell" *namaskar,*(salutation). framed it and placed it in Swami's chair. Yesterday wonderful miracle occurred and the photo was blessed with vibhuti – confirming to us ALL that Baba may have left us in physical form but will ALWAYS be around us and protect us." File: *//1Sri sathya Sai baba Namakar Photograph Miracle in UK 2011.htm*

In the recent issues of *Sanathana SarathI* –the official monthly jourrnal os Sri Sathya Sai Sadhna Trust, Prasanthui Nilayam, several eminent Sai devotees from the different parts of the world have published their thrilling experiences of having received Sri Sathya Sai miraculous grace in their own lives. Inqusitve readers are suggested to procure the following issues of *Sanathan Sarathi* borrowiung from their Sai friends, or available in the nearby Sai Centres in their places/countries:

1 *Sanathana Sarathi.*;.May, 2011

• 'Love unbounded'- *R.J.Ratnakar,* Trustee, Sri Sathta Sai Central Trust

Sanathana Sarathi (Special Issue)'Memories of Bhagavan Sri Sathya Sa Baba', Nv.2012

- Bhagwan is always withus; *R.J.Ratnakar*, Sri Sathyta Sai Central Trust
- 'Human facets of Swami:';*Prof, Sashidhara*. Sri Sathya Sai Institue of Higher Learning
- A goldmine of divine experiences:*Sheen Peculllel*. Zone Chairman, Russsiaan-speaking countries, Sri Sathya Sai Internatioinbakl Organizations
- Life's journeYr with my Sai: *Dr.J.Geeta Reddy, Minister*, Abndhra Pradesh

Sanathana Sarathi, June 2013

- Miraculous escape from disaster:Group Captain V.Mehta,
- A goldmine of divine experiences:Steen Peculllel
- A most miraclouds gift drsamuel sndweiss;

Sanathana Sarathi, June 2013

- How Swami providd direction to my life: Dr.V.K.Ravindran,, Chairman.Zone 4,Sri SathyaSai International Organization

Sanathana Sarathi, Sept.2013

- 'Love is the basis of all creations': Rabbi David Zeller, Welknown teacchor of Jewish spirituality and meditation
- 'A tragic event changed in to a blessing': Prof.U.S.Rao, Former Principal Prasanthi Nilsya,m Campus, Sri Sthya Suin Institut of Higher Lerning, Prasdantghj Nilayam

Sanathana Sarathi Oct..2013

- 'Different religions express the same truth': Tehseen Dhall, assistant director, institueof Sathya sai education, austrralis

Sanathana Sarathi, March 2014

- 'Journey with Lord Sai: *Maj. Gen.(Retd.) Shivdev Singh*, Sri Sathya Sai international Centre for Sports
- *A mre touvh of Baba cured polio* Dr.Charanjir Glool

Sanathana Sarath Nov.,2014

- 'There is no fear when Swami is with us.: *R.J.Ratnakar*, Trustee, Sri Sathta Sai Central Trust

Innumerable miracles of Sri Sathya SaI Baba are availa\ble in thearchives of Sai Radio website. Many miracles of Sri Sathya Baba have been and are stil happening at at many places throughout the world even after his physdcal departure from the world in Apirl 2011. They have been rand are still being reported on the Internet.

I too have observed many Sai miraces hapening with others, and I too experience his miracles. He saved my life and that of my wife notonce but maqny times, ans he helped helped me at my professionl career and in facing the vissitudes in the very difficult situations in life. He told me inmy first interview at is Brindavanm *ashram* in June 1974 "I am with you always." And I have hound it to abouluely tru tiin this time in 2014. I have mentioned asaany 22 such mirackles of his divine help in my life. I have recorded thrm in my book '*The Triple Incarnations of Sai Baba*'.

PROMINENT SAI MIRACLES
OFFICIALLY REPORTED ON LINE

Reported on the web site of Sri Sathya Sai Cerntral Trust

'DEVOTEES' EXPERIENCES - MIRACLES AND EXPERIENCES

Miracles and *leelas* (Divine sport) are in the very nature of the Avatar and a source of delight and bliss to His devotees. From a very young age, Bhagawan was known to possess miraculous powers, producing objects from an empty bag as gifts to His classmates and often demonstrating paranormal powers of omniscience. As more and more devotees gathered at the Divine Feet, the number of such instances grew. Thousands of people from all over the world have experienced the divinity of Bhagawan in a number of ways. Some have been miraculously saved from dire situations or calamities while others have had spiritually illumining experiences. The specific instances may vary, but they all make us aware of the undeniable presence of God in our lives.

The miracles of Bhagawan are a manifestation of His divine powers of Omnipresence, Omnipotence and Omniscience. But, Bhagawan points out that His most potent power is His Love which can melt even the stoniest of hearts and fill the mind with the peace that 'passeth all understanding'. Bhagawan calls miracles His visiting cards and says that His *Chamatkars* (Miracles) draw people to the Divine presence for undergoing the process of *Samskar*(Refinement). This refinement brings about an attitude of *Paropkar* (Service). By serving one's fellowmen, one earns the grace of God and reaches the ultimate goal of *Sakshatkar* (Self-realization).

The scriptures set great store by contemplating on the miraculous deeds of the Lord. In the *Shri Sai Satcharita*, the author records the words of the Sai Baba of Shirdi on the great spiritual merit that can be acquired by listening or reading about the story of the life of the Lord come in human form. He says,

"The pride and egoism of devotees will vanish, the mind of the hearers will be set at rest; and if the devotee has wholehearted and complete faith, he or she will become one with the Supreme Consciousness".

In these pages, we have presented some of the experiences of devotees of Bhagawan. The accounts are based on the narration of these experiences in books on Bhagawan that are approved for sale at the Sri Sathya Sai Sadhana Trust (Publications Division). Read on to get a glimpse of the glory of our beloved Bhagawan.

I. Transformation of the Heart

The Testimony of Dr. Frank Baranowski, an aura expert

The Rainbow Man
A sceptic is convinced of Bhagawan's divinity

The Story of Kalpagiri
How Bhagawan brought about a change of heart in a criminal

II. Resurrection

Resurrection of Mr. Walter Cowan
How Baba brought Walter Cowan back to life

Sri Radhakrishna – the 'Lazarus' of our times
How Baba gave Radhakrishna a new lease of life

"Now you can go!" - Ticket to Eternity
How Baba extended the life of Sri Seshagiri Rao

Subbamma: What a deliverance!
Bhagawan fulfils His devotee's last wish

III. Materialization

The Miraculous Flow of Vibhuti
How Bhagawan would cause Vibhuti to flow from an empty vessel

The Sacred 'Lingodbhavam' Wonder
How Baba materializes and brings forth Lingas from His Being

The Manifest visits the Unmanifest
How Baba 're-charged' the Badrinath Shrine

IV. Miracle Cures

The Gift of Sight and Light
Bhagawan restores Dr. Ravi Kumar's eyesight, twice!

Special Saving Grace
How Smt. Shyamala Devi's nephew was saved from the jaws of death

The Magic of Lord's Blessing
A dumb and lame child is miraculously cured

All-Encompassing Compassion
How the cancer of a devout Christian was cancelled

"I got your two telegrams"
How Baba answered the prayer of Sri S N Singh

X. The Same Baba: Shirdi Sai and Sathya Sai

The Cure and the Confirmation
How Baba proved to Mr. Dixit that He is the same Shirdi Sai come again

The Shirdi Link
Baba reveals His Omniscience to the Rani of Chincholi

The Assurance and the Fulfillment
How Baba had prophesied His advent to Smt. Sharada Devi

XI. The One appears as Many

"Don't Worry; The Instrument is With Me"
How Baba assumed multiple forms to save a devotee

The 'Jodi Aadipalli Somappa' Miracle
How Baba appeared as three villagers to rescue his devotee

The Lord – Ever Alert for His devotee
How Baba appeared as an old man to save Dr. Padmanabhan

God is present in every Being
How Baba came as an old beggar to Shardamma's house

XII. Manifesting in Multiple Locations

The Virupaksha Miracle
Young Sathya appears in the sanctum sanctorum of the Virupaksha temple

"Baba Appeared in front of My House"
How Baba was there in Venkatagiri and Manjeri at the same time

XIII. Transcorporeal Journeys
The Lord rushes to the Devotee
How Baba blesses His devotee in her last moments

"I just had an increase in temperature"
How Baba saved Mrs. Sushila from burns

"My Shoulders Are Aching"
How Baba saved Mr. Radhakrishna from a watery grave

XIV. The Miraculous Vibhuti

A Child Shall Lead Them
How the faith of little Mayan gave her a new life

The Gift of Grace
How Shiv Kumar regained his sight, speech and movement

The Unbelievable Cure
How Vibhuti allowed cricketer Sunil Gavaskar to play in Australia

The Divine Prescription
How the Aerodome Officer's Cancer was cancelled

The details of each of these miraculous experiences of devotees may be known by clicking on the miracle the readervis interested in.

In the recent March,2015 issue of *Sanatana Saraathi* a very moving account by Leonardo Gutter of Argentia has been published under the title 'I WIIL NEVER DISAPPOINT MY DEVOTEES' in which he has graphicazlkly narrated how Sri Sathya Baba had cancelled his cancer, miraculously.

Sri Shirdi Sai Baba and Sri Sathya Sai Baba both have again for the four the time saved my life on 27.2.2014 when I suddenly lost my breath in late evening. I had to be ambulanced to the, Sarvodaya hospital immediately, put on the ventilator throughout the night and treated in the ICU for five days and was discharged on 5.3.2015 on my great insistence..The doctors have told that that if I had not been rushed to the hospital immediately and put on the ventilator within 5 minutes I would certainly have and only divine help saved my life in such a precarious condition.

I am now on complete bed-rest and trying to complete my mission of completely mending books' under publication.

- Earlier Sai Baba had saved me from likely car accident in 1974, then In 1997 when I had heart attack and then I had a serious attack of coronary thrombosis and paralysis on the left side in September 2007, and had to be on complete bed rest and medical treatment for three years. Although since then I cannot legibly speak, hear from left ear stand, walk, travel,, and do any physical activity, yet by Sai Baba';s grace I have been able to resume my spiritual writing work since 2012. and I have been able to edit and prepare for publication my six books and get them published and thereby; trying my best to complete the mission of my life.. I have been most eagerly trying to get the following six books prepared and published by good publishers during the last three years 2013-15;

1. How I Found God

- *- Role played by Fakir Shirdi Sai Baba and the Spiritual Masters in my*
- *Spiritual Training resultng in my God-realization* (By; Yogi Minocher.K.. Spencer), New Delhi; New Age Books, 2013
- ISBN 978-081-722-352-00

2. Shirdi Sai Speaks to, Yogi Spencer in his Vision.. Bloomington,USA,: Partridge India Publishing Co..Jan.,2015::

   ISBN: Paper back 978- 1-4828- 2 ISBN: e book; 978-1-4828-4362-5

3. Essentials of Foundations of Education- *New Useful Modern Concepts of Education Teachers Under B.Ed.Training.* Bloomington,USA,:. Partridge India Publishing Co..Jan.,2015.:

   ISBN:Paper back 978- 1-4828- 6
   ISBN: e book; 978-1-4828-4362-9

4. Select Spiritual Writing of Yogi Spencer- *Harbinger of the new Age of Spirituality.*,
   Bloomington, USA,: Partridge
   India Publishing Co.:
   ISBN:928-2-
   4828-4362-6 (*Under publication*)
   n Seach of Sai Divine -*Exploring Sathya Sai Baba's Mystery and Unique Contributions to Humanity as the Harbinger of the New Sage of Spirituslity.*
   Bloomi ngton,USA,: Partridge India Publishing Co..(*Under publication*)
   ISBN:Paper back 978- 1-4828- 3
   ISBN: ebook; 978-1-4828-4362-6

5. The Triple incarnations of Sai Baba—Sri Shirdi Sai Baba,Sri Sathya Sai Baba and Future Prema Sai Baba IS BN: Softcover 978-1-4828-2293-9 IiSBN; e Book 978-1-4828-2292-2

6. In Search of Sai Divine—Exploring Sri Sathya Sai Baba's Mystry and Unique contributions to
   Humanity as the Harbinger of New Age of Spirituallity

Although I have been having all these serious ailments, by essings of my spiritual masters and so instead of bearing grave exploitation and injustice of a publisher in India who has been publishing and selling worldwide as many as my 36 books of mine, out of which 20 books are in English bearing ISBN, and were advertized and sold by many prominent web sites for the over 15 years and still not paying my due royalties on them, I have taken the inspiration from Lord inspiration from Lord Krishna's great message in Bhagvat Gita; Do not bear injustice, don't be impotent, and coward but do your legitimate *Karma* - fight for your rightful claims keeping God';s name in your heart constantly and leave its fruit in the hands of God., I filed a case against the publisher in Delhi High Court in 2012,. the High Court has on 14.8.2014 appointed the sole Arbitrator to, settle this Royalty claims dispute, the, arbritration proceedings are going on and its may be known in the next few months..

All the above are sole due to the miraculous grace of Sri Sathya.Sai Baba in my life.

- I have been most eagerly trying to get the following six books prepared and published b good publsheres durin the last three years 2013-15;
- e 1. How I Found God - *Role played by Fakir Shirdi Si Baba and the Spiritual Masters in my Spiritual Training resulting in my God-realization*(By;Yogi Minocher.K..Spencer), New Delhi;New Age Books, 2013. ISBN 978-081-722-352-0.

2. Shirdi Sai Speaks to, Yogi Spencer in his Vision. Bloomington,USA,: Partridge India,2015:: ISBN: Paper back 978- 1-4828- 2 ISBN eBook; 978-1-4828-4362-5

3. Essentials of Foundations of Education- *Introducing New UsefulMoidern Concepts of Education to Student Teachers Under B.Ed.Training.* Bloomington,.USA,: Partridge India Publishing Co..Jan.,2015: ISBN:Paper back 978-1-4828-6 ISBN: ebook; 978-1-4828-4362-9

4. Select Spiritual Writings of Yogi Spencer- *Harbinger iof the new Age of* Bloomington,USA,: Partridge India Publishing Co.: ISBN:928-2-4828-4362-6 (*Under publication*)

5. In Search of Sai Divine -*Exploring Sathya Sai Baba's Mystery and Unique Contributions to Humanity as the Harbinger of the New Age of Sprirituality.*Bloomi ngton, USA,: Partridge India Publishing Co.. (*Under publication*) ISBN:Paper back 978- 1-4828- 3
ISBN: ebook; 978-1-4828-4362-6

5. The Triple incarnations of Sai Baba—Sri Sjhirdi Si Baba,Sri Sathya Sai Baba and Future Prema Sai Baba ISBN: Soft cover 978-1-4828-2293-9 ISBN; e Book 978-1-4828-2292-2

6. In Search of Sai Divine—Exploring Sri Sathya Sai Baba's Mystery and Unique contributions to Humanity as the Harbinger of New Age of Spirituality

Although I have been having all these serious ailments, by the blessings of my spiritual masters nstead of bearing grave exploitation and injustice of a publisher in India who has been publishing and selling worldwide as many as my 36 books of mine, out of which 20 books are in bearing ISBN, and were advertized and sold by many prominent web sites for the over 15 years and still not paying my due royalties on them, I have taken the inspiration from Lord Krishna's great message in Bhagvat Gita; Do not bear injustice, don't be impotent-, a coward but do your legitimate *Karma* - fight for your rightful claims keeping God';s name in your heart constantly and leave its fruit in the hands, of God. I filed a case against the publisher in Delhi High Court in 2012.the High Court has on 14.8.2014.the court then appointed the sole Arbitrator to settle this Royalty dispute, the arbitration proceedings are going on and its judgment may come in the next few months.

All the above are solely due to the miraculous grace of Sri Sathya Sai Baba in my life.

Chapter - 7

CONTRIBUTIONS OF DEVOTEES AND SCHOLARS OF RELIGION

"I shall protect all My true devotees no matter what difficulties the world may face, You have come within My fold and this is My Divine assurance"

- Sri Sathya Sai Baba's
Discourse on *Guru Purnima* day, July 13, 1994

Sri Sathya Sai Baba (1926-2011) was unique divine personality—an incarnation of God amidst us. He has given to the mankind a rich gift of religious and spiritual ideas, moral code, teachings and an enlightened world view. His followers talk of "Sai Religion", although Sri Sathya Sai Baba himself said that He had not come to establish any religion or cult of his own or to disturb any existing faith.

The basic traits of Sai Religion are:

- Belief in One God:He (Sri Sathya Sai Baba) is the God Incarnate who is *Sawadevataswaroopam* (All Gods and Goddesses rolled into one)
- There is only one caste—the caste of humanity; there is only one language—the language of love; soul is immortal; belief in the essential bond between one's *Karma* and rebirth;
- The five foremost values—Truth, Righteousness, Peace, Love and Non-violence must be followed by all; there should be 'Unity, Purity and Divinity' observed by devotees;
- *Namasmaran* (Repetition of Lord's Name) and *'Manav Seva'* (Service to man) should be done by every one for his or her salvation; die-hard rituals, dogmas and superstitions ought to be discarded, and the *'Golden Age'* for humanity is to dawn soon for which Sri Sathya Sai Baba is exercising his divine powers.

Baba's discourses and writings are woven around these basic elements of his religious thought. Most of these traits are essentially those of the ancient '*Sanathana Dharma*' of the Aryans. Almost all these have been emphasized by all the world religions. Baba has integrated and revitalized them and cast them into His unique model of integrated and secular religion suited to the modern times. His religion thus unites and transcends all religions. It presents the essence of the highest teachings of all religions. Baba said that not only He but each one of us is God, the only difference being that while He knew that He was God, we do not know this. Baba sought to unite all mankind and lead it to divinity. His mission carries the symbol in which the symbols of the five great religions of the world are included. Baba emphasized the observance of the usual modes of worship of different religions by their respective followers but insists that the religion of humanism ought to be emphasized. He does not want people to change their religion after seeing Him. Countless people of different faiths and races have been drawn to Him. They regard Him as God, and they have become His devotees.

What unique thing have devotees discovered in Baba? This has to be understood. Every devotee has had some unique experiences with Baba, but not all devotees have recorded them in print. Only a few devotees have presented their experiences and perceptions relating to Baba in their books and articles. A brief content analysis of the books written by Baba's devotees reveals some very interesting things about him.

The main thrust of these devotee-writers' contributions has been on these four aspects:

1. Baba's charismatic personality;
2. Baba's miracles;
3. Baba's interaction with H his devotees,
4. Baba's revelations on the past, present and future.

Let us briefly review the devotees' writings on these themes:

Baba's Charismatic Personality:

Most of the devotee-writers have been struck by the physical features of Sri Sathya Sai Baba. He was 5 feet 3 inches high, 108 lbs in weight and slim. He had a crown of hair, broad deep eyes and very delicate and beautiful hands and feet. Some close observers like devotee authors like Hislop (1979)[1] and Jayashree Menon (1990)[2] have revealed that Baba's skin color changed from various shades of blue, dark to golden. Menon wrote in '*Our Sai Beyond Miracles*' (1990):

"Our Swami at first glance to a person who has neither seen Him before nor known Him is not very beautiful. But once a person sees this physical form, he is instantly attracted and enraptured by the beauty of the form. We have never seen anything more beautiful than this form. Why? Because He is the Creator... He represents the totality of creation. From the vibrations of love, His form is the most beautiful on our planet within creation.

In the astral or in certain dreams and in certain *Darshans,* those who have experienced the beauty know it. Facial expression of Swami changes because of changing of deities or other departmental Gods. Some see different colors' or different lights or sometimes Swami appears dark in complexion or golden in color; His body actions are regulating the cycling creative and destructive forces. He has to do the action because others' human consciousness is present."[3]

This description of Baba's skin color provoked the following comment from Ustad Tarik Knapp, a German Muslim devotee of Sai Baba, in his personal letter to the present author in 1992 wrote as under:

"... I should like to point out that the notion of beauty has no objective basis at all and is purely subjective according to the cultural and physico-racial standards and traditions of the various ethnic units of a certain civilization. The Kaukasian races (Indo- Germanics, "Arians", Semites, Hamites) in a naive-natural, and not at all civilized habit, feel that the physiognomic pattern of the races they belong to are "beautiful", "noble" etc., and that members of coloured races (East Asians, Black Africans, Dravid, Papuas, American-Indians, Australian Aborigines etc) are only beautiful as far as they resemble the Kaukasain standard. Only the Semites were taught by their prophets expressly that racism is a great sin; they have been educated and, in this respect, civilized. Not so the "Christian" Europeans, who by their technical and political superiority have fostered racism since their circumnavigation of Africa (in 1498 ad Vasco da Gama arrived in Calicut/Kerala) and their "discovery" of America (in 1492 ad Columbus landed in Guanahani): they managed to foster racism even in the minds of the "colored nations", a mental poisoning that has now to be washed out of the body of mankind. This knave, but self-conceited conviction of today, when unity of mankind is so necessary, cannot stay uncontested.

It certainly is not accidental that the physiognomy of Sri Sathya Sai Baba is so "negroid", although in a much spiritualized way. The Bhagavan's outward appearance immediately makes him trustworthy within a second to all non-Kaukasians in the world, because it does not give the impression of belonging to one of the "master-races" who since centuries have conquered the Southern and Eastern continents and subjugated the non-Kaukasian inhabitants.

I am *alhamadul'illah*. I am in a special social position by birth to be able to recognize the advantage of a physical appearance as *Bhagavan* has. His face already "Black is beautiful" is a consoling and convincing message to all human beings now thinking they are the "forgotten children of God" under the terror of the European races."[4]

All those who have had invaluable opportunities of seeing and knowing Baba from close quarters have found him to be a paragon of virtues, an ideal human being. He was loving by nature; his love is genuine and is more than that of a thousand mothers' love. He is compassionate, kind, affectionate, polite, altruistic, caring and considerate. He had sense of humor. His 'jasmine humor' has been reported by Gokak (1975)[5], Kasturi (1982)[6], Sitapati (1990)[7]a, and Peggy Mason *et al* (1995) [7]b.

Baba showered his love and grace on his chosen devotees so much that tears of ecstasy flowed from their eyes. He endeared his visitors and devotees by his sweetness, poise, grace, cleanliness, and elegant style of walking, talking and gestures.

Devotees have reported in their writings that Baba's eyes penetrated their hearts, and even in silence he was sen speaking. He wss secular in the most modern and liberal sense. Considerations of one's faith, caste, and race did not affect him at all. "Not only is the secular and integrated personality of the Divine Superman, *Brahmana* or *ParaBrahma* before us, but He is ever present to melt away the rigidities, vanity, megalomania, egoism and follies of all those who parade themselves as great religious authorities or champions of their 'best' religions, all-knowing physical scientists and social scientists, with the help of not only his super intelligence and super wisdom, but with the help of his myriad kinds of thrilling miracles." (Ruhela, 1991).[8]

Some devotees like Ra Ganapati (1990)[9] and Kasturi (1982)[10] have recorded that Baba sometimes would burst into anger and it so happened often that the person with whom he showd his anger or from whom he showd his withdrawl or silence, could not understand the reason of Baba's angry behavior. Ra Ganapati (1990) has mentioned "...Even many a humble and generally unquestioning devotee has given expression to the writer to his doubts whether Swami is partial—over- bountiful to certain people and over harsh towards certain others. This goes against our general conception of the Divinity as equal-visioned towards all."[11]

Baba seemed to be like an over-indulgent father who defends his chosen or close devotees and organizational leaders and bosses with a great deal of emotion. He as authoritarian in his style of benevolent leadership. His sense of discipline was very rigid. He relied more on his appointed leaders; workers and devotees under the leaders did not have any direct access to him to present their grievances, if any, although they all believe that as omnipresent divine being He might be knowing all. It was experienced by many devotees including the present author that Baba often assures or promises certain things to his devotees, but they did not materialize. None was ever sure when the promised thing or event would really happen, or was it only his joke or an empty assurance just to please the devotees? Devotees thus ultimately rationalize that is it his divine *Leela*. Annie-marie Marwaha observed, "The question of not keeping his promise does not arise at all but the time factor is always a big question with Baba often promising something but we do not know when the promise will be fulfilled."[12]

Almost all devotees have the innocent belief that if Baba touched anything in a devotees' hand, it must be taken as blessed by him and it must then prove to be good and fortunate thing for him. But this was not necessarily so, as several devotees including the present author himself had experienced a number of times. Baba perhaps touched these objects just by way of courtesy to please the anxious devotees, but it did not necessarily imply that he had really blessed them. This often came as a real shock afterwards to people; they could do nothing but to rationalize it as His divine *leela*. People were often at a loss to understand this *leela*.

Ra Ganapati (1990)[13] had noted a number of inconsistencies or contradictions in Baba's behavior which also he himself rationalized by saying; "God as God does not come to the world but mixes with human traits when incarnating; "Jewels cannot be made out of pure gold. Only when a little proportion of copper is alloyed it lends itself for jewel- making."[13]

He concluded "Swami, in His day to day life is like a rose. Its form of beauty is the orderliness in his actions; its fragrance, His love. Just as the rose carries invisibly within it honey, He has latent within Him the essence of Divine powers."[14]

Ganapati noted Baba's uncertainty or unpredictability and extolled it as his divine virtue which lended to charm to his charisma. He differentiates between Sthoola Sai (Gross Sai) and *Sookshma Sai* (Spirit Sai) and holds that the latter aspect of Sai is free from inconstencies.[15]

The writings of Kasturi (1961-80)[16],Gokak(1975)[17],Ra Ganapati(1985)[18], (19990)[19], Ruhela (1976)[20a],(1994),[20b], M.N.Rao(1985)[21] and many other devotees have revealed that Baba led a simple life. He ate very little food without butter and sugar. He liked neatness, orderliness and artistic and colorful decorations, dance, drama, music, *bhajans*, etc. On festive occasions he showered his love on his students, teachers, workers and devotees by giving gifts of sweets, clothes and other articles. His discourses were full of great charm, eloquence, wisdom and interesting stories from Indian scriptures and lives of great men of different religions. The magnetism of his charisma attracted every one, and devotees long to have his *darshan* again and again, and still they remained thirsty for his darshan. Such was his divine charisma.

Devotees like Kasturi and Gokak, who were privileged to live and work in very close proximity to Baba for several years, have revealed that Baba was a hard taskmaster. He was like a flame that burns and it was really difficult to live very close to him. One had to be extremely alert, ideal, moral, sensitive, egoless, all the time fearful and full of great reverence and silence in his company. Sometime Baba mightt cut jokes with his devotees, but the *vice-versa* was just not possible. In the interview room he spoke very endearingly to devotees, but as soon as the interview was over, he becomes totally dethatched and distant from those devotees, which sometimes amazed them.

In his remarkable memoirs *'Loving God'*, Kasturi has mentioned:" discovered a new fact of Baba's personality - the rarity, the clarity and the validity of His understanding of the contemporary condition[6].

Anne-marie Marawaha testified, "He answers our mental calls much quicker than any call from our lips. No human mother can be so considerate and generous."[22] Dianna Baskin has on the basis of her long experience observed "Swami's love and compassion are so deep that if we, each, could develop but a small amount of it towards our fellow men, we would instantly be in the *"Golden Age."*[22] Italian Catholic Priest Mazzolini (1994)[23] has testified that Baba is "full of goodness and sweetness, but without being effeminate or weak...His life is free of struggle or interior or exterior conflicts."[24] He concludes by saying. "The qualities that anyone can see in Sai Baba's personality demonstrate His holiness and His Divine Essence with absolute clarity."[25]

Many devotee-writers have corroborated in their writings what Joy Thomas had observed in her '*Life is a Dream: Realize It*' (1992); "...Our Baba is not a distant God. He has come not only to enlighten us, but also to bring love and joy in our daily lives..."[26]

In '*Pathways to Peace: Prasanthi*" (1988), Kasturi presented the quintessence of his assessment of Baba in these words:

"Swami is the embodiment of the Consciousness that energizes the infinite Cosmos, the One which science is seeking with intermittent success and which religion seeks and sees as energizing the infinitesimal too. Swami leads us to the awareness of the One, in all ideas, ideals, objects, waves and particles. He has come to teach the Truth of Unity, for that Truth alone frees us from fear and the death it breeds...To those who fight against each other waving holy books and flags he declares that every religion is a facet of the same Truth."[27]

In '*Bhagavan Sri Sathya Sai Baba: My Divine Master* (1994)[28], the Swedish Sai devotee Curth Orefjaerd has mentioned:' 'In the multi-splendored personality of Bhagavan Baba, one notices an unruffled equanimity, an unchanging and continued awareness and bliss." The writing of several devotees like Nagmani Purniya (1976)[29] Neeta Roy (1973)[30], T.S. AnanthaMurthy (1974)[31], S.P. Ruhela (1991)[32], Charles Penn (1981)[33], (1991)[34], Ra Ganapati (1984, 1985)[35-36], S. Balu (1983)[37], V. Balu (19850)[38],(1993)[39]. R. Lowenberg (1980)39-41,M.N. Rao (1985)[42], Peggy Mason & Ron Laing (1982)[43], Anne-marie Marwaha(1985)[44], Phyllis Krystal (1985)[45],, R.M. Rai (1987)[46], Diana Baskin (1990)[47], S. Palanivelu(1990)[48], Sai Usha (1990)[49], Sudha Aditya (1990)[50], C.L. Sahni (1985)[51], Jagthesan (1980)[53], P.P. Arya (1992)[54], V.I.K. Sarin (1993)[55], Little Heart (1993)[56],John Hislop (1978)[56], Joy Thomas (1989, 1991, 1992)[57-59], Rita Bruce (1981)[60], Judy Warner (1990)[61], Mazzolini (1994)[62], M.R.Kundra (1994)[63] and N. Bhatia(1994)[64], and several others [65-83] invariably mentioned about Sai Baba's genuine love and deep human feeling for the devotees inherent in Baba's charismatic divine personality.

Sai Baba's Miracles:

In 'We devotees' (1983), Indu Lai Shah wrote as under:

"Our story:, Devotees that we are, commences with hearing or reading about Sri Sathya Sai Baba. We are drawn towards Him primarily by the account of the miracles characterizing His life right from His early boyhood at the primary school, mainly in the form of 'materializing' fruits and sweets, erasers and pencils for his small companions. During the subsequent years, these miracles grew fast with the swelling stream of devotees, both in their number and variety. Very often, we meet our friends or relatives, who thrilled us by narrating their first-hand experiences of Baba's Divinity when they visited Prasanthi Nilayam. Many of us could witness these manifestations of Baba's Divinity in our own native place, thousands of miles away from Prasanthi Nilayam, when Baba made His presence felt through *vibhuti, kumkum* and amrit appearing on His portraits in some devotees' homes. Finally, we ourselves felt a growing urge to meet Baba and we ourselves went to Puttaparthi."[87]

This shows that Baba's miracles mainly most of the people towards him.

Sri Sathya Sai Baba is well known for his miracles all over the world. Sociologist Lawrence A. Babb has also observed:

"It is largely because of the miracles that devotees are drawn to him in the first place. The miracles, however, seem to play a vital role in sustaining the allegiance of his devotees. Miracles are the staple of any conversation about Sathya Sai Baba among his devotees, and are the principal topic of the literature concerning him as well, any attempt to understand his cult, therefore, must try to come to terms with the miraculous," [85]

The earliest book on Baba's miracles entitled '*The Divine Leelas of Bhagavan Sri Sathya Sai Baba*' (1976)[89] was written by Nagamani Purniya who had come to Puttaparthi village as a bride and stayed there witnessing the miracles done by the then village miracle boy Sathya Narayan Raju (the present Sathya Sai Baba) about seven decadfes years back. Baba's biography '*Sathyam Sivam Sunderam.*'[90] written by Kasturi after collecting materials from Baba's family members, childhood friends, villagers, devotees and from his own observations, provided a mine of information about his miracles of all kinds. Murphet's first book '*Sai Baba: Man of Miracles*' (1972) [91] which was an impressive catalogue of Baba's miracles experienced by several Indian and foreign devotees, vigorously publicized Baba as a miracle man throughout the world.

Baba's miracles have been recorded by devotees who were not so highly educated but just housewives and ordinary worldly people, as also by highly educated people like Prof N. Kasturi, Prof V.K. Gokak, Prof M.N. Das76, Dr Hislop, Charles Penn, M.V.N. Murthy, M.N. Rao, J. Jagathesan, R. Lowenberg, Judy Warner, Sarojini Palanivelu, and even jurists like Justice V. B. Eradi, Justice Khastgir, and so many other well known public personalities in India and abroad.

The various kinds of miracles, happenings, co-incidences created by Baba have been classified in my book '*Sri Sathya Sai Baba and the Future of Mankind*'

(1992)89. Not only *Sanathana Sarathi* - monthly journal from Baba's *ashram*, but all magazines, books and newsletters published by Sri Sathya Sai Seva Organizations in many countries like UK, USA, Australia, Malayasia, South Africa, France, Italy, etc, have been publishing thrilling miracles witnessed by devotees all over the world.

R.D.Awle, an outstanding researcher and worldwide informer of Sri Sathya Sai Baba's numerous very thrilling miracles has published them on the internet in the last deade, 'Ghandikota V. Subba Rao has published the most thrilling Sai miracles happening with him in an interesting book '*Sri Sathya Sai Avatar of Love*', published by Prasanthi Socierty in Novembrer 1993.

The present researcher had himself witnessed quite a number of thrilling miracles done by Baba at Prasanthi Nilayam and Brindavan (Whitefield) *ashrams*. He had witnessed the miraculous creation of '*Atma Linga*' and the Divine *Jyoti* (Flame) changing colors' with the Lingam on the occasion of Maha-Sivaratri in February, 1974 in the Poornachandra Hall at Prasanthi Nilayam. Eruch B. Fanibunda had vividly described that thrilling event in his book '*Vision of the Divine*' (1976)90 and also the historic declaration made by Baba in course of his short discourse on the inner significance of that *Lingam* in the dawn:

"You have had the good fortune of looking at the Divine Vision. You have also seen the Divine significance of the Lingam and that will grant you complete salvation. So far as you are concerned, you have attained complete salvation and there are no more rebirths for you. Why is it that of all the crores of people in the world only you have seen this manifestation of Divinity? It is a piece of great good fortune for you. Some of you have seen this manifestation as a specific form, some as a light and some only as a streak or a flash of light; but it does not matter in what form you have seen the generation and manifestation of this *Lingam*. What you have really seen is the secret of creation."

The researcher has during the last four decades had seen Baba creating *Vibhuti* (holy ash), gold and silver chains, rings, rosary, sugar candy etc. Baba gave white diamond ring set in gold, silver locket and a small *lingam* to the researcher's friend Mohd. Farah Aidid, Ambassador of Somalia in 1986 and 1987. On 20 December 1987 Baba materialized a number of His visiting cards showing his photo and address in the interview room and lovingly gave a copy each to the researcher, Aidid, his wife Khadija, the well-known Congress (I) leader and a former Union Minister Ambika Soni, her husband, and Ramchandran (the well known Gandhian and Education Minister of Tamil

Nadu), and to a number of foreign devotees and IAS officers of Andhra Pradesh in his interview room at Prasanthi Nilayam. The researcher also witnessed Baba materializing gold chain and other jewellery for Vice-Chancellor Prof S. Sampat's daughter in her marriage ceremony performed in the hall at Brindavan (Whitefield) and the materialization of a diamond ring set in gold for the famous musician Bhimsen Joshi soon after his musical performance in the Summer Course in May, 1992. He has seen the materialization of *Vibhuti, kumkum, honey*, etc, at the houses of some devotees and in the shrine built by B.Halagappa at Srirangapatanam (Mandya District). Karnataka, where honey constantly materializes from the two small lockets given by Baba to Halgappa several years back.

Vibhuti had indeed materialized twice or thrice on Baba's photos in the researcher's house at New Delhi also several years back. Innumerable miracles showing Baba's omnipresence, omnipotence and omniscience were narrated to the researcher by his friends like Prof A.P. Tripathi, (Late) Prof R.N. Safaya, D.D. Gupta, Dr M.Siddiqui, former Education Officer, Municipal Corporation of Delhi, Dutch devotee Dirk Van de Wignaard, and many other devotees. Dirk sent him a photo in which Baba's face materialized on a wall adjoining an open space where he was standing.

A Sai devotee from Madras (Late) M.R. Raghuramanaathan had sent him some photos showing Baba's thrilling miracles. One of those photos was taken at Guntur (Andhra Pradesh) while a procession of devotees went through the streets singing Sai Bhajans and carrying lamps in their hands. Baba miraculously made the flames of these lamps to rise and go upwards as if they were reaching heaven. In the second photo, Baba is shown with a green parrot sitting on his shoulder. The parrot is blocking Baba's right eye from us, but surprisingly Baba's right eye is still clearly visible to us through the parrot's neck. This carries the meaning that nothing can be hidden from Baba wherever he is; nothing can block Baba's eyes from seeing us or anything anywhere. In the third photo, Baba's face with the crescent (Moon) attached to his head in the background of Nag Sai Temple of Coimbatore is shown. The photo reveals that He is Shiva. In the fourth photo Baba's face is occupying the entire building of Prasanthi Nilayam, showing his '*Vishwaroopa*' (Cosmic Vision).

Many devotees in India and West have several other miraculous photos of Sai Baba. None of them are photo tricks; all are genuine manifestations of Baba's miraculous grace and love to make his devotees happy and help then realize his divinity.

The researcher witnessed *Vibhuti* and some other materialization at the places of the well-known lady S. Saiamma, authoress of '*Sri Sathya Sai My Loving Son*'[91] in her room in Prasanthi Nilayam and at her house at Madras. She had mentioned some of the thrilling miracles of Baba experienced by her in her book.

A well-researched book '*Miracles are My Visiting Cards*'(1987)[92] by Dr Erlundur Haraldsson, Professor, Department of Psychology, University of Iceland, had established that Baba's miracles were genuine; there was absolutely no element of fraud, magic or any shady business in them.

In the background of all this collective testimony of devotees, intellectuals and that of the researcher's own, which emphatically establishes that Baba's miracles are genuine divine materializations aimed at inculcating love and strengthened faith towards his divinity in the hearts of these devotees, the attempts of the so-called rationalists who weren trying to do adverse publicity about Baba's divinity and His miracle-making powers, did not cut ice. There are many video films like '*Aura of Divinity*' 'and others showing Sai Baba's miracles, in the homes of Indian and foreign Sai devotees and they can be seen and studied by scientists and experts in photography.

Baba's following quotations about his miracles clarify all doubts raised about them:

"...You believe in such things (miracles) when they are related to Rama and Krishna or others, for you feel that belief does not impose any obligation on you. But in the case of the (Sai) incarnation before you, you apprehend that when the divine is recognized, certain consequences follow, and you try to avoid them."

"I shall tell you why I give these rings, talismans, rosarise etc. It is to signify the bond between Me and those to whom they are given. When calamity befalls them, the article comes back to Me in a flash and returns in a flash, taking from Me the remedial grace of protection. That grace is available to all who call Me in any name or form not merely to those who have these gifts. Love is bond that wins grace."

"*Leelas* are occurring throughout India in tens of millions of homes. Swami keeps them down so that publicity about My *leelas* will not spread..."

"They are not intended to demonstrate or publicize; they are merely spontaneous and concomitent proofs of My divine majesty"[84]., Some objects Swami creates in just the same way that he created the material universe. Other objects, such as watches, are brought from existing supplies. There are no invisible beings helping Swami to bring these things. His *sankalpa*, His divine will, brings the object in a moment. Swami is everywhere. His creations belong to the natural unlimited power of God and are in no sense the product of yogic powers as with *yogis* or of magic as with magicians. The power is in no way contrived or developed, but is natural only."

Baba's Interaction with Devotees:

Baba interaction with people who are very close to him is distinctly of a very high degree of intensity of divine love and care. Many women devotees worship him as Mira Bai worshipped her God Krishna, as *summum bonum* of their life, as 'friend, philosopher and guide, as divine lover, husband, father, mother, Some like Sakuntala Saiamma love Baba as her loving son. Male devotees love him like Surdas, Tulsi, and such celebrated saints. How Baba responds to such feelings of his earnest devotees, is indelibly imprinted in the personal memories of such devotees forever.

Here are some of their clinching testimonies:

Anne-marie Marwaha has recalled: "On his (Baba's) face was an unearthly look of love, bliss and compassion. Both His hands were half-raised as if He was lifting all of us. He stood for quite some time like this and his vibrations touched my soul. It was breath-taking for me; I felt that my own soul was standing there. I never experienced anything like it before."[93]

Diana Baskin observed: "Swami so well describes the relationships between God and His devotees with the analogy that He can be liked to electricity and we to light bulbs. We all have different voltage and vibrate at various levels. When we are plugged into Swami, He charges us with the proper voltage that our physical frames can handle and the current flows steadily and smoothly."[94]

"Thomas Bruce has stated:

"The most precious stories are never told because they are too deeply personal to share."[95]

Many others also have mentioned about the unique bonds of love existing between Baba and the devotees and how endearingly Baba expresses his love through gestures, words and all other kinds of grace.

Baba's Revelations about the Past, Present and Future of His Devotees:

Just as Sri Shirdi Sai Baba had revealed that his devotees Mlahasapati, Nanasahib Chandorkar, Raghubir Purandhare, G.C. Narke, Hemadpant

Upasani Maharaj, Chandrabai Borker, Pishya, Anna Saheb Khaparde, Lakshmi Khaparde, etc, 102-103 had been with him for the last several births and told them many facts of their past lives. Similarly Sri Sathya Sai Baba has also personally disclosed the facts of the past lives of some of his devotees in personal interviews or dreams.

Sri Sathya Sai Baba revealed that Shirdi Sai Baba's faithful servant Abdul has been reborn as the Canadian citizen Ken of Japanese origin. He has reportedly disclosed that Vivekananda has been reborn and in near future he would come to help Baba in looking after his educational institutions and missionary activities, He has revealed that Prof N. Kasturi –Baba's biographer and very esteemed devotee, would be the mother of Prema Sai Baba. He has already disclosed to a number of devotees like Laxmi Deshpande, Dr D.J. Gadhia and some others that they would be reborn to serve him in his next incarnation as Prema Sai Baba.103 In a dream in December 1975 Baba had revealed to the present researcher that he was a school teacher and author in his previous life.

A very thrilling incident has been mentioned by M.N. Rao in his book '*Sri Sathya Sai Baba -A Story of God as Man*'[96]. Baba told one person (RR) that in his past life he had been poisoned at the age of 40 by his young wife in connivance with the village Karnik named Raghuvulun and reborn n as Raja, and that he would be meeting them just "on the day after tomorrow." And truly RR met a truck accident and was shifted to a village home in an unconscious state and there he was attended by an old lady, his young wife who had poisoned him in his past life and saw Raja as a dog there..

In some personal interviews Baba revealed that some of the blind visitors had been dacoits in their previous births who had not only looted certain travellers but even mercilessly taken out their eyes. He revealed to a panting mother that her only son had drowned in Tirupati Devasthana tank because in his previous life he had a keen desire to sacrifice his life at Tirupati. Many such rare and invaluable revelations of past lives have been made by Baba to several persons. Baba had prophesied about the future of a number of individuals and of certain nations. Fanibund testifies that in the Summer Course at Ooty in 1976 Baba had materialized "a beautiful map of India in silver, mounted on a black polished wooden base about 4" in diameter;...Around the periphery of the emblem, a circle of large precious stones was present and from each stone was issuing a silver line pointing to various places in India. *Bhagavan* then explained these lines were pointing to His future centers and the names of the people who would be in charge of these centers was also mentioned here."

Baba told an East African leader Ambassador Mohd. Farah Adid that his long time wish to become the President of his country would be fulfilled. Indeed Adid could become the President of Somalia in 1995 but only for a short time as his shot dead by an unknown rival.

It is quite popular among many Sai devotees that about 35 years or so back Baba had predicted to the present Prime Minister Narasirnha Rao that he would become the Prime Minister of India. Later he has told that the then Karnataka Chif Minister also thatr he would be Prime Minister of India, Both indeed became Prime Minister in their lives. Baba had told some of his German devotees that East and West Germany would soon be united into one.

A noted Guajarati Sai devotee settled in Uganda Late Dr. G.C. Patel whom Unganda's tyrant Adi Amin knew personally, revealed to the present researcher that Baba had told him and some Indian devotees in Kampala (Uganda) in July 1968 that a turmoil in Uganda was going to take place in very near future and it was advisable for them to leave Uganda to themselves. Baba had told that the Chinese aggressors would withdraw from the Indian territory.

A wonderful compilation of Sai Baba's miraculous message - entitled "*Sai Messages for You and Me*"[97] by a British Sai devotee Lucas Ralli, published in five volumes, reveals how Baba was vigorously working, using his devotees as instruments in his divine hand, to usher in the *Golden Age* "When the *Golden Age* dawns there will be harmony throughout the world and love will flow everywhere... the arrival of the *Golden Age* will be heralded by a New Coming as well as some upheavals, sufficient to uproot the evil that is so prevalent today."

Baba had in several privet conversations and discourses revealed about his future incarnation as Prema Sai who would be reborn at the Gunparthi village in Mandya district of Karnataka in the second half of the 21st century.

In the ancient scriptures of the Hindus, the advent of Kalki Avatar as the tenth Incarnation of Vishnu in this age of Kali had been predicted. Several Sai devotee-writers like Hilda Murphet[109], Ra Ganapati[110], Sarojini Pelanivelu[111] and the present author[112], Taba[108], hold the belief that Baba himself is the Kalki Avatar who came to rescue the mankind and inaugurate the era of 'unity, purity and divinity'—the *Golden Age* of humanity which would flourish and expand by the contributions of Prema Sai Baba..

A unique, highly intimate diary of an of a blessed anonymous foreign lady devotee writing under the pseudonym of 'Little Heart' given to her by Baba, entitled '*Unique Graciousness*' (1993)[113] revealed that she (the Australian widow staunch devotee of Sri Sathya Sai Baba who was living in Prasanhthiu Nilayam in the 1990s, was in one of her past births about 5200 years back had actually been born as the only younger brother (Sri Dama) of Krishna's beloved Radha of Barsana village in the *Dwapar Yuga*—. Baba repeatedly showed her visions and dreams of herself as Radha's brother playing with child Krishna and both lovingly fed by Radha. Baba has, in so many spoken words, fully confirmed this relationship in July 1982, saying, "You are peculiarly Mine." and also on several other occasions later on.

The renowned American Sai devotee authoress Phylis Krystal's moving memoirs '*The Ultimate Experience*'(1985)"[98] provide thrilling revelations of Baba's omnipotence, omnipresence and omniscience and his greatest of miracles, love for the mankind in general and for his devotees in particular.

These writings are authentic testimonies of love between the living Divinity and his devotees and they are unsurpassed in their intrinsic sincerity and devotion, as are the devotional epic 'Ramayana' of Tulsi das and the devotional songs of Mira Bai who was keen to merge with her only dear lord '*Girdhar Gopal*'.

In '*Third Eve and Kundalini-*,[99], B.S.Goel had presented his unique experiential account of the mercy of Guru Bhagavan Sri Sathya Sai Baba in awakening his *kundalini* and elevating him from dust to divinity. This great book is a re-affirmation of the timeless yogic truth of all religions of the world that the grace of Guru/God can descend on any one pursuing the path of spirituality, and further, that once the grace descends, the *sadhaka* (Spiritual aspirant) will be automatically uplifted from the lower plane of most gross existence to the highest plane of *Sat-Chit-Anand*."

Goel's intrinsic experiences as a *Sadhaka,* on whom Sri Sathya Sai Baba's had fallen so abundantly, convincingly prove that Sri Sathya Sai Baba is 'The Eternal Witness', 'The Shiva', 'The Divine Father and Mother of All.'

Goel's monumental work clarifies some very important points of doubts prevailing in the minds of innumerable devotees and devotees of Sri Sathya Sai Baba:

Many people, mostly non-devotees, often treat Sathya Sai Baba as a mere miracle man, a controversial god man and a saint patronizing the rich and highups in politics. They do not realize that he is in fact the God Incarnate, the Cosmic Ruler who can uplift us spiritually and even grant *Moksha*. Goel revealed how Baba, as Guru of the real Sadhakas, is God guiding their advancement in spirituality.

Many people believe that a Guru grants his authority to his devotees through word of mouth or appointment as teachers, *avadhoot* etc. Goel testifies that "A true Guru (as Sri Sathya Sai Baba is) can appoint Presidents, Secretaries, Conveners etc, through the word of mouth for organizing the work on the social, economic and other levels. But a true Guru will always grant God-realization at the inner level to a disciple to make him a true Guru in order to put him on the right spiritual path.

There is a widespread impression created by Baba's organization that without seeking the patronage, approval or permission or grace of *Sai Samiti* president, boss or leader, one cannot have Baba's grace. Goel's experiential account categorically discounts it. He has written thus:

"I had also this firm opinion on the basis of my knowledge about individuals who were getting immensely rich and varied experience is in diverse fields through the mercy of *Bhagavan* Sri Sathya Sai Baba that many of them would bring up independent institutions to work in those fields making spirituality to be the base of their thinking. While they and their institutions would not be in any way connected with the *samitis*, they will nevertheless be acknowledged all over the world as institutions of *Bhagavan* Sri Sathya Sai Baba."

In *'Man to Divinity My Life History in Brief'*(1987)100 A.T. Kariappa revealed how, he, then an ordinary householder, was suddenly in the evening of 18 September, 1967 addressed by the spirit of Sri Sathya Sai Baba saying "…I am an invisible and subtle Supreme Spirit. I am known as *Eswara, Shiva* or *Shankar* (various names of God) and also I am known by various names and forms in various religions. I am the creator of the universe. If you have any doubts, take the *Bhagavat Gita* and verify My statement relating to My presence as the *Atman* of all beings…I have incarnated with full majesty and glory in the name of and form of Sri Sathya Sai Baba at Puttaparthi to establish *Dharma* according to My previous Sri Krishna Avatar's Spirit manifesting in Me. This attracted me towards the present incarnation's name and form of Sri Sathya Sai Baba of Puttaparthi (even before I had seen that form or that place of Puttaparthi)."

Sri Sathya Sai Baba made the humble house-holder A.T. Kariappa a God man overnight by his grace. Kariappa established Sri Sadguru Sai Shanker Trust and Prasanthi Nilayam *Ashram* at Ponnempet.

The writings of (Late) B.S. Goel who was later on known as Siddheswara Baba, and A.T. Kariappa (Late *Sadguru* Sai Shanker) unmistakably establish Sri Sathya Sai Baba's identity as God incarnate. These two writings are of utmost importance to anyone who is really keen to know who Sri Sathya Sai Baba really is, but the pity is that most devotees still have not come across these rare and genuine writings and they have not gone to see the unique spiritual work being done in their ashrams under the divine and subtle guidance of Sri Sathya Sai as Guru/God. Anyone who seriously studies these two testimonies can be fully convinced that Sri Sathya Sai Baba is in fact God amidst us, and it is stark ignorance and wrong and unwise on anybody's part to think that Baba was just like like some other false controversial Godman, tantrik or jet age Swami of whom we have scores at present.

Jack Shemesh, a Canadian devotee of Sri Sathya Sai Baba, in his learned treatise '*When God Walks the Earth*'(1992)[101] had analyzed thoroughly the divinity of Bhagavan Sri thya Sai Baba. According to him, Swami's *Mandir* at Prasanthi Nilayam is a replica of the Creation ind reveals all the Vedic Truths; in one pictures Swami grants liberation to those who know that their conscience is not yet free, but have fully surrendered; Shiva and Shakti are both in Sathya Sai; He is pivot, Unbalance of the three worlds in past, present and future; the miracle of the emergence of *Lingas* from Swami's mouth shows that He is the Supreme Creator of all creation: He is God of Gods without a second. Shemesh has ably shown why and how Vedic religious truths, which are demonstrated by Swami by his divine personality and teachings, must be grasped by all true seekers of spirituality throughout the world who seek liberation.

A book '*Uniqueness of Swami and His teachings*'[102] by Dr A. A. Reddy is a very comprehensive book on Sri Sathya Sai Baba.

Thus we see that several Sai devotee writersn - from humble academic qualifications to highly qualified ones, have discovered many traits of divinity in the personality of Sri Sathya Sai Baba as a God man. The observations of each one of these devotee-writers are genuine and unique. Their writings have been based on their earnest and perfectly honest and close personal observations for many years, so they cannot to ignored or dismissed by any one saying that these are figments of imagination and devotees can not be called scientists. This sort of myth and on the part of ignorant people and loud mouthed critics need to be just ignored. Let us point out that observation method is the most crucial and essential method of research adopted by all physical scientists and social scientists.

References

1. Hislop, John S., *My Baba and I.* Prasanthi Nilyam: Sri Sathya Sai Books & Publications Trust (Year of Publication not mentioned).

2. Menon, Jaishree D., Our Sai Beyond Miracles. Prasanthi Nilayam: Authoress, 1990.

3. *Ibid.*

4. Ustad T. Knapp's personal letter to S.P. Ruhela in 1993.

5. *Gokak, V.K., Bhagavan Sri Sathya Sai Baba: The Man and the Avatar. New Delhi: Abhinav Prakashan, 1975.*

6. *Kasturi, N., Loving God. Prasanthi Nilayam: Sri Sathya Sai Books & Publications Trust, 1982.*

7a. *Sitapati, M. 'The Multi-facted Glory of Sai-The World Teacher' in Sathya Sai- The Eternal Charioteer. Hyderabad: Sri Prasanthi Society, 1990, pp. 84-85.*

7b. Mason, Peggy et al, *Sai Humonr.* London: The UK Sai Orgasization, 1995.

8. Ruhela, S.P. *Sri Sathya Sai Baba and the Future of Mankind.* New Delhi; Sai Age Publications 1991, p. 182.

9. Ganapati, Ra, *Avatar Verily*: Reproduction of the newly added 46th chapter in BABA: Satya Sai (Part-11), 1990, p. 89.

10. Kasturi, *Op Cit.*

11. Ganapati, *Op. Cit.*

12. *Ibid.*

13. *Ibid.*

14. *Ibid*

15. I*bid*

16. Kasturi, N., *Sathyam Sivam Sundram*: The Life of Bhagawan Sri Sathya Sai Baba (Vols. I-*IV). Prasanthi Nilayam: Sri Sathya Sai Books & Publications Trust, 1961- 1980.*

17. *Kasturi, Loving God, Op. Cit.*

18. Gokak, Op Cit.

19. Ganapati, Ra, *BABA: Satya Sai.* (Part 1) Madras: Sai Raj Publications, 1985. (II Ed.); (Part II) 1990.

20. ((i).Ruhela, S.P. & Robison, D. (Eds), *Sai Baba and His Message*: A Challenge to Behavioural Science. New Delhi: Vikas Publicshing House, 1976.

20. (ii) Ruhela, *Sri Sathya Sai Baba and the Future of Mankind*. New Delhi: Vikas Publishing House, 1993.

21. Rao, M.N., *Sri Sathya Sai Baba: A Story of God as* Man. Prasanthi Nilayam: Author, 1985.

22. Marawaha, Anne-marie,....and the Greatest is Love. New Delhi: Authoress, 1985.

23. Baskin, Diana, *Divine Memories of Sathya Sai Baba*. Prasanthi Nilayam: Sri Sathya Sai Books & Publications Trust, 1990.

24. Mazzolini, Son Marlo, *A Catholic Priest Meets Sai Baba*. Faber: Virginia: Leela Press, 1994.

25. *Ibid.*

26. Thomas, Joy, *Life is a Dream: Realize it*. California: Ontic book Publishers, 1992.

27. Kasturi, N., Pathways to Peace: Prasanthi. Prasanthi Nilayam: Sri Sathya Sai Books & Publications Trust, 1988.

28. Orefjaerd, Curth, *Bhagavan Sri Sathya Sai Baba: My Divine Master*. Delhi: Motilal Banarasi Das, 1994.

29. Purniya, Nagmani, *The Divine Life of Bhagavan Sri Sathya Sai Baba*. Banglore: The House of Seva, Banglore, 500067, 1991 (III Ed.;) (I Ed. 1976).

30. Roy, Neeta, *Sai Darshan*. New Delhi: Authoress, 1973.

31. Murthy, T.S.A., *Divine Life and Mision of Bhagavan Sri Sathya Sai Baba*. *Banglore:Author (140, 8th Main Road, Malleswalam), 1974*.

32. Ruhela,S.P.,*Sri Sathya,Sai Baba and the Fututre of Mankind,*),*Op* Cit.

33. *Penn, Charles, My Beloved*. Prasanthi Nilayam: Sri Sathya Sai Books & Publications Trust, 1981.

34. Penn, Charles, *Finding God: My Journey to Bhagavan Sri Sathya Sai Baba*. Prasanthi Nilayan: Sri Sathya Sai Books & Publications Trust, 1991.

35. Ganapati, Ra, *BABA: Satya Sai* (Part-I), *Op. Cit.*

36. Ganapati,Ra, BABA: Satya Sai (Part-II), *Op. Cit.*

37. Balu, Shankuntala, *Living Divinity*. Banglore: SB Publications 1983.

38. Balu, V., *Divine Glory*. Bangalore: S.B. Publications, 1985.

39. Balu, V., *The Glory of Puttaparhi*. Delhi: Motilal Banarasi Das, 1993.

40. Lowenberg, R., *The Heart of Sai*. Bombay: India Book house, 1990. (I Ed.1981).

41. Lowenberg, R., *At the Feet of Sai*. Bombay: India Book House, 1990. (I Ed.1985).

42. Lownberg, R., *The Grace of Sai*. Bombay: India Book House, 1990 (I Ed. 1985).
43. Rao, M.N. *Op. Cit.*
44. Mason, Peggy & Laing Ron, *Sathya Sai Baba: The Embodiment of Love*. London: Sawbridge Enterprises, 1990. (IV Ed; I Ed. 1982).
45. Marwaha, Anne-marie,....*and the Greatest is Love*. New Delhi: Authoress, 1985.
46. Krystal, Phyllis, *Sai Baba: The Ultimate Experience*. Prasanthi Nilayam: Sri Sathya Sai Books & Publications, Trust, 1985.
47. Rai. R.M., *Satya Sai Avatar: Glimpses of Divinity*. New Delhi: Sterling Publishers,(l Ed. 1987).
48. Baskin, Op.Cit.
49. Palanivelu, Sarojini, *Sri Sathya Sai's Miracle & Spirituality*. (Three Parts). Madras: Sarojmoor Publications, 1990.
50. Usha, Sai, Holy *Mission Divine Vision*. Madras, Authoress, 1990.
51. Aditya, Sudha, *The Sai lncarmaion*. Madras, 1990.
52. Sahni, C.L., *Sai Darshan*. New Delhi: Authoress.
53. Jagtheeshan, J., 'Sri Sathya Sai Baba: The World Phenomenon' in *Golden Age*, Kadugodi, 1980.
54. Arya, P.P., *Love of Sai*. Punchkula, Author, 1992.
55. Sarin, V.K., *Face to Face with God*. Prasanthi Nilayam: Saindra Publication,1993.
56. Heart, Little, *Unique Graciousness*. Banglore: Authoress, 1993.
57. Hislop, John, *My Baba and I, Op.Cit.*
58. Thomas, Joy, *Life in a Game: Play it!* California: Ontic Book Publishers, 1989.
59. Thomas, Joy, *Life is a Challenge: Meet it!* California: Ontic Book Publishers, 1991.
60. Thomas, Joy, *Life is a Dream: Realize!* California: Ontic Book Publishers, 1992.
61. Bruce, Rita, *Vision of Sai* (Parts I-II) Prasanthi: Nilayam: Sri Sathya Sai Books & Publications Trust, 1991.
62. Warner Jidy (Ed:), *Transformations of the Heart*: Stories by devotees of Sathya Sai Baba. Long Beach: Marine (U.S.A), Samuel Weiser Inc., 1990.
63. Mazzolini, *Op.Cit.*
64. Kundra, M.R. *Is Sai BabaGod '!* New Delhi, 1994.

65. Bhatia, N., *The Dreams & Realities: Face to Face with God*. Prasanthi Nilyam: Author, 1994.

66. Arora, Kamla, "This Sai Incarnation" in *Souvenir* published by Sri Sathya Sai Seva Organization, Delhi, on the Ocassion of the Golden Jubilee Celebration of the Announcement of Avatarhood by Sri Sathya Sai Baba, on 20th October, 1990, at New Delhi, pp. 1-7.

67 (i), Joshi, Sarala, *Kaliyug ke Tirthsthal*. Pune: Saryash Publications, 1990 (In English/ Hindi).

67 (ii). Joshi, Sarala, *Path Pradeep*. New Delhi: Frank Educational Aids Pvt. Ltd., 1989. (In Hindi).

68. Kakde, R. & Veerbhadara, A, *Shirdi to Puttaparthi*. Hyderabad, Ira Publications, 1988.

69. Kanu, Victor, *Sai Baba: God Incarnate*. (Part I). London. Sawbridge Enterprizes,37, Sydney Street).

70. Kanu, Victor, *Sai Baba: God Incarnate*. (Part II). Prasanthi Nilayam: Sri Sathya Sai Books & Publications Trust, 1990.

71. Kulkarni, S.D. *Sri Satya Sai: The Yugavatar* (The Scientific Analysis of Baba Phenomenon).Bombay: Shri BhagawanaVyasaItihasa Samsodhana Mandira,(Bhisma, B-7-8, Shreepal Apartments, Thane), 1990.

72. Kulkami, S.D., *Shri Sathya Sai: The Fount of Vedic Culture*. Bombay: Shri Bhagaawana Vedavyasa Itihasa Samsodhana Mandiram 1992.

73. *Love in Action*, Germany, 1993.

74. Maheswaranand. Swami, *Sai Avatar*. Panaji, Goa: Shantihai S Tailor, 1988. (In Hindi).

75. Maheswaranand, Swami, Sai Baba and Nara Narayan Gufa Ashram (Part-I) Prasanthi Nilayam: Shanti Bhai S. Tailor, 1990.

76. Maheswaranand, Swami, *Sai Baba and Nara Narayan Gufa Ashram* (Part-II) Madras: Prasanthi Printers, (29, Rameswaram Road, T. Nagar), 1990.

77. Menon, Jaishree D., *Our Sai Beyond Miracles*. Prassanthi Nilayam: Authoress, 1990.

78. Menon, Jaishree D., *Self Realization*. Prasanthi Nilayam: Authoress, 1990.

79. Menon, Jaishree D., *Sai Consciousness*: (Freedom). Prasanthi Nilayam: Authoress, 1990.

80. Murphet, Howard, *Sai Baba: Man of Miracles*. Madras: Macmilln Co. of India, 1972.

81. Murphet, Howard, *Sai Baba Avatar*. Madras: Macmillan Co. of India, 19?8-

82. Murphet, Howard, *The Glory of Avatar*. Madras: Macmilan Co. of India, 1982.

83. Murthy, M.V.N., *The Greatest Adventure - From Sai to Sai*. Prasanthi Nilayam: Sri Sathya Sai Books & Publications, 1983.

84. Ramarao, N.B.S., *Dreams Visions & Divine Experiences with Baba*. Madras: Prasanthi Printers, 1991.

85. *Shah, Indulal, We*, the Devotees.Bombay: M.D. Rahjans Topographic, 1993.

86. Singh, I.D., *Gagar Main Sagar Sai*. (In Hind). Bihar Sharif: Poonam Prakashan, 1987.

87. Singh, T.B., *Sathya Sai Baba*. New Delhi: Hind Pocket Books, 1976.

88. Shah, *Op. Cit.*

89. Babb, Lawrence A., 'The Puzzle of Religious Modernity" In *India: 2000: The Next Fifteen Years* (The Papers of A Symposium Conducted by the Centre for Asian 'Studies of the University of Taxes at Austin as Part of the 1985-86 Festival of India in the Unted States), (Ed) James R. Roach. New Delhi: Allied Publishers, 1986,

90. Purnia, Nagmani, The Divine Life of Bhagavan Sri Sathya Sai Baba.,op cit,

91. Kasturi, *Sathyam, Shivam, Sundram, Op. Cit.*

92. Murphet, *Sai Baba Man of Miracles, Op. Cit.*

93. Ruhela,S.P., *Sri Sathya Sai Baba and the Future of Mankind, Op Cit.*

94. Fanibunda, E.H., Vision of the Divine. Bombay: Author, 1976.

95. *Ibid.*

96. *Saimma, Sakuntala, Sri Sathya Sai My Living Son. Madras: Ganesh & Co., 1993.*

97. *Haroldsson, Erlendur, Miracles are My Visiting Cards-An Investigative Report on the Psychic Phenomenon Associated with Sathya Sai Baba. London: Century Hutochinson, 1987.*

98. Kovoor, *Begone Godmen: Encounters with Spritiual Fauds*. Bombay: Jaico Publishing House, 1991 (I Ed. 1976) (Ch. 3).

99. Marwaha, *Op. Cit.*

100. Baskin, *Op. Cit.*

101. Bruce, *Op. Cit.*

102. Ruhela, S.P. *Sri Shirdi Sai Baba: The Universal Master*. New Delhi: Sterling Publishers,1994.

103. Ruhela, S.P., *What ResearchersSay on Sri Shirdi..* New Delhi, M.D. Publications, 1994

104. Rao, M.N. *Op.Cit.*

105. Fanibunda, E.H., 'I am Here But I am Here', in *Sai Vandana* (ed) S.N. Saraf.Prasanthi Nilayam: Sri Sathya Sai Institute of Higher Learning, 1990, pp. 28-29.

106. Ruhela, *Sri Sathya Sai Baba and The Future of Mankind, Op. Cit..*

107. Ralli, Lucas, *Sai Messages for You and Me.* (Vols. I-IV). London, 1987-93.

108. Ruhela, S.P. *The Sai Trinity.* New Delhi: Vikas Publishing House, 1994. (I Ed. 1993).

109. Murphet, *Sai Baba Avatar, Op. Cit., pp. 90-95.*

110. *Ibid*

111. *Ganapati, BABA: Satya Sai* (Part-I), *Op. Cit.*

112. Palanivelu, *Op. Cit.,* (Part-2), P. 141.

113. Ruhela, S.P., *Sri Sathya Sai As Kalki Avatar.* Delhi: B.R Publishing Corporation, 1996.

114. Little Heart, *Op Cit.*

115. Krystal,Phyllis, *Op.Cit.*

116. Goel,B.S., *Third Eye and Kundalini.* Kurukshtra; Third Eye Foundation, 1985.

117. Kariappa, A.T., *From Man to Divine: The Life of Sri A.T. Kariappa in Whom Sri Sri Sri Sai Shanker Manifested.* Ponnempet: Sri Sadguru Sai Shanker Trust, 1987.

118. Shemesh, *Op.Cit.*

119. Reddy, A. A., *Uniqueness of Swami and His Teachings, Prasanthi Nilayam: Sai Sathya Sai Books & Publications Trust, 1995.*

Post Scipt::

The following three books on Sri Sathya Sai Baba wriiten by perceptive eminent Sai devotees,which could not be included in this review due to oversight,, are very also very significant to understand Swami:

120. Vasantha Sai, *Sathya Sai Baba 10 Avatars in 1.* Royapalyam: DSri Vasantha Sai Books and Publications Trust, 2009,

121. Ramamurthy,Karunamaba, Sri Sathya Sai Ananddaiyi.Bangalore:Sri Sathya Sai Publicatiions Society,Sudama House, Chickpet,,2001.

122. Iyer,Promilla,   a,e,i,o,u.Pune:Pomilla   Iyer,Sahil   Apartments. Pariharhowk,Aundh.
Email promillaiyer@yahoo.com Mobile09422034085/ 94230 08594.

- Vasantha Sai's about four dozen books and some e books on Sri Sathya Sai Baba, Prema Sai Baba and divine secrets reveal a lot of new and very important information. They may be had from:

Vasantha Sai Publications Trust,
Mukthi Nilayam,.
Royapalyam Village B.O.,
Tirumagalam S.O.,
Madurai-irudagar Road.
MadraiDistrict,Tamil Nadu.Pimn Code -625 706
Email mukth
inilayam@gmail.com

- Books,*Sanatha Sarathi* monthly journal.VCDs and CDs of *Bhajans* may be had from ri SathyaBba's Prasanthi Nilayam *ashram*:

Sri SathyaSai Sadhna Trust, Pujlicatioi Division), PrasanthiNilayam,-515134 Anantapur District, Andhra Pradesh.
E Mail:enquiry@sssbpt.org
Website www.sssbpt.org

Chapter - 8

CONTRIBUTIONS OF PHILOSOPHERS

"He who reveals Himself all over the Cosmos,
He who is ever near those who pray,
He who installs faith and guards the faithful,
When He has come to Puttaparthi,
How does it happen, you keep Him away from Your heart?"

- Sri Sathya Sai Baba[1]

I

In the words of Seneca, a great philosopher of Europe, philosophy is "the love of wisdom and the Endeavour to attain it". In pursuance of their love for wisdom, as has been rightly pointed out by Dr. S. Radha Krishnan, "the philosophers are concerned with all sorts of abstract questions of knowledge, logic, ethics, morality, values, ideals and the "widening experience of humanity". The philosophers, thus, according to Plato are "lovers of truth."

The philosopher's approach, as explained by Josiah Royce in his article 'The Spirit of Philosophy', New York Times (2 Dec.1945) is critical:

"You philosophize when you reflect critically upon what you are actually doing in your world. What you are doing is, of course, in the first place, living. And life involves passions, faiths, doubts and courage. The critical inquiry into what these things mean and imply is philosophy."

A proper study of the philosophy of a great personality like Sri Sathya Sai Baba, must seek to research into two aspects-one, a content analysis of the discourses and writings of such a divine personality in order to identify the concepts involved, and, two, a close observation of his example of living.

Researchers in Sai Philosophy

Thirteen scholars have contributed to the clarification, understanding and popularization of Sri Sathya Sai Philosophy. A brief review of their contributed is presented below:

I. Kasturi (1960-1980)

1. Baba is a votary of *Advaita* philosophy. "This interpretation (*Advaita* or non-duality) satisfies the most complex demands of the intellect and reconciles all the discoveries of science. *Advaita* awareness of the one in full measure, in all things, at all times. When you know that the 'many' is a figment of your own imagination born out of your incomplete knowledge, you become sole Master and all fear vanishes; you are free from the thralldom of from the many-faced *Samsara.*"

2. He (Man) is the child of immortality, heir to Divinity destined to be the master of the mind and its waywardness, the crown of creation. He is not a monkey that has taken a few steps towards civilizations. Realize the God that is immanent in the Universe, that is calling out for recognition from every flower, every dew drop, every star that twinkles in the sky; realize Him as the Him as the source of the *Ananda* (joy) that you project on the objects around you, so that you may enjoy them,..that realization will render death a pleasant passage to birth-less-ness

3. My mission neither is to raise the consciousness of man to a level at which he neither\oices nor mourns over anything. In that supreme state, one is going through rebirth and re-death and each moment, for these acts are one and the same, emerging from the formless into form, merging from the form into the formless. Then there is no success or adversity, no joy or pain. When the devotee attains this oneness, his journey towards Me ceases. For, he will be with Me endlessly.5" "The real "you" is innocent of falsehood. The real 'you' will not accept the imputation. The real 'you' is Goodness, Joy, Happiness, Auspiciousness, *Sivam....* *The* real 'you' isBeautySundaram... You are the *Atma* and you resent when the deformities and defects of the physical vehicle are attributed to you."

2. Balasingha, D. (1972)Balasingham, a Ceylones advocate, a scholar in Hindu philosophy and an ardent devotee of Sri Sathya Sai Baba, in his valuable study *'Sai Baba and the Hindu Theory of Evolution'* (1972) has contributed this most revealing point: "...Hinduism sees that drama of evolution as a deliberately planned process to confer liberation on the individual soul or for the manifestation of the divinity latent in man. This is the sup[reme *leela* (sport) of that omnipresent, omniscient and omnipotent sat-chit-ananda which guides and controls this entire universe through *hiranya-garbha*.

...When Bhagavan Sai Baba says the fact is worship of the worship of the Lord in any form, in any name, is the worship of 'Sai' or that He who grants all boons irrespective of the God to whom you make your supplication, what is meant is that the power that operates in and through the Sai is identical with the power to which you pray. In these instances the use of the word 'I' refers not to tlx physical body but to the absolute power which is functioning through the body7".

This central idea clearly shows that there is only one God who responds to the prayers of all.

3. White Charles S.J (1972)

Prof. White, an eminent professor of Philosophy in the Department of Philosophy and Religion at the American University, Washington, D.C. (USA) and a pioneering scholar in Sai philosophy contributed these findings of his research study in his research paper "The

These various research findings lend credibility to White's thesis that both the Sai Babas seem to resemble or represent the Nathpanthi yogis.

4. Murthy T.S.A. (1974)

Murthy, a retired judge of Bangalore and an ardent devotee of Sri Sathya Sai Baba, brought out two interesting books in 1974 -*Life and Teachings of Sri Sai Baba of Shirdi'*[2] and Divine Life and Mission of Bhagavan Sri Sathya Sai Baba.[3] In the first book, on the basis of his deep research study he revealed that Sri Shirdi Sai Baba had extra ordinary love for his devotees and he described the various thrilling miracles, activities, procession of Baba. This was the first book in which Sri Sathya Sai Baba's disclosure about the parentage, circumstances of birth and early childhood of Sri Shirdi Sai Baba made to Prof V.K. Gokak and some other close devotees in February199. It was mentioned at length by Prof. Gokak in his Foreword.

In the second book[14] Murthy described briefly the life of Sri Sathya Sai Baba and presented the gist of Baba's discourses in the Summer Course on Indian Culture and Spirituality, 1973,[15] in which Baba had explained the meaning and implications of Adi Sankaracharya's *Bhaj Govindam'*- the famous fourteen stanza verse. Murthy discovered Baba's mission was rooted in the concepts of 'Self inquiry', 'Advaita' and 'God as all pervading *Atma'*—the key concepts which had been so beautifully mentioned by Sankaracharya. Murthv found that while explaining the stanzas of *Bhaj Govindam*, Sri Sathya Sai Baba made a number of very revealing philosophical points, the mostsignificant ones of them are:

- "..*Eswara* (God), *Prakriti* (Nature) and *Jeeva* (man or creature) are not distinct entities. To imagine these three conceptions to be distinct is an illusion of mind. To discover their oneness is Advaita."
- "...When God is available in the form of a Guru, people undertake useless pooja and pilgrimage and so on and put themselves to trouble. If you cannot recognize holiness or God in the person of the Guru, how can you recognize it in images, photos and so on?"
- "If you can feel that the same *Atma-tatva* (Soul element) dwells in you and in every other creature and act on the basis of such a feeling, you will have reached the goal of spiritual endeavour."
- "Those persons, who have no faith, will not be able to see God when He is shown to them. God or Atma pervades the universe, but the eye of wisdom is needed to perceive it."

5. Gokak, V.K. (1975)

(Late) Professor V.K. Gokak was a renowned scholar of English and Kannada languages and a great spiritualist. He was an ardent devotee of Aurobindo and later on he came to the fold of Sri Sathya Sai Baba. He was the doyen of Indian literary personalities. As the first Vice-Chancellor of Sri Sathya Sai Institute of Higher Learning, he had lived and worked in close proximity of Baba. He spoke and wrote extensively on Baba's Avatarhood, and his philosophy, educational thought, mission and the wonderful features of his divine personality. In his article 'Baba and the Intellectual' published in *Swarna Pushpanjali*, a publication of the Kerala State Sai Organization in 1971, Gokak very clearly and emphatically stated as under:

"Baba never indulges in making hair-splitting metaphysical distinctions though he can do so as well as any pundit, alive or dead, if only he is required to go in for them. He is the savior of the common man, and he has formulated his philosophy for the common man. Its central message is that what the individual requires is not information, but transformation. He has often said: "My life is my message. We don't have to ask questions about the here-after but live the life given to us as well as we possibly can.

...His philosophy is a simple and universal formulation based on the psychology of man, the philosophy of Truth, Right Actions, Peace, Love and Non-violence. He is a prophet by virtue of this new formulation and an Avatar because he lives it Himself and has the power to persuade the individual and collectivity to live in the light of this philosophy.

...The rationale of the Avatar consists in the fact that He comes down to teach human beings how to make themselves divine. The democratic ideal animating the Sai movement demands that the whole of human society should be an oak instead of our having a shrub or brier here and there."[16]

In his another masterpiece contribution 'Baba and the Path to Reality.'[17] Gokak mentioned his discovery of the following two basic attributes of the Sai philosophy:

a) There are six Upasanas or approximate disciplines that Baba speaks of for an experience of integral Reality:

i)   *Sathyopasana*: The pursuit of Truth;
ii)   *Anyavati:* The approach of Beauty;
iii)   *Anyavati:* The essence of Goodness;
iv)   *Savitri*: The approximate discipline of Power the Adi Shakti;
v)   *Prabhavopasana:* The approximate discipline of light, illuminated introspection or *Dhyana;*
vi)   *Nidhanavati Upasana*: The approach to Reality through Love. All these six approaches are illumined by intimation, which is Love.

b) Naitikta: Morality is the stepping stone to spirituality.

Prof. Gokak's contribution is well-recognized also for his systematic formulation and presentation of the 'Theory of Avatarhood' in his book on Baba[18] and a number of booklets and articles. In Indian philosophy, the concept of *Avatar* has been there since long, but Prof Gokak has advanced the full theory of Avatarhood while analysing the significance and role of the contemporary Sai Avatar.

According to Gokak, 'Baba's philosophy, in one sense, is a philosophy of 'Pragmatic Transcendentalism'.

Being a keen participant observer of the Sai Avatar's activities, Gokak very aptly concluded this about Sri Sathya Sai and his philosophy:

"It is as a prophet and the inaugurator of a new social order that we think of Baba in his overall role. But it is equally true that he is the deity in the bosom of every individual, a presence constantly to be felt in our innermost hearts. It is from that centre that he guides, corrects and protects us. His presence is there because he is one with the World Soul or the Oversoul and the soul of each one of us."[19]

Thus it is evident that Prof Gokak's contribution to Sai Philosophy was profound. He could discover and highlight those sophisticated philosophical points which scholars before him had not been able to catch.

6. Hislop. J. (1973)

Dr John Hislop, born and educated in Canada, served as College Professor in USA. He is a distinguished academician, businessman, administrator and philosopher. A very close devotee of Sri Sathya Sai Baba since 1968 Hislop is known for his great contribution *Conversations with Bhagavan Sri Sathya Sai Baba*[20] in which he recorded his penetrating questions of philosophical, spiritual and religious nature to Baba and Baba's answers to them. Hislop's other book 'My Baba and I'[21] and a number of articles on Baba published in souvenirs, magazines, etc., are also important contributions in trying to understand Baba and his divine philosophy.

Hislop's philosophical research contributions in the field of Sai Philosophy are very substantial. He was able to draw out from Baba though his research questions a number of philosophical and spiritual secrets and thoughts. He gathered from Baba that:

1. The concept of *Moksha* is not elitist; it is not some sort of rare honor for only a few. "It is something that all must achieve, whether they are heroic or not. Moksha is when you have lasting joy and lasting peace."

2. The concept of *Dharma* does not really mean duty; what it really encompasses is both reason (in which there is freedom) and duty (in which there in no freedom).

3. "The most subtle aspect of Swami's teaching is love. The circle around that subtle point, in order to realize it, is spiritual practices."

4. "Happiness is essential for God realization. It is one of the major gates to divinity."

5. "*Bhakti Yoga* is the direct path to God. It is the easy way. All others are useless."

6. "The Ramana Maharishi's inquiry (Self Inquiry) is not good. It must be combined with meditation."

7. "The human form is unique in that the divine force is as much as 80 per cent present. In the animal only 15 per cent. Man can raise himself to God, whereas the animal can never be free of its natural state."

8. There are differences in the lives of individuals due to two reasons: one; each person is unique; two; because of action and reaction consequences of past actions account for that apparent unfairness in life about which we tend to protest; the major events which occur in our lives have their roots in the distant past. Events are like the fruits of a tree, a seed takes time to sprout, grow, mature, and distribute its fruits.

9. Baba tells us again and again in his discourses that God alone exists, the duality of oneself and the world is an illusion; the understanding of duality and unity will transform our lives if we do not allow a host of predetermined concepts to hold us as prisoner.

10. The direct way to God realization is love. 'Baba tells us to let love come first, and the direct realization of our Truth will inevitably follow'

11. Bhagavan enlightens us about. our real nature;

"You as a body, mind or soul are a dream but you really are in existence, knowledge, bliss. You are the God of this universe. You are creating the whole universe and drawing in it."

7. Narasappa, A.P. *et al* (1979)

In their interesting book 'Garuda Purana and Sai Teachings 'Different Worlds and World Religions (Fourteenth Chapter' (1972)[22] three Medical

Doctors Dr A.P. Narasappa, Dr Radha Narasappa and Dr Seethalakshmi of Bangalore, have remarkably shown how Sri Sathya Sai Baba has descended on earth as *Avatar,* and what religion he preaches, and how all his teachings and role performance are in agreement with the teachings of Lord Narayana to Garuda, the divine bird on which the Lord takes his seat.

These three translators of the Garuda Purana, Narasappa and others say, "As a response to the cries of the suffering pious men all over the world, the omniscient, most merciful God has assumed a human form half a century ago in the name Sai Baba, to teach mankind, the world Religion. We as scientists make this statement after critically studying for the last sixteen years. For, we have found that He possesses all the powers and qualities attributed to God by all religions of the world, viz., power of creation, power of preservation, power of transformation, ommpotence, uniform love towards the entire creation etc. right from His childhood."[23]

The contributors quote Baba on *Garuda Purana:*

"Garuda is the symbol of *Karma* with the two wings of *shradha* and Bhakti, the bird on which the Lord will take His seat, the Hridaya vihaga."[24]

"In the Garuda Purana, Sri Hari instructs Garuda about the daily decline of human life, and the attacks that Death deals with him, with his army of diseases, accidents and natural calamities. You have earned this human body by the accumulated merit of many lives as inferior beings and it is indeed very foolish to fritter away this precious opportunity in activities that are natural only to the inferior beings"[25]

In *Garuda Purana*, the Garuda asks the Lord the question, What are the dimensions of the World of Yama? How does it look like? Who hascreated it? How does the Court-hall of the World of Righteousness look like? Who are present there in it?

In reply to these searching spiritual questions, the Lord reveals the following:

i)   There are two important aspects of God—the Merciful Teacher, and the merciless King of Justice. The Lord is the Merciful Teacher, while Yama is the Merciless Judge;

ii)   In all religions the concept of God as Judge finds a place;

iii)   There are four paths to go to the city of the King of Righteousness, three paths- eastern and others for the virtuous people, while the southern path is for the sinners.

Along the eastern path, proceed sages, merited, blemishless, saintly kings, groups of celestial dancers, magicians and serpents; those who worship deities, those who indulge in devotion, those who provide water on roadside during summer, and those who give the gift of firewood in summer; those who provide shelter to the ascetics during the rainy season, those who give solace by good words, and give shelter to the afflicted; those who follow the truth and righteousness and have left anger and greed, those who have devotion to father and mother and indulge in service of their teachers; those who give gift of land, gift of house, gift of cow and gift of education, those who preach and listen to the stories of scriptures and those who indulge in reading sacred books; these and other doers of good deeds enter through the eastern gate. These persons of good character and pure minds go into the Court of Righteousness.

Along the northern gate travel the scholars of scriptures, worshippers even of uninvited guests, the devotees of protective and resplendent aspects of God and those who bathe in sacred waters on auspicious days, those who die while fighting righteously, those who die during observance of fasting, those who die in Kashi, in the fight for protection of cattle, and accidently in the sacred waters of pilgrim centers those who die for the sake of a person who has the knowledge of divine, or while performing the work entrusted of idols of God or during the practice of Yoga, and those who worship the deserving good persons by giving great gifts daily. They enter through the northern gate and go to the Court of Righteousness. The third is the western path through which pass those who keep away from harming others and others' property and unnecessacy arguments from others, who are true to their wives, who are the holy ones, who offer oblations to fire and study the scriptures;

The *Garuda Purana* states that "having obtained the human body which is difficult to get, he who does not perform the spiritual exercises daily, goes to the terrifying hell. Who else is more foolish than he?"

It is the thesis of the contributors Narasappa et al that Sri Sathya Sai Baba has also been teaching almost the same sort of teachings to his followers and so there is a great similarity between the philosophy of the Garuda Purana and Sai Philosophy. They have proved this by quoting Baba's discourses wherein He has often referred to Chitra Gupta, the God of Justice in Heaven, the *Punya* (good deeds) and *Papa* (sins), one's duties towards one's mother, father, motherland, society and God. Earlier Baba had declared that he would be present 'wherever and whenever his glory is sung'; now he is declared that he would be present 'wherever service to mankind is done by his devotees'.

The contributors have revealed that the Symbol of World Religions designed by Sai Baba and used by all the Sathya Sai Seva Organizations all over the world has many points of significance:

i)   All the five symbols represent God.
ii)   The five symbols represent five paths to become God: the Cross represents killing the ego; the Fire represents burning the desires; the Wheel represents following the words of God, that is, righteousness, the Moon and Star represent steadfast faith in God, and the Om represents the highest spiritual exercise that is the meditation on soul.
iii)   The incorporation of these five symbols clearly indicate that the basic principles of all religions are the same;
iv)   Their incorporation in the emblem of World Religions also indicates that the World Religion is the confluence of all religions.

Narasappa has developed a 'Theory of God' which has been appended to this interesting work. Life is a mixture of Life-atoms. Consciousness of the human being is greatest on earth because his Life-atom is heaviest. Forces which act upon a life-atom have two opposite type of components- A and F. Consciousness resulting from them can be analysed into two opposite types of feelings, viz. happiness and unhappiness. The world is God as perceived by the human mind through the senses. The law of action and reaction is applied to life-atoms.[26]

8. Swallow, D.S. (1982)

In his research paper 'Ashes and Powers: Myth, Rite and Miracle'[27] (1982), Swallow has revealed the spiritual and social significance of Vibhuti materialized and given by Sri Sathya Sai Baba to those who come to seek His grace and physical, mental, and spiritual help.

9. Sholapurkar, G.R. (1985)

In his book 'Foot-Prints at Shirdi and Puttaparthi'23 Sholapurkar has drawn not only from the ancient texts but from the writings of Baba and devotees' experiences to reveal the secrets of Avatarhood and Baba's teachings.

He has concluded that both Sri Shirdi Sai Baba and Sri Sathya Sai Baba are essentially one.

He poses the question: Can God be intellectualized? He goes on to reply this question in these words:

"Man possesses many latent powers and there are no physical limitations to his inner vision and his psychic faculties know no barriers of space and time. Within his natural faculties are dormant powers which vibrate in consonance with the cosmic consciousness and thus get some idea of the cosmic creation and its management."

...He rightly comments: "The two Sais have been pedagogic in their approach towards religion or philosophy. Their approach has been pragmatic so as to instil! love and devotion amongst their followers.

10. Bashiruddin, Zeba (1985)

Zeba Bashiruddin, Professor of English at Sri Sathya Sai Institute of Higher Learning, Anantapur Campus, is an ardent devotee of Baba. As a Muslim she is fully conversant with the Holy Quran and Sufi literature. Her unique contribution lies in the fact that she has been able to discover the following:

i) In her research article 'Hazarat Mehdi and Baba: Truth of a Prophecy,19 she has referred to a rare Arabic book of the 16th century Bihar-ul-Anwar' and revealed how Sri Sathya Sai Baba perfectly fits in the description of attributes of the future great saint Hazrat Mehdi whose coming had been prophesied by the Holy Prophet fourteen centuries back.

ii) In her article 'Sai Baba: Mercy to the World,' she has described how the miracles and love of Sri Sathya Sai Baba have deeply touched her.

iii) In her article 'The One is All' (1990), she vividly described how she has come to discover, being an associate of Baba, that the teachings of Islam and Gita are the same and the concept of God being One as preached by Baba is commonly shared by both Islam and Hinduism.

iv) In her article 'Sai and Sufism'(] 985)32 she has shown how the philosophy of love propagated so extensively and intensively by Sri Sathya Sai Baba, had been the philosophy of Sufi saints like Rumi. She concludes:

v)   "A careful and minute study of Rumi's philosophy of love shows his affinity to what Baba says about the religion of love. In Rumi's life and his spiritual development one can find a case history as authentic and detailed as any Sai devotee's account of his or her progress, after meeting with Baba."33

These research articles and her recent booklet 'Sai Baba and the Muslim Mind'M (1993) constitute a unique contribution of Prof Zeba Bashiruddin to Sai Philosophy. She has been able to establish clearly how the essence of Islam and Sai philosophy are essentially the same.

Dr Kamla Arora in her unpublished Ph.D. Thesis on *'A Philosophical Study of Shri Sathya Sai Baba in the Context of Contemporary Religio- Philosophical Milieu'*5 (University of Delhi) has mentioned that the spiritual mission of Sri Sathya Sai Baba is very significant. "...It needs a lot of superhuman courage to take up such a mission which could be within the reach of God himself. The only other instance we can find in the history of the world is that of Krishna who had announced and accomplished a somewhat similar mission for protecting the virtuous and for the annihilation of the wicked...Shri Sathya Sai is also engaged in battle like Krishna but he does not have to fight battlefield but he is fighting it in the hearts and minds of people.'

According to her:

Sai Baba's Philosophy has four components:

A) Religious Philosophy,

B) Concept of Love,

C) Educational Philosophy,

D) Social Philosophy.

A) The highlights of Baba's Religious Philosophy are:

i)   The common man needs not 'information' but 'transformation';
ii) From *Danavata* (Animality) man has to move up to *Manavata* (Humabity) and thence to *'Madhavta'* (Divinity).

If he does not realize the deity, the *Shivam* in him, he is no better than *Shavam* (corpse);

iii) To combat the disease of discord and disharmony that has undermined human relations, love is the paramount panacea;

iv) *Sanathan Dharma* is the remedy for all the ills of the world;

v) Baba synthesizes the three philosophies of *Advaita, Vishist Advaita* and *Dvaita*. The three stages of *Dvaita, Vishist Advaita* and *Advaita Vedanta* are explained by Baba as "You are in the light. The light is in you. You are the light."

In the words of Baba:

"From milk, butter and butter-milk emerge milk which contains all is *Dvaita*; after that is separated, the buttermilk that remains is Vishist Advaita. But though their tasks differ the color of all these is the same always. This, which is the same in all, is the *Nirguna Brahma* (Formless Divinity)."

vi) All things and beings are sweetened (like sugar) by the same principle God;

vii) Each man is divine. The only thing is that he has to realize it;

viii) Baba says, "Follow the Master; Fight the devil till the end; Finish the Game";

"The Master is Conscience purified or Buddhi or Intellect- Intellect through which purified Buddhi speaks. The devil is temptation; fight till the end' - the fight is to overcome temptations, attachments and ignorance must continue till we reach the ultimate truth. 'Finish the Game' is overcoming the cycle of births and deaths through self-realization";

ix) Baba asks us to know who we really are;

x) He gives great emphasis to Bhakti Yoga (Devotion) as compared to other Yogas, as he thinks it is the easiest path. He repeatedly tells us that the path of *Bhakti* is also the superior path. In the words of Baba;

"More than the adherents of the path of *Karma*, and *Jnana Yoga*, the follower of the path of *Bhakti* is declared to be fortunate and superior. He is better than the *Yogi*, the *Sanyasi*, the *Jnani* and *the Sadhaka* who takes up the discipline of *Karma*."

xi) Baba holds that Guru is necessary to a common man to progress in the path of spirituality, but he prefers the man to be his own Guru. It is basically God who is within everyone who can be the real Guru;

xii) Baba binds the entire humanity in common bond and exhorts us to see God in everyone.

xiii) Baba synthesizes all *yogas*; he equates the different yogas to different paths which lead to the same goal;

B) Love: We should love all; through love alone one achieves happiness and liberation.

C) The highlights of Baba's Educational Philosophy are:

i) Integral education is needed. It means the cultivation of secular as well as spiritual values.

ii) "There are two aspects of *Vidhya* (knowledge): *Gyan* (knowledge) that you have to master, and *Vigyan* understanding the world around us; and also *Pragyan* - the higher being, the art of controlling the inner fears and many layers of consciousness."

D)The highlights of Baba's Social Philosophy are:

i) The very purpose of human life is to seek unity with God.

ii) Everyone should be a *Karmayogi* in society—he should do his allotted task to the best of his ability realizing his *Swadharma*iii) Science and technology should be used for the welfare of mankind;

iii) Man should participate in social life, interact with others and perform his role fully to achieve peace and happiness.

iv) Baba defends the four *Varnas* which are the part and parcel of the Hindu social structure. But he gives a new interpretation to the *Varnas*. It is the duty of every one to stick to his *varna* and perform what is the true nature of his varna. He says:

v)   Baba defends the four *Varnas* which are the part and parcel of the Hindu social structure. But he gives a new interpretation to the *Varnas*. It is the duty of every one to stick to his varna and perform what is the true nature of his *varna*. He say:

"If a thorn sticks to the leg, does not the body bend and hand remove at the command of the self?"

Sai Baba and the Other Saints Dr.Arora has compared other saints with Baba as under:

i)   Buddha and Baba: Both have stated the same truth about the true nature of man. Buddha said that the true nature of every human being was *Buddh* iwhile Baba says that it is *Brahma*n; the difference between the two appears to be only one of semantics rather than any real difference.

ii) Kabir and Baba: According to Kabir, the final goal of every soul is the union with God. Baba reiterates the same.

iii) Nanak and Baba: Nanak exhorted his disciples to discard trust in external forms, remove differences of caste and wealth and to cultivate inner devotion.

Baba is doing the same for the degraded and suffering humanity all over the world. Like Nanak Sri Sathya Sai Baba is busy spreading the message of love.

iv) Ramakrishna Paramhansa and Baba: We can clearly conceive in Sai Baba, Ramakrishna as far as catholicity and universality or harmony of all different religions is concerned. Both of them have shown the path of *Bhakti* and Love. Both of them are alsc similar in their attitude which is quite modem as happening in modem times.

v)   Swami Vivekanand and Baba: Like Vivekanand Baba is also laying emphasis on *Daridranarayan seva* (service to the poorest of the poor).

vi) Baba has gone a step forward in laying great emphasis on rtiml development taken up on a fairly large scale by his organization. Both have given due place to *Karma Yoga*. Both want that people should lead the normal life of household and they can achieve realization through *Karmayoga* as well. Both emphasize the 'Brotherhood of men' and the 'Fatherhood of God.'

vii)   Sri Rnmana Maharishi and Baba: The only areas of similarity between the two are that both of them

viii) have derived their teachings from *Vedanta* and therefore in essence are similar.

Dr Arora concludes that "Baba can be placed in the class of world teachers. His appeal is for the masses including the contemplative types for he wants every man to follow a path which is according to his nature and temperament. He has been teaching that all paths lead to the same reality. Sri Sathya Sai Baba's appeal also transcends the religious and geographical boundaries and is most relevant to the present age....He has been able to influence not only the Indians but also the westerners."

The researcher has recalled a very pertinent description of the spiritual revolution launched by Sri Sathya Sai Baba in the modern age as given by Baba himself:

"A Revolution - more powerful and persuasive than any that man has undergone so far – neither political, economic, scientific, nor technological but deeper and more basic is now in. It is Spiritual Revolution.

The Revolution has love as means and ends. It will awaken the springs of Love all over the world in the fields of Education, Morality, Law, Politics, Commerce and Science. It will inspire man towards service, revealing the 'Brotherhood of Man and the Fatherhood of God'. Everyone, wherever he lives, whatever his status, and whichever his faith, can share in this Revolution and be an instrument for the liberation of mankind from its own ignorance.

It sharpens the inner vision of man so that he can see his *Atmic* Reality; its impact will surely develop and enrich all human communities and transform mankind into a stream of *Sadhakas*, flowing smoothly to the limitless sea of Divinity. India was, for centuries, teaching the world the ideas of unity, peace and tolerance and again she has to take the lead in this spiritual revolution."

In *an article 'Sri Sathya Sai Avatar' pu*blished in a Souvenir in October 1990, Kamla Arora phi*losophic*ally analyzed the significance of Sri Sathya Sai *Avatar* in these words:

"'When at any period of human development or the evolutionary pilgrimage of man towards Godhood, the moral standards and moral values get degraded and evil forces become rampant, whenever out of the four Purusharthas, that is *Arth, Kama,*

Dharma and *Moksha. Dharma* and *Moksha* are completely neglected and *Arth* and *Kama* are pursued for their own sake whenever a Ravana or a Kamsa are in the ascendant, then God out of His compassion for suffering humanity comes down to this earth for (i) the protection of good, (ii) the destruction of wicked, and (iii) the re-establishment of *Dharma.*"

But why does the Divine have to take a body to redeem the miseries of mankind? Why cannot He just by his *Sankalpa* (determination) these evils and ills away? Since He is omnipotent "May the wicked perish' should be enough to bring about the annihilation of the wicked. Bhagavan Baba Himself answers the question thus;

There are two ways in which the *Avatar* can help people. An instant solution as against a long term one. Any instant solution would go against the fundamental quality of nature itself, as well as the *Karmic* law of cause and effect. Most people live in the material world of their desires and egos which is governed by this Law. They reap the fruits of their actions and this brings about their evolution and devolution. If the *Avatar* intervenes instantly to solve their problems, it would stop all action, development, even evolution. "This can even lead to very disastrous results." Once a person asked Baba –"Swami can you change the whole sea water into oil?

Swami replied" Yes, I can." The seeker requested—"Then Swami please do that, because that will solve the problem of oil in the world." Swami replied smilingly," Yes, I can do it, but then there are more chances that a person like you might stand on the sea-shore and bum a cigarette and after burning the cigarette might throw the burning stick into the sea. Can you imagine what will happen then?" ' The questioner did not know which side to look. The crux of the problem, then, seems to be our basic nature that should be changed.

Therefore, Bhagavan Baba suggests a long term solution, whereby the *Avatar* leads the people themselves to a higher level of consciousness to enable them to understand the truth of spiritual laws, so that they may turn towards righteousness and steadfastly work for better conditions. That means that the crisis in which *Avatar* incarnates, though appears to us ordinary people as a crisis of events and great material changes, but is, in fact, in its source and real meaning, a crisis in the consciousness of humanity and for the sake of humanity, it must undergo real modification. When the modification or change required for a crisis is just intellectual and practical, then the intervention of *Avatar* is not required.

Bhagavan Sri Sathya Sai Baba is the first *Avatar* of the Age of Science. He first came in the form of Shirdi Sai and is now in this form of Sri Sathya Sai. He says he will come again as Prema Sai. He encourages people not to accept anything without proper inquiry. He invites people to come, see, examine, experience and then believe. He is not averse to scientific inquiries. On the other hand, he wants people to make full use of these and derive maximum benefit from science but at the same time He does not want people to be infected by the insanity of science and wants the scientists to humanize and spiritualize the science. He says, "We should evolve a method of channelizing sciences towards spirituality". Sri Sathya Sai Baba again says, "Science and spirituality are the two legs that enable man to progress towards his goal".

Scientists have started recognizing this point of view of Swami. Dr. R. Millikon, Nobel Laureate in Astro-Physics who says, "It seems to me that the two great pillars upon which all human well-being and human progress rests are, first, the spirit of Religion and second the spirit of Science and Knowledge. Neither of them can attain its highest effectiveness without the other. To foster the latter, we have universities and research institutions. But the supreme opportunity for everyone, with no exception, lies in the first." In this 'Age of atom', 'Space Age, Jet Age' or 'Computer Revolution', as it is described by different people, science has conferred innumerable benefits on man and has filled his life with conveniences and comforts. But all the hopes raised by science about building a better world order have proved dupes. A study of the international scene would show that most of the countries live under the shadow of internal revolts or external aggression; very many times war clubs in some part of the world or the other have been sounding a threat of world conflagration." The whole world is on fire. I have therefore, come to put down, that conflagration." In these words Sri Sathya Sai Baba sums up the world crisis and gives an assurance of securing man from self-destruction by showing him the right path. To a world steeped in materialistic pursuits Sri Sathya Sai Baba suggests for the welfare of the world at large, the conscious awareness of God in everything. In awakening this consciousness of the living reality of God in the minds and hearts of millions of people, all over the world, Sri Sathya Sai Baba is effecting a spiritual transformation or Revolution of a kind unknown in the history of mankind. It is a revolution which goes a step further than the revolution brought about by Gandhi. This revolution does not only aim at *Sarvodaya* but aims *at Sarvatmbodhaya*. He demonstrates this profound teaching by living in his life, "My life is My message," He says, and his life is indeed a miraculous expression of love in the form of gentleness, protectiveness and kindness which he extends to ail his devotees.

Bhagavan Baba says that Bharath, which has been the *Yogabhumi* (the land of *Yoga,* self-control, sense-control, mind-control), *Tyagabhumi* (the land where he who renounces is revered) the land of personality integration (the cultivation of spiritual intuition), has also been infected by the insanity for hard and capitalized sciences of the West have filled the people of our sanctified land with emptiness, loneliness and desperation. Materialism of the Charvakas seems to have come back to us. We see people holding the Charvaka view. "Enjoy life to the fullest, as long as you live, do eat sumptuous food, even by borrowing money, if need be. How will the body (that you are) once burnt to ashes come again to this world?" Even in this holy land of ours, a land of saints and sages—the finer qualities like charity, selfless love, compassion and self-sacrifice seem to have been replaced by greed, hatred, corruption and cruelty, etc. India has, for centuries, been the spiritual leader of all mankind. Bhagavan Sri Sathya Sai Baba is determined to have a spiritually resurgent India as the torch-bearer of the New Era of Renaissance. Bhagavan Baba has already started his spiritual resurgence in India through the thousands of Sathya Sai Seva *Samithis*, the *Seva Dal*, the *Bal Vikas*, the *Mahila Vibhag* etc. Not only in India but nearly in 90 countries of the world these Sai organizations have spread their wings and are fulfilling the task for which the *Avatar* has incarnated.

Like other *Avatars*, Baba also has the same mission of *Vedaposhana, Vidwathposana, Bhaktarakshana* and *Dharmarakshana*. By *Dharma*, Swami does not mean any particular religion or creed but according to Him *Dharma* means Righteousness—it is a system of life in full accord with the Truth of one cosmic consciousness in all beings. He advocates Sanathana Dharma not in the sense of Hindu Religion. He says that *Sanathana Dharma* is *Sanathana* or eternal because it encompasses all religions of the world. He says, "Those who follow Christianity, those who follow Islam and so on, all of them describe that part of *Sanathana Dharma* which is appropriate to their respective religions. Each one is describing a fragment. No one is describing the totality. Therefore, if you want to understand and establish the total picture what you have to do is to make a synthesis of the essence of all religions. When we are able to bring and put together the ideas of everyone, the moral laws supported by all religions and the truth that is in all religions, we will have a picture. Spontaneous the cripple got of *Sanathana Dharma* and overflowing love, enchanting and melodious voice and his concern for his devotees reflect his Shakti aspect. He is complete in himself like Shiva-Shakti.

Besides the Shiva-Shakti aspect, Love is the most significant aspect of Baba's personality. His entire mission is based on Love; His message is Love; He lives Love «nd is the very embodiment of Divine Love. He addresses his devotees as *"Premaswaroopa"*- embodiments of Love for He wants them to realise that they all are the sparks of the same Divine. Out of his Love, he wills miracles for his devotees, for it is through these miracles that they are attracted towards him in the beginning. Baba's miracles are like the miracles of Christ and Rama which are the acts of God for the love and benefit of his devotees^ The *Avataras* attach very little importance to miracles. But they still perform miracles, for those are the acts which easily pull people towards them. They are concessions made by the Divinity for people to understand them and benefit from them. They are in a way a form of disclosure of God to man. According to Baba they are His visiting cards. "The card says here among us is a God man who uses his power to help us to make us happy, to bring us bliss." The direct and integral impact of a single miracle can produce a life time conviction in a man which no amount of persuasion, argument or discourse can ever bring. Just to cite an example from Dr Gokaks book 'Sri Sathya Sai and the Culture of India and the World, ' Dr Gokak says, "I was present in Whitefield when a group of thirty or forty Italian devotees came to see Swami. They could not speak a word of English, nor understand much of it. They came all the way from their homeland to see the Godman, who had appeared on the human scene. They all sat crowding themselves into Swami's interview room. I also sat in a comer. After smiling to all of them and speaking a few words to one or two who knew a little English, he asked a cripple among them who had kept a couple of his crutches near him to hand over his crutches to him (Baba). When he did that Baba said smilingly to the cripple, "You can now walk towards the Bhajan congregation gathered outside", waiving his hand to him. The cripple got up and, with real hesitation, started moving his leg. He could move them. Like a child learning to walk, he walked with slow but sure steps towards the *Bhajan* gathering. This sight of the cripple making his own way through the people around him excited his fellow countrymen and they all exclaimed. "Jesus has come." They tried to say it with gesticulations also to the Indian devotees who gathered around them. The fact that Baba was a God man was clear to them from this single incident". According to him, *Sanathana*

Dharma is like the ocean where all the religions of the world merge. Not only Bhagavan Baba materializes pictures of various Gods for his devotees belonging to different religions but he also seems to have given visions of different gods to devotees belonging to their respective religions. No wonder people from more than 90 countries of the world are His devotees and all of them see in him the form of their own God. The Christians- see in him their Jesus, the Muslims see in him their Allah, the Parsees see in him their Zorashtra and the Hindus see in him their Krishna. Therefore, he becomes the synthesis of all the Gods - a *Purnavatara*. But unlike other two *Purnavataras* of Rama and Krishna, the mission of Sri Sathya Sai Baba is much more complex in nature and wider in scope.

As Sathya Sai has been playing a complex role of not only helping millions of his devotees in their spirituals upliftment but has been equally busy in bringing about a synthesis between science and spirituality as well as unity among all religions. In fact, He is doing all that is good for the entire humanity. Prema Sai will be the culmination and fulfillment of the mission of the Sai Avataras.

Like Lord Krishna in the *Gita,* he also says, "I have a vow to lead all who stray away from the straight path, again into goodness and save them. My mission is to foster all mankind and ensure for all of them life full of Ananda". Again he says, "Many hesitate to believe that things will improve; that life will be happy for all and full of joy and that the *Golden Age* will recur. Let me assure you that thus *Dharmaswarupa*—this Divine body has not come in vain. It will succeed in warding off the crisis that has come upon humanity. While Sai Baba has to play the role of three Avataras (Shirdi Sai, Sathya Sai and Prema Sai), He in his own capacity as Sri Sathya Sai Baba is a joint manifestation of Shiva and Shakti. This has a very special significance like Shiva destroyed the *Kama*, the Lord of desires, Baba is destroying the ego, the pride, the jealousy and hatred from the hearts of his devotees and is thus helping and guiding them on to the path of good and God.

Sri Sathya Sai Baba can be easily termed as the Avatara of Love. He comes to us as a cool breeze in the hot and burning world of hatred, greed and jealousy. Sad though it might seem, but out of billions of human beings, how many of us have been able to see through the veil of Maya and cognize the descent of lord in human form? Let us all pray to Him that He be merciful on all of us and in His Shiva aspect destroy the ignorance from our minds and in his Shakti aspect fill our minds with His Divine Love".[36]

7. Singh, S. (1990)

Dr. Sarvajit Singh, a Member of the Indian Administrative Service, former Secretary of Uttar Pradesh Public Service Commission, and later on a Collector in Uttar Pradesh, is an ardent devotee of Sri Sathya Sai Baba. He did his Ph.D. in Philosophy from Allhabad University on the topic *'The Philosophy of Sri Sathya Sai Baba of Puttaparthi* '1 which was published in book form in 1990.

Dr Singh's whole endeavour has been to explain the basic tenets of Sai Baba's philosophy in a coherent, unified and understandable manner. He has done a comparative study of Sai Baba's ideas with the basic truths contained in ancient Indian scriptures like Bhagavadgita, Upanishads or Indian saints and spirituals seekers like Adi Sankaracharaya, Ranade, Aurobindo etc., as well as with several western and Chinese scholars and men of wisdom.

i) He has competently demonstrated that the roots of Sai Philosophy lie in the *Smritis,* the Upanishands, the Gita, the Puranas, the Brahmsutra and such ancient holy scriptures of *Sanatana Dharma.*

"I think there is not a single discourse of Baba or his conversation or advice where he (Baba) has not made a reference to the Upanishadic literature. His references to these texts are so spontaneous and frequent that one unacquainted with this may have the conclusion that Baba is using nothing but those which had been given in those texts."

"...As a matter of fact, Baba has a direct and immediate communion with all the angles of reality, he has an inspirational fountainhead to visualise and express whatever becomes necessary to fulfill his Sankalpa. He rather originates from the same roots of spiritual awakening fromwhere sprang the seers like Yagnavalkya, Janaka, Acharya Shanker and so on. That is why, smi'iar and almost identical references are found in all these philosophies."

ii) Exploring the 'Ontological Framework of Sai Philosophy' Singh mentions the following:

"Agreeing with *Upanishadic* wisdom Baba takes man as a precious jewel encased in a five-fold box, a treasure preserved with the five *Kosas* (sheaths) - *Annanmaya, Pranamaya, Manamaya, Vijnanmaya* and *Anandmaya.*

...According to Baba, the Lord (*Brahaman* or Absolute) is immanent in everything, in every being. He is within and without. Being the inner core of everything He has filled everything. All are He and He is all. Epistemologically Sathya Sai Baba appears to take the same stand which was taken in the Upanishadic literature...that it would not be possible for us to know the self in the technical meaning of the word "Knowledge". Baba does not agree with the Kantian version that God and self are unknowable and that they are mere matters of faith. He rather agreeing with Upanishads holds that it is true that God and self are unknowable but they are not merely objects of faith; they are objects of mystical realization. Baba does not regard the self as unknowable in the agnostic sense of the term, it is rather unknowable from the stand-point of philosophical humility.

iii) Baba holds the view that 'Brahman' is an unchanging, nondual entitity; the world is illusion, man's real nature known as Atman is not different from Brahman (the Ultimate Reality). Baba has brought this Advaitic vision to Reality to a dictum which could be narrated thus: the Advaitic metaphysics. Epistemology, ethics and exiology are variations upon the common theme of the reality of non-dual Brahman.

Like Shanker, Baba maintains that there are no necessary and sufficient conditions and guaranteed ethical or religious conduct for realising liberation.

iv) The researcher has discovered striking similarities between Baba and Shanker in the context of their life stories, their methodology, their approach to the studies of Sanathana Dharma and, above all, their philosophies. For both, Advaita is the ultimate reality. They both take philosophy as a practical means, a way of life, a style of how to love life and how to awaken the divinity in man. It appears that Baba recapitulates what Adi Shanker had established long back- "The knowledge of Brahman results immediately in realization of *Brahman*".

The researcher discovers tnat there is one very significant distinction between Baba and Shanker: Baba does not refute any tenets of religion as fault. As a matter of fact, Baba believes in the unity of all religions and faiths. So he needs no dialectical methodology to refute any.

v)   The Sai Philosophy is an all comprehensive one as it includes all the existing philosophies like Vaishnaism, Saivism, Christianity, Islam etc.

Under the theme 'Unity of Faiths', it is brought out that Sri Sathya Sai Baba upholds the unity of all faiths and advocates the Religion of Humanity which is the sum and substance of all faiths. Baba has descended as Avatar at the critical time in the history of humanity to set right the social and moral imbalance or decadence. Baba emphasizes the truth contained in our scriptures about the law of harmony existing in the cosmos which should be adopted as the be-all and end all of all human ways.

vi)   Baba is endeavouring to develop a new man—a value structured person. Baba's approach to all problems is practical, demonstrative, possible and sublimative. His methodology to unite science and spirituality, religion and science, reason and poetry, and, above all, the various faiths with one Advaitic Reality is a singular, unprecedented and unique effort in the history of mankind. He does it with profound conviction, absolute confidence and invincible pronouncement".

i)   Unfolding the Axiological dimension of Sai Philosophy, the researcher reveals that Baba emphasizes love as a disinterested sacrifice of the heart in the service of man. Baba prescribes a code of conduct for the spiritual aspirant - duty, discipline and devotion, and ethics. Sai ethics prescribes three ways of saving oneself—*Pravarthi* (external action to sublimate the instincts and impulses), *Nivrithi* (detachment or internal quiet), and *Prapathi* (surrender). Baba says, "Do and dedicate, work and worship, plan and protect, but do not worry about the fruit. This is the secret of spiritual succeeses." In the fashion of Badranarayana's style and much too close to Shankara, Baba refers to the cultivation of Tapas which includes virtues like austerity, simplicity, profoundity etc.

ii)   Baba is a unique mystic. His 'New Mysticism' is a prctical mysticism. "No one can understand My mystery. The best you can do is to get immersed in it; it is no use your arguingabout its pros and cons—dive and know the depths, eat and know the taste. Develop *Sathya* and *Prema* and you need not even pray to Me to grant you this and that. Everything will be added to you unasked". Baba has declared that He is "all forms ascribed to the Almighty". "I am being Awareness, Bliss, Atma, the One without a second; Truth, Goodness, Beauty". Baba time and again assumes an invisible presence being "Antaryami" (Inner Dweller) who watches on thoughts, deeds and words. "This super mysticism of Baba is so subtle and unscrutable that each of the devotees feels that he is secretly watched or spied on. Such constant universal awareness makes devotees alert so as to guard their talk, they keep control when they feel that a concealed microphone is recording all that they say, this is the posited 'Inner' presence which can censor our thoughts. Baba really is such a presence even when He is physically absent. Boundless love is the other most important element of Sai mysticism.

The researcher quotes Emerson to describe the New Mysticism: "The seer in this ecstatic vision has an access to the secrets and structure of nature by some higher method than by experience—being assimiliated to this original soul by whom and after whom all things subsist, the soul of man does then really flow into it. "This description truely fits unique contemporary mystic Sri Sathya Sai Baba.

15. Ruhela, S.P. (1992)

The researcher, a sociologist by training and a teacher educator by profession, has searchedout from the Sai literature the following points as the predominant features of the Sai Philosophy:

1. Belief in the existence of one God who is omnipresent, omnipotent and omniscient.
2. Equality and unity of all people of the world on the principle of the oneness (sameness) of *Atma* (Soul).
3. Fatherhood of God, and Brotherhood of all men.
4. Universal values of Truth, Righteousness, Peace Love and non violence.
5. Spiritual elevation as the supreme desirable goal of human life.

6. Fusion of modern knowledge of science and technology and moral and cultural traditions of India which is the Spiritual Guru of the world.
7. Secularism, Liberalism and Humanism.
8. Unity of all religions and faiths — there is only one religion—the religion of Love.
9. Freeing the human soul and mind from all kinds of irrational, die-hard, hackneyed, dysfunctional customs, rituals, systems practices and bondages.
10. Man should basically follow the *Atma-Dharma*, not merely his Swadharma and Paradharma; he should behave morally, lovingly and conscientiously in the spirit of universal humanism and altruism.
11. Present time is the most important among past, present and future.

These points constitute the comprehensive gist of Sri Sathya Sai Baba's innumerable divine discourses and writings of Sri Sathya Sai Baba.

Thus we find that Sri Sathya Sai Baba's philosophy is profound, all inclusive and functional to the moral and spiritual transformation of man.

In the end, let us recall Yogahanda's valuable piece of advice:

"Right behind space is Intelligence. And right behind you is God. Live no longer in ignorance of His presence. Churn the darkness with your mediation. Don't stop until you find Him. There is so much to know; so much to see within".39

References

1. Sri Sathya Sai Baba quoted in: Penn, Charles, 'The Agony of God' in *Garland of Golden Rose*. Prasanthi Nilayam: Sri Sathya Sai Central Trust, 1975, p. 30.
2. Kasturi, N., *Sathyam Shivam Sundaram*. Prasanthi Nilayam: Sri Sathya Sai Books & Publications Trust, 1961-80.
3. *Salya Sai Speaks* (Vol. II). Prasanthi Nilayam: Sri Sathya Sai Books & Publications Trust, p.75.
4. *Ibid*, p. 75.
5. Ibid, p. 200.
6. Ibid, (Vol. Ill), p. 111.
7. Balasingham, D., *Sai Baba and Hindu Theory of Evolution*, Bombay: Asia Publishing House, 1972.

8. White, Charles, S.J. 'The Sai Baba Movement: Approaches to the Study of Indian Saints', *The Journal of Asian Studies*, Vol. XXXI, No. 4, Aug., 1972, pp. 863-878.

9. *Ibid.*

10. *Ibid.*

11. Hemadpant, *Shri Sai Satcharita*. Shirdi: Shirdi Sai Sansthan, 1982 (X Ed.) pp. xxiii - xxiv.

12. Murthy, T.S.A., *Life and Teachings of Sri Sai Baba of Shirdi*. Bangalore: Author, 1974.

13. Murthy, T.S.A., *Divine Life and Mission of Bhagavan Sri Sathya Sai Baba*. Bangalore: Author, 1974.

14. *Ibid.*

15. Summer Showers in Brindavan. Prasanthi Nilayam: Sri Sathya Sai Books & Publications Trust, 1973.

16. Gokak, V.K., 'Baba and the Intellectual' in Suvarna *Pushpanjali* (Souvenir). Kerala State Sai Organization, 1975, pp. 1-4.

17. Gokak, V.K., *Bhagavan Sri Sathya Sai Baba: The Man and the Avatar*. New Delhi: Abhinav Prakashan, 1975.

18. *Ibid.*

19. Gokak, V.K., *The Advent of Sri Sathya Sai*. Guwahati: Sri Sathya Sai Prakashan,1975.

20. Hislop, J., *Conversations With Bhagavan Sri Sathya Sai Baba*. Sri Sathya Sai Books & Publications Trust, 1979.

21. Hislop, J., *My Baba and I*. Prasanthi Nilayam: Sri Sathya Sai Books & Publications Trust.

22. Narasappa, A.P. et al., *Garuda Purana and Sai Teachings: Different Worlds and World Religions*. Bangalore: T.A. Appaji Gowda, 1955 (II Ed.).

23. *Ibid.*

24. *Ibid.*

25. I*bid.*

26. *Ibid.*

27. Swallow, D.S., 'Ashes Powers: Myth, Rite, and Miracle in an Indian God Man's Cult', *Modern Asian Studies*, 16, 1982.

28. Sholapurkar, G.R., *Foot-Prints at Shirdi and Puttaparthi*, Delhi: Bhartiyatiya Prakashan, 1989.

29. Bashiruddin Zeba, 'Hazrat Mehdi and Baba: Truth of a Prophecy; Sanathana Sarathii, Nov., 1991.

30. Bashiruddin, Zeba, 'Sai Baba: Mercy to the World'. (Article)

31. Basiruddin, Zeba, *'The One is All'*, (Article)

32. Bashiruddin, Zeba, 'Sai and Sufism' in *'Human Values* and Education, (ed) S.P. Ruhela, op. col, pp. 105-112.

33. Ibid.

34. Bashiruddin, Zeba, *Sai Baba and the Muslim* Mind. Anantapur: Authoress, 1993.

35. Arora, Kamla, A Philosophical Study of Shri Sathya Sai Baba in th Context e of Contemporary Religio-Philosophical Millieu. Delhi: University of Delhi, Department of Philosophy, 1989. {Unpublished Doctoral Thesis in Philosophy).

33. Arora, Kamla, 'The Sai Incarnation' in Sai Avatar: *Sonvenir,* New Delhi:. Sri Sathya Sai Seva Organisation, 20 Oct., 1990, pp. 1-7.

34. Singh, Sarvajeet, *The Philosophy of Sri Sathya Sai Baba of Puttaparthi.* Allahabad:Kitab Mahal, 1990.

35. Ruhela, S.P., 'The Educational Theory of Sri Sathya Sai Baba', *University News* (Indian Association of Universities, New Delhi), Sept. 21, 1992. pp. 4-10.Also published in: Ruhela, S.P., *Sai System of Education and World Crisis.* New Delhi: M. D. Publications, 1996, pp.20-38.

Chapter - 9

CONTRIBUTIONS OF SOCIOLOGISTS

"What *has sociology or the social sciences to do with the science of the spirit or the inquiry into the human spirit?.. No society can find its fulfilment, No social ideal can fructify without the blossoming of the spirit of man*".

- Sri Sathya Sai Baba

Sociology is the scientific study of society. Sociologists are concerned with the study and discovery of the reality of social and cultural phenomena in human society. They study all causes, forms, aspects and consequences of social action. Roles played by social beings, called social actors, and the functioning of social groups, social processes movements, organizations, changes, as well as disorganization and impacts are emphatically and critically studied by them. They use various approaches, like historical, comparative, structural-functional, ideal type-analysis, survey etc, and methods and techniques like observation, interview, case study, questionnaire. Critical incidents technique, content analysis etc are also undertaken by them.

When a God man, prophet, saint or spiritual personality acts as a social actor in society assuming the role of a spiritual teacher, preacher, reformer, leader, harbinger of change, originator or promoter of a cult or religion, or a moral socializer, various kinds of social relationships, interactions, power equations, socio-religico institutions, associations and value structures emerge. His charismatic personality, role set and style of functioning and impact become matters of sociologists' concern.

German sociologist Max Weber, one of the Founding Fathers of Sociology, was the first one among sociologists to study the phenomenon of Prophet or spiritual personality sociologically. He defined a prophet in these words:

"Prophet is an absolute personal bearer of a charisma who in virtue of his mission announces a religious doctrine or a divine command. It is essentially immaterial whether he announces an ancient revelation, or one regarded as ancient, in a new manner, or delivers an entirely new message; he may be the founder of a religion or a reformer. Nor is it conceptually necessary that his actions give rise to a new community or that his disciples should be personally attached to him, or to his teachings alone. The determining factor is his personal vocation."[2]

Since then, Sociology of Religion has emerged a well developed discipline in its own right, and sociologists like Talcott Parsons, Robert Bellah, Bryan Wilson, Claries GlOck and many others have studied religious ideologies, new religious consciousness etc.

Sociologists' Interest in Sai Baba

Sri Sathya Sai Baba claims to be God Incarnate, Sociologists may, therefore, take him to be a 'Prophet' in the Weberian terminology. He is accepted as an Avatar, a supernatural or divine personality, a great miracle man, a great Guru of the world by millions of people of all races, countries and religions. His 'Sai Mission' or 'Sri Sathya Sai Seva Organization' is a global organization through which his teachings are spread and social service activities in many fields like charity, social welfare, rural development, education, feeding of poor, health and hygiene and chanting the Name of God are conducted by his inspired and dedicated devotees, volunteers and office-bearers of his mission. During the last 55 years, that is since He declared his Avatarhood in 1940, the range of the activities of his mission and his influence have grown in an unprecedented dimension throughout the world.

As a great spiritual personality Sri Sathya Sai Baba, and as the biggest social and spiritual movement his mission ought to have attracted attention of sociologists worldwide. But this has unfortunately not happened. Modern sociologists are much more concerned with the burning problems of society than religious and spiritual phenomena.

Only five sociologists have tried to study Sri Sathya Sai Baba and his divine activities, namely Duane Robinson, S.P. Ruhela, R.P. Rastogi, Lawrence A. Babb, and Krishna Bhardwaj. Some non-sociologists have also given interesting sociological information on Baba. Among them, the contributions of N. Kasturi, M.K. Rasgotra, M. Venugopal Rao and M.N. Rao are significant.

We briefly highlight their contributions:

Duane Robinson, (1976,1980)

Dr Duane Robinson, Professor of Social Work at George Williams College, Illinois, USA, authored two papers "Building a World Community"[3] and "Building the Sai Community"[4] published in *Sai Baba and His Message: A Challenge to Behavioural Sciences* (1976) and the third paper 'The Sathya Sai Era; Glimpses of A Spiritual Movement'[5] published in *Golden Age* (1980).

In these papers, Robinson presented a masterpiece analysis of the growing impact of Sri Sathya Sai Baba's spiritual mission, the highlights of which are:

(i)   In the contemporary world crisis in which not only severe moral, social and ecological decay but destruction and even elimination of mankind is being feared, Sai Baba's principles of brotherly love, peace, mutual sharing, and mutual service can save us. "To build a world human community is to meet and serve some of man's deepest needs and desires. It requires dedication, some skills that can be learned and practised and some awareness of the great challenge such building offers to humans. Sai Baba has presented this challenge unmistakably."[6]

(ii)   ... "The task emerges for followers of Sai Baba, and for various seekers for awareness of divine intention, of building the Sai community, a community based upon the principles of truth, right conduct, peace and love, and striving for the goals of spiritual consciousness, openness with the Divine and service to the community..."

... "Sai Baba says that the spiritual bliss and joy available to the Sai family members is a possibility for the extended family, the tribe, the village, the neighborhood, the city and the region, and for the nation, and the world as well. This profound challenge exists to those who follow His teachings. The challenge is to learn how to bring it about, with the help, remember, of His omnipotence and omnipresence."[7]

... "Building the Sai community requires of devotees the discipline of responsible action, attention to the complex and dynamic forces and processes at work, and skill in expanding one's energy most effectively in the service function integral to community building. Such activities also bring to the builders the immense rewards of reflecting in some very small way the divine light and inspiration of the Teacher and Master."[8]

(iii)   ... "Human populations ignore their Divinity and their destiny and hurry along self-destructively... In this age of confusion, turmoil, terror and defect, Sri Sathya Sai has come with his message of truth, righteousness, peace and love.

...The Sri Sathya Era, this era of spiritual revolution which we seem to see emerging, has had a period of foundation laying... In teaching us humans to live according to the principles of peace and love, Baba has defined three paths to follow Work Worship and Wisdom.

... "A critical requirement for us, it seems to me, is for us to understand clearly, first, what role each of us might play in the Divine design and what part our Teacher is playing, to the extent that he wishes to share a portion of that immeasurable element with us."

...Our task is to find our personal place in this movement. Perhaps Sai will lift mountains, stay the clouds of atomic debris, hold back the waters, sometime, someplace. But is it our role to just watch the cosmic? display. Only in action can we really begin to follow Baba's teachings, by working, by serving, in His name. It is for each of us to assume our minute share of the Spiritual Revolutionary task of building a world based on love."[9]

Thus we find that Robinson has competently analyzed the role of Sai devotees in the spiritual revolution launched by Baba on the global level.

1. Ruhela, S.P. (1976,1980,1983,1992)

(i)   In his paper 'Educational Reconstruction in the Sai Age'[10] presented in the Summer Course on Indian Culture and Spirituality at Sai Baba's Brindavan Ashram, Whitefield in June, 1974, Ruhela identified the following ten points of differences in the currently dominant views of Sociology and Social Sciences and those of Sri Sathya Sai Baba about the nature of man and society:

Differences in the currently dominant views of social sciences and those of Bhagvan Sai Baba about the real nature of man and society:

(1) The overall impression one gains from the study of the sociological, psycho-analytical and socio-psychological conceptions about man is that he is basically an animal having debased nature, full of hatred, envy, egoism and ashanti. While an earlier school of psychology considered him to be a mere creature of instincts, the most popular modern school of psychology treats him as a creature of motives and drives, most of which are egoistic and hence unsocial or unethical. It is this distrust about the basic nature of man which has been the latest guiding principle in education. Since long, in actual practice most of our teachers and parents have dealt with the child or the student, thinking him to be a nuisance, or a mini devil. Our methods of disciplining the child and of examining the students, betray this hidden principle fraught with horrible consequences. The school has become, in Dr Zakir Husain's words, "an invention of some devil". Isn't it the root cause of the widespread intergenerational conflict today?

Bhagavan Sai Baba totally rejects this conception of man when He proclaims:

> "You should not delude yourself by imagining that you are the centre of disquiet and untruth, know that you are the embodiment of peace, that love is the very blood in you, that your very nature is joy. Realise this by actual practice and experience". (Baba)
>
> "...You enquire of another the reason why he is depressed; you are not worried if he looks happy, why? Because depression is unnatural; it is against man's real nature." (Baba)
>
> "...Man is divine, take it from Me; he is really here on a holy mission, for divine purpose. Man must earn his birthright, namely *Santhi*. *Asanthi* is for him the unnatural state. His real nature is Santhi." (Baba)

(2) The most dominant school of thought about society in Sociology today is what is called the 'Conflict School of Thought' or the 'Conflict

Model of Society', according to which "the basic condition for social life is dissension, arising through the competition for power and advantage between the two groups." The Marxian contributions to the sociology of social stratification and sociology of knowledge are based on the theory of tension or conflict among the social classes, which has created endless distrust and tensions among people of different social class origins. This theory has led Marx to decry religion as "an evidence of resignation in face of oppression, or opium of the poor". I hope I am not exaggerating in remarking that more than half of the current Sociology (as well as Political Science) is nothing but the glamourized picture of the theories of class tension and group- conflicts authored by Marxists, Marxists-Leninists, Neo-Marxists and the like. There is perhaps no room for God in this conception of the world built up by these theories. We social scientists have but to feed ourselves on the currently fashionable diet of these theories of conflict, which generate asanthi, tension, violence and all sorts of disjunctive social processes. We have become habituated to derive hedonistic pleasure out of these tensions. So great is the force of these Fascist tendencies in the sphere of sociology of knowledge.

Which way will this conception of human society passed on to us by Marxists and the other votaries of the Conflict school of thought ultimately lead us to\? This is a fundamental question for us all to ponder over. I personally have no political leanings and so I have no answer to give to this question.

Bhagvan Sri Sathya Sai Baba has already some eight years back given an emphatic reply to it to one of my friends and an erstwhile colleague Dr B.S. Goel, Lecturer in History of Education in the National Council of Educational Research and Training, New Delhi, in course of the early stages of his meditation. Dr Goel was a very staunch and extrovert or turbulent type of Marxist of several years standing. But then, inspired by Baba in his meditation and guided by Him at every stage, he has greatly changed and for the last several years he has been writing a monumental work entitled Psycho-Analysis and Meditation: The Philosophy and Religion of Life.1 In this he reveals to the world at large in a grand manner how Karl Marx and Freud have failed to lead man to the reality of his existence, and how through meditation the modern man can in fact achieve the supreme goal of his life. This is what Bhagvan Sri Sathya Sai Baba distinctly spoke to my friend Dr

Goel (later known as Siddheswar Baba of Bhagaan) in his meditation in early 1970's :^

> "...Do you know why I made you a Marxist? I made you a Marxist so that you may understand its language, its dialectics, and its real meaning as are being preached and practised by a number of people in the world. I kept you to be a Marxist for ten years for this purpose.
> "...The Marxist thought and the psycho-analytical thought are spreading fast among the people. They do not represent Me. They represent ignorance about the original human nature. None guided by these thoughts will ever reach Me. None would become happy in the real sense by these thoughts. You tell the suffering people all this. You expose the limitations and untruth of these streams of thought. You tell the people to return to Me again to fulfill themselves.."[8]

Our ruling politicians and our so-called radical educationists and educational planners and administrators, who are mere puppets in the politicians' hands, are today bent upon injecting Communist ideologies in the content of education to be provided to the children of our nation in the name of "socialism through education". What will be the future of our younger generation, for Bhagavan has emphatically proclaimed "None guided by these thoughts will ever reach Me ? The conclusion is very clear—we as a nation are destined to be doomed unless we correct our perspective at the earliest.

While all this talk of Godlessness, social class tensions and asanthi in the fashionable world of ideas is the current fad, Baba's prescription is:

> "It is only when God is the Goal and Guide, that there can be real Peace, Love and Truth"
> "It is the duty of man to see in society the expression of Divinity and to use all his skills and efforts to promote the welfare and prosperity of society".
> "...The brotherhood of men can be translated into life only on the basis of the Atmic vision. All are one *Atma*". (Baba)

Baba has repeatedly instructed us not to hate or envy people on the basis of their wealth, position, religion, caste or social or cultural status. This enjoins upon us all teachers and students to leave aside our social class prejudices in our mutual interactions and to work sincerely in the direction of developing a healthy, pious and non-violent social context of teaching and learning in our schools, colleges, universities, homes and in all other agencies or areas of socialization.

(3) Freud, the great psycho-analyst of the world, (who considered libido or sex instinct to be the driving force of all human activities) reached upto this climax only in his thinking that to meet death is the only ultimate desire of a man. Sai Baba's philosophy and psychology of meditation, on the contrary, enjoins upon us to believe that since every person is a divine spark born out of the Supreme Soul, his or her highest or ultimate desire is to merge with the Supreme soul, that is, God or the Supreme Ananda. And, that is why, in meditation, great emphasis is laid on performing the backward journey at the completion of which "you will turn your face towards the cosmic energy, or God again would be transcended and the gates of the sense would be closed, as Jesus said".[9]

(4) The current Sociology and Social Psychology very heavily rest on a theory called the "Theory of Reference Groups." According to it, it is not the individual who can freely decide his role-performance or behavior, but it js actually the whole mass of the expectation- positive or negative of this reference group that is people or groups surrounding him cognitively or mentally, which dictates his choice of behavior or role-functioning in the society. The importance of the individual in chartering his own course of action freely and intelligently is thus belittled in this connection.

On the other hand, Sai Baba lays a great deal of emphasis on the inner promptings of one's soul, conscience or God, which must be cautiously heard in one's prayers and meditation, and which must become the main levers or springs of social action. Man should exercise his own viveka (sense of discrimination) and act with a high sense of responsibility; he must have the dignity of an enlightened leader and be dedicated. He must refuse to be a mere pawn, slave or scapegoat in the hands of others.

Baba instructs us thus: "Do not shape your conduct according to the opinion of others. Instead, follow bravely, gladly and steadily the rational promptings of your own awakened conscience, your own inner self". (Baba)'

(5) The overall emphasis of Sociology has been on treating society; it is the basic unit of analysis. According to it, it is the society which provides the basic incentive, guidance, help and control for the social actions of individuals, and hence society is more important than the individual. In Political science, there has since long past been a somewhat similar controversy going on: whether the state is for the individual or the individual is for the state? And now we practically find than the individual has clearly been degraded to considerably lower or inferior position than society and state in both these perspectives, of sociology and political science, and this has created problems of serious imbalances and tension.

Baba's writings emphasize a balance between the individual and the society for both are inextricably inter-twined. However, Baba seems to emphasize that the individual must be the basic unit of analysis, action, reform, reconstruction or development of society. All strength to society, all changes in society, must necessarily flow from the introspection and meditation of the individual on the society.

To quote Baba:

"What has sociology or social sciences to do with the Science
of the Spirit or the inquiry into the human spirit?
...No society can find its fulfillment, no social ideal can
fructify without the blossoming of the spirit of man".

(6) Sociologists generally start with the main point that a commonality of interests (vested interest) usually bind people in the society. That is the basis of their social solidarity. Although this seems to be true to an extent, let us not forget that the extent, depth or strength of this sort of social solidarity in social groups whether they are political parties, bureaucratic cliques, friendly circles, caste groupings or while

communities, are bound to be limited, shallow and elastic or flexible. According to Baba, the Atmic principle is the only true, reliable and permanent principle of social solidarity.

(7) Modern physical sciences as well as social sciences lay great emphasis on empiricism, that is elieving only in "*pratyaksha*" and rationality. We have almost been indoctrinated by these sciences to believe in only what we can see or experience with the media of our senses, and what we can reason out logically.

Baba has, through His innumerable miracles (which have baffled scientists all over the world) as well as through His analyses and in His divine discourses, very convincingly demonstrated that we have actually hitherto relied upon very unreliable notions of empiricism and logic or rationality, for the spirituality or knowledge about the soul, God and the related super-human matters cannot be understood thereby.

> "Do not be misled by what you see; what you do not see with your eyes is much more significant." (Baba)
> "...Scientists, on account of some selfish aspirations and with a view to acquire certain advantages for themselves, have introduced in their methodology a disbelief in God. You should not accept such rules and say that nothing can be truth unless you are able to have "prathyaksha" as your authenticity.

Social Psychology and Sociology are expressing their pride by demonstrating their researches as to how the ego-identity of the individual can be formed and expanded. Erik Erikson's writings on the subject of identity formation and individuation and the writings of social scientists on the subject of personality development impress educators very much.

Baba's instructions are that if everlasting Santhi (peace) Ananda happiness) and Iswaranugraha (God's grace) are to be achieved, by ran, he must constantly strive to reduce his ego till it is completely estroyed and thereby he attains *Moksha* or salvation. Clearly, the eduction of ego has hitherto remained a subject outside the ken of the iterest of the social scientists and educationists. Our present-day power politics — whether it is in families, palaces of work, administration, social work or anywhere else and its consequences in the form of vergrowing tension, conflicts, miseries and complexes of various kinds, are the results of our emphasis on inflating the man's ego.

(8) The modem craze of social scientists to run after the elusive concept of modernity has led them to lay disproportionately greater emphasis on pseudo or false modernization. We in India have been indoctrinated by many foreign as well as Indian social scientists to believe that modernity and tradition are necessarily antithetical or contradictory to each other.

Baba has demonstrated the fallacy of this stand of the so-called scientists. He has shown how many of our traditional values, practices and knowledge can lay the solid foundations of a really happy and cohesive social living and social progress in our society by synthesizing the desirable modern values and practices. Our traditional and modern values must supplement each other. We are not at all safe if we tend to reject one set of values totally and follow the other rashly. We will have to strike a healthy balance between the two. Many of our social scientists in India are so far only paying a lip service to this proposition; they are not making any conscious and concrete effort at this. The result is that we are still engulfed in the multiple dimensions of value- conflicts relating to tradition versus modernity.

(9) Professor A.K. Saran, a great sociologist of our country, had rightly remarked, "The New social science will be based on a dynamic concept of social relationships. Relationship between the two human beings will be based on swadharma, that is on the dramaturgical ideas of the roles in which they find themselves".10 This shows that the traditional social sciences do not yet have a dynamic concept of social relationship.

Baba has since long been emphasizing this very point and explaining to different role-actors the need of understanding their swadharm and of following it with the high sense of discrimination, devotion and duty.

These differences clearly reveal that our faulty conception or perspective of the reality of a man's life in this society has been basically responsible for giving a wrong direction to our educational thinking and our educational efforts.

(10) In his paper *'The Sai Baba Movement: A Sociological Profile'* presented in the seminar on the subject given in the Department of Sociology, Indian Institute of Technology, Kanpur, chaired by Professor R.P. Rastogi in 1983. Ruhela analyzed Sai Baba's spiritual movement sociologically on the basis of the following nine points:

1. Genesis
2. Functions.
3. Ideology.
4. Leadership and Organization.
5. Social Base and Reference Groups.
6. Social Control.
7. Significance or Impact.
8. Critics. Future.

According to Ruhela, "Sai Baba seems to be developing four Utopian orientations" (a term contributed by Karl Manheim, an authority in the Sociology of Knowledge):

(1) Development of human society based on the belief in the existence of God and the universal values of truth, duty, peace, love and non-violence, and unmitigated by the considerations of differences in sex, community, class, caste, region, nation, etc.

(2) Promotion of understanding and appreciation of the concept of 'Human Religion' which is a unique amalgamation of the finest teachings of the major religions of the world.

(3) Social service to be the essential part or built-in device of the followers' faith, devotion and commitment towards this movement in general and its origination in particular propelled by Baba's Divine Will. "The secret of the steady progress of this great moral and social movement lies in its being ncillu i aggressive nor defensive, but in its tendency to go on progressing with strong faith in the truth Sri Sathya Sai Baba and his mission stand for."

(4) In his paper 'Baba: A Challenging Sociological Phenomenon[12] published in *Golden Age* (1980), Ruhela analyzed Sai Baba's "charisma which is always at work" in mobilizing human as well as the material resources of the vast community of his followers for organizing social welfare

activities of tremendous proportions. In his view, "In the history of social revolutions and movements, the Sathya Sai revolution is bound to find a unique place, for it is entirely a spiritual movement which is not vitiated by any tinge of bigotry, fanaticism, violence, unholy or immoral values. It is unique in this sense that one personality controls it despite its ever-owing frontiers, and that control is exercised through the self-discipline in the millions of followers of the Sai movement."

(5) Ruhela content-analysed Baba's teachings and identified the following basic elements of 'Sai Sociology' in his research paper 'The Educational Theory of Sri Sathya Sai Baba' (1992).13:

1. Principle of divinity inherent in every person and creature.
2. Principle of love as the basis of all human relationships.
3. Principle of sharing.
4. Principle of commonality.
5. Principle of peaceful co-existence.
6. Principle of balance and synthesis between tradition and modernity.
7. Principle of selfless service for the common good.
8. Principle of obliging people.
9. Principle of self-discipline.
10. Concept of progress, which means development of a God-fearing, moral, human and forward-looking society.
11. Principle of happiness, which emphasizes that happiness can be obtained only by cultivating a state of mind which is detatched-unaffected by fortune-good or bad. In his book Sri Sathya Sai Baba and The Future of Mankind' (1992)14 Ruhela analyzed the sociological causes for which people believe Sri Sathya Sai Baba to be God and go to him in large numbers. These factors have been discovered by him after interviewing devotees informally for several years.

In the same book, he has sociologically analyzed how Baba communicates with his devotees and followers and persuades them as a moral socializer, through a variety of his strategies of roie playing. The role of Sri Sathya Sai Baba as an Avatar has been highlighted in a sociological perspective using structural-functional analysis and social survey approaches.

9. Rastogi (R.P. (1986,1993)

In his paper 'Reconstruction of Social Systems' (1986)15 R.P. Rastogi, Professor of Sociology, Indian Institute of Technology, Kanpur, analyzed the malfunctioning of existing social systems and showed how a really functional social reconstruction can be brought about by applying into practice the four great values — Sathya, Dharma, Shanti and Prema preached by Sri Sathya Sai Baba. According to him, "This framework of Sathya, Dharma, Shanti and Prema is superordinate and super-rational in so far as rationality is usually defined in subjective terms by groups and persons. It is rational in an absolute and universal sense. The process of social reconstruction follows logically and systematically from the foregoing super-rational values. Its focus lies in the transformation of individual... The process of transformation is deemed to start from individual 'I' in a gradual manner. I's internalization of four super-rational values changes his psychic orientation towards himself, his family and the outside world".

Greatly impressed by Sri Sathya Sai Baba's scheme of social transformation through adherence to these super-rational values, Rastogi has concluded that 'It (social transformation) is essentially a process of self-directed and socially supported spiritual change within the individuals, its quintessence lies in the man's true knowledge of himself."

In his another paper 'Moral Regeneration of the Somali People"*' published in '*The Preferred Future Development in Somalia*' (1993), Rastogi again emphasized that moral regeneration of a people can be affected by understanding the foundations and sustenance of moral values, specially universal love (Prema) and inner serenity (shanti) emphasized by Sri Sathya Sai Baba.

10. Babb. Lawrence A. (1986)

In his two sociological research papers—Sathya Sai Baba's Miracles (1986)17 and 'The Puzzle of Religious Modernity' (1986)n, Bebb has analyzed Baba's miracles and their impact on his devotees and how he organizes and controls his followers in his vast spiritual empire. The highlights of his sociological analysis in these contributions are:

1. "Sri Sathya Sai Baba's dominant identity is Shiva, and He is conographically portrayed in association with linga and vibhuti."

2. "The raison d'etre of his cult is the worship and service of this living God"., the cult has rather a narrow—but socially and culturally very influential—constituency, which is drawn from urban India's English educated elites."

3. "One of the most remarkable features Sri Sathya Sai Baba's cult is that he has managed to serve the imagery and atmosphere of a purely personal constituency, despite the fact that many of his devotees see him rarely, and often only from a distance. The cult-in-the world is a kind of devotional empire, far flung, but totally dependent on the authority of its sovereign".

4. "In contrast to the Radhaswami and Brahamakumari movements the cult does not consider itself to be in tension with the religious usages of the surrounding community. The cult does not have prescribed rites that might conflict with other ceremonial requirements, nor does it see its tenets as it adds in any way with what it said to be true essence of other religions. Given Sathya Sai Baba's divine identity, all worship of God - in whatever form- is actually worship of him in any case."

5. "One can participate in the cult at practically any level - family, samiti, community, ashram, form of address etc."

6. "Sri Sathya Sai Baba's doctrines are 'basically an eclectic blend of elements drawn from a variety of well-known philosophical and devotional traditions'. Auspiciousness. Under the rather cluttered eclecticism of Sathya Sai Baba's teachings are a few consistent themes. One is a persistent note of cultural rationalism of a kind that sometimes verges on nativism. Although he welcomes foreigners as followers, he regards Western cultural influences as highly destructive in India. He believes that many Indians have sold themselves to the West and have become alienated from their own heritage." Sathya Sai Baba's harsh judgement of the Westernization of India, which is expressed repeatedly in his discourses, is not a minor theme."

7. "His discontent with the state of present day India does not mean that he advocates radical reforms of existing economic or social institutions. For example, he is against strikes; for him the ideal social order is one based on non-competitive complementation, a view deeply conditioned by the ideology of caste.. Sri Sathya Sai Baba urges his followers to treat others with decency and charity, but he does not advocate the upsetting of existing hierarchies. He is no feminist, but by his own

lights he has a deep concern for women's education.. His views on the innate characteristics of women are a piece with his views on caste, and are hardly enlightened, at least from a feminist point of view."

8. "...For most devotees Baba's teachings are little more than a tambura-like background—drone. For them what is important about what he says is not its content, but the fact that he is the one saying it".

9. "It is largely because of the miracles that devotees are drawn to him in the first place. The miracles, moreover, seem to play a vital role in sustaining the allegiance of his devotees. Miracles are the staple food of any conversation about Sathya Sai Baba among his devotees, and are the principal topic of the literature concerning him as well. Any attempt to understand this cult, therefore, must try to come to terms with the miraculous."

In his paper 'The Puzzle of ReligiousModernity" Babb has presented these sociological observations:

1. "At one level he is a religious teacher. Although he has no "system" of his own,' 'his teachings embody a coherent indistinctive religious outlook' '.

2. His fame rests "not on these teachings but on the miracles with which he is credited."

3. His miracles are "projections of Sathya Sai Baba's character as a deity. One of the most obvious features of this deity saint's person is his utter unpredictability. He is loving and generous, but also trickster-like: mercurial, mischievous, full of fun.

Although this aspect of Sathya Sai Baba's character may puzzle Euro-Americans, it is consistent, with certain Hindu concepts of divinity. His accountability is only a delusion arising from human limitations. It is true, for example, that he frequently fails to reward those whom the world regards as virtuous. It is true, too, that he frequently fails to ameliorate the misfortunes of the apparently innocent, and it cannot be denied that he sometimes lavishes his favours on those who appear too favoured already by a corrupt world. But the impression of moral chaos arising from these apparent facts is really only a product of the narrowness of human moral insight. Human beings do not even know their karmic past, to say nothing of those of others. Sathya Sai, however, knows every thing, "past, present, and future". In this context the dry opacity of his behaviour becomes a reinforcing evidence of his divinity. The seamlessness of this logic is an important ingredient in the strong sense of reassurance and confidence that devotees gain from their contact with Baba.

4. Baba presents "the total symbolic package, of which the magic is only one element, resonates with what in many of his devotees is a deeply entrenched hopefulness. There is something fundamentally confident about the "Sai" outlook on the world. For his devotees the world is suffused with his love, a place in which nothing is impossible, and in which events always serve a benevolent purpose. This view embodies a kind of optimism that is consonant with the attitudes of those most rewarded by a social and economic order still being born".

In his paper 'Sathya Sai Baba's Saintly Play' 19 (1987), Babb describes the Avatar's divine ways.

5. Dr. Krishna Bhardwaj (1995)

A young sociologist, Dr Krishna Bhardwaj's research study which sas published under the title 'Social Change in India: Change, Religion and Individual (1995)."[20]

In her research she has compared Radha Soami and Sri Sai Sathya Sai organizations at Jaipur taking a sample of 70 families each of the two sects, comprising of both males and females Lecturer in Sociology, Government Arts College, Alwar (Rajasthan) had conducted her doctoral study in Sociology at the University of Rajasthan, Jaipur and people of five age groups—20-30, 31-40, 41-50, 51-60, 61 plus, and of different age groups. The objectives of her study were:

(i)   to examine the role of modernization in the emergence of religious sects in India;
(ii)   to identify the elements of modernity in the ideologies of sects;
(iii)   to observe the process and pattern of recruitment of members of the sects;
(iv)   to find out the levels of modernization and traditionality of the members;

(v)   to know the consequences of modernity in individual's life and find their religious involvements;

(vi)   to see whether the extent of participation in sects and the sect ideologies influence the role behavior, role satisfaction and commitment of an individual to his duties.

The findings of her interesting sociological research study are:

(1) The comparison of the traits of the followers of these two sects creates an impression that they are opposite to each other. But this proves only to be an illusion if we probe the issue of the relation of modernity and tradition.

(2) The organizational structure of these sects proved to be equally suited for the purpose of missions abroad as well as for the purpose of spreading modernization in India as they allow everybody to adopt a new way of life but he may as well continue his traditional way of life taking up only new interpretations.

(3) The pictures of these sects explain their emergence in modern society. They both emphasize on love and devotion. Their founders have essentially made it a faith of actual practice and behavior. Sathya Sai sect focuses on the experience of this world whereas Radha Soami sect emphasizes both the experience of this world and the other world. However, the practiced form of both the sects is intended to facilitate the living in the contemporary modernizing society.

(4) The respondents were mostly influenced by the philosophy and teachings of the faith and by the Guru.

(5) Most of the followers experienced a change in their way of looking at life after they joined the sect. Some of them reported to have become less materialistic; others thought they have turned more spiritualistic. There were also experiences of more humanitarianism and some experienced an overall change in their personalities. Most of the followers reported increased confidence after joining these sects.

These facts reveal a close relationship between religion and society.

6. Kasturi, N. (1961-88)

The writings of N. Kasturi, Baba's closest and longtime devotee, are full of very intimate and authentic information about His personality, habits, miracles, activities, and impact as a unique God man on all those who visit him. In his books 'Sathyam Sivam Sundaram (Baba's official biography in four parts)21, Eswaramma; 198822, Loving God (1982)23, and Prasanthi and articles like 'The Interview He Grants' (1975)24 etc. Kasturi has revealed, rare sociological information based on his participant observation for over two decades in close proximity of Baba.

Kasturi quoted Baba telling an American, "I know not only what happened 7000 years ago at the historic battlefield of Kurukshetra but what happened 70,000 years ago, too. I read no books. When you run on the first gear, the car goes forward; shift to reverse gear, you go backwards. I can go forwards and backward in time, and know anything I wish. Time and Space can impose no limitations on Me.'

He also recalls Baba telling Hislop about the halo around Baba's head, "Thousands have seen the halo. You must be both near and dear to Me so that you can see it."

Kasturi records how Baba is omnipotent, omnipresent and omniscient, and how humane, compassionate jovial, exemplary he is while dealing with his devotees. Kasturi's writings are indispensable for anyone who wishes to understand Baba from religious, philosophical and sociological perspectives.

7. Rasgotra, M.K. (1975,1980).

A distinguished career diplomat and Baba's ardent devotee, M.K. Rasgotra has contributed a number of articles on Baba in sociological perspective which are of much interest to keen sociologists.

(i)   In his earliest article *'Baba: The Hope of Mankind'* (1975)24, Rasgotra wrote:

"The only way to understand Sai mystery, as Baba himself says is to merge in it, No small task that; success in which might, besides, find one engulfed in a vast area of silence. In writing about him the most one may attempt is perhaps a chronicle of certain events of his life or the more easily comprehensible manifestations of the power and purpose, or, by way of homage or tribute, a narrative of one's own experiences of his grace."

Rasgotra testified:

"Embodiment of Love. That is what Sathya Sai Baba is: the *Avatar* of Love whose task is to release mankind from the vicious grip of fear, ignorance and hate."

(ii)   In his article 'An Avatar's Reality, His Powers and His Mission (1980)[25], Rasgotra recalled that his first acquaintance with Baba was in March 1972, and in early February, 1994, Baba asked one of the members of the group, which included Rasgotra, in the interview room, "You have doubt? Do you want proof that I am Avatar? What kind of proof will satisfy you? What do you want from God? "At that point he held out his right hand, fore arm bare, palm open and empty and facing upwards; he then closed the palm saying. "All the three worlds (*lokas*) are here in this hand. Tell me what you want and I'll give it to you here and now — gold, riches, diamonds, anything. I shall produce for you here and now anything you ask for."

(iii)   In his Convocation Address26 at the VIII Convocation of Sri Sathya Sai Institute of Higher Learning in November 1989 and also in his article 'Sri Sathya Sai Mission For the Right World Order'21 published in Sai Vandana (1990), Rasgotra portrayed the disturbing socio-political world context and highlighted the following:

"Sathya Sai Baba is re-awakening India to her divine heritage
so that India may fulfil her mission of revealing to the world
the path to the divine".
by side in the Sri Sathya Sai Institute of Higher Learning...".
S. Rao, M. Venugopal (1976)

Rao presented a Marxist analysis of Sai Baba's ideas in his article 'Synthesis between Spirituality and Materialism'[21] published in the (Blitz Weekly) on October 16, 1976, and commented that Baba's ideas to solve the problem of inequality and mal-distribution in society through spiritual means do not seem to be practicable.

"To achieve the end of rehabilitation of our economy, Baba said "One has to rid the people of the disease of individuality, greed and selfishness. Every individual must be taught to think and work in the broader concept of society and its needs." While accepting that distribution of wealth and property is not taking place properly, Baba contended that the doctrines of Equality and Socialism have not succeeded in this aspect and that spiritualism alone can bring about equality in the desires of the people. "We must persuade the rich that desire and its fulfillment in material wants is an aspect of the monkey-mind which can only harm them and put them under bondage. That alone will solve the problem of inequality and mal-distribution."

This spiritual means seems to be a permanent solution. If it is possible to change the psychology of the individuals by mere persuasion, then Karl Marx's innocuous utopia—the withering away of the state will become a fact, and equality in the true sense of the term will exist. This process of perfecting the psychology of the people is, however, an eternal one, since it is an endless continuation that the passing away of the existing generation will be followed by the coming of posterity.

Can the Wealthy be Persuaded?

Moreover, the fact that in spite of the strenuous efforts of innumerable spiritually enlightened acharyas, swamis and babas, from time to time, to persuade people to tread the path of spiritualism, mankind is still badly in need of spiritual enlightenment, which again emphasizes that the Endeavour to enlighten the people is unstrained. As such, under this ceaseless process of spiritual persuasion of the people, there is no definite guarantee of when "the rich will give up their extravagant wants, the poor will get what they need and a little more. "All this talk of persuasion of the rich is nothing but asking the poor to wail for their material betterment till the rich get persuaded, so that the latter should come to share their ill-gotten fortunes with the poor. It is awkward to teach philosophy or morality to the poor with hungry bellies. Irrespective of spiritual matters, first of all, the poor must be given the indispensable essentials of life—back and belly, shelter, education and work.

...He (Baba) did not take into consideration the scientifically proved socialist truth that it is the capitalist mode of production and distribution and its myriad evils regularly indulged in by the capitalists in exploiting the nation which are the root causes of the misery of the majority of the toiling masses.

Spiritualism Ys Marxism

As Karl Marx observed: "The restless, never-ending process of profit-making alone is what he (capitalist) aims at. This boundless greed after riches, this passionate chase after exchange-value, is common to capitalist and the miser; but while the miser is merely a capitalist gone mad, the capitalist is a rational miser."

It is this "boundless greed after riches" that the bourgeois minds should be cured. For this purpose, as Baba contended, "the healing touch of spiritualism" is the only permanent panacea, which also, must be administered permanently. So, besides spiritualism, some materialistic devices are to be implemented to clean the bourgeois minds of insatiability and to infuse also a sense of self-reliance and complacency in the minds of the people.

These measures should be such as to make everybody realize that it is absolutely impossible for him to act as an exploiter and that his pe-sonal good is involved in the common good of all. Is it sane to provide the individual with all the evil means to commit all the atrocities, and then try to persuade him not to do what is undesirable?"

The author's conclusion, as contained in the opening para of the article is:

"Though I dare not suspect the divine missionary zeal of SathyaSai Baba, I was confused by his prescription of the means of Spiritualism for the material betterment of mankind, in particular of the poor"

9. Rao M.N. (1985)

Rao's study *Sri Sathya Sai Baba - A Story of God as Man'* (1985)[28] is a remarkable sociological study of Sri Sathya Sai Baba. The researcher collected a treasure of rich sociological information about Sri Sathya Sai Baba as a person in his early life, his ashram, mission, miracles and the organization and educational transformation engineered by this unique Godman. His description is based on his close observation as a participant observer in Baba's Prasanthi Nilayam, Ashram and his interaction with a number of functionaries in Baba's mission and ashram and eminent devotees.

Rao's sociological profile of Baba as a Godman par excellence is very thrilling for it highlights very intimate authentic data about Baba. Thus, for instance, he informs us that Baba uses no cosmetics or scents and yet there is a natural fragrance in his crown of hair; he does not use any ha5*- dye nor did a barber visit him for more than two decades, Baba's dietary habits are not too rigid, he is strict vegetarian, he does not take any milk, curds, cheese or butter, he has an exclusive kitchen, he is a poor eater. He works all alone, his simple office consists only of a chair and a writing table; no telephone, no files, no reference books, neither a secretary nor a typewriter. He himself opens hundreds and thousands of letters received daily; he knows the contents of all letters even without opening them, as has been empirically verified by a devotee. Baba writes all his letters himself in English or Telugu. He is a light sleeper.

The researcher has presented an ethnographic account of Baba's daily routine, activities, festivities and celebrations in his ashram, and mentions some of his most thrilling miracles like creation of vibhuti and other articles, multiplication of food and sweets, transmutation, informing about lost possessions and secret treasures, surgical miracles, and telling one's past, present and future most accurately.

According to the researcher, "Swami (Baba) is conversant with the latest in all subjects and in all sciences" Rao has given examples from Public Health Engineering, Anthropology, Ariel Trick Photography, spiritual sciences, languages etc. Baba's Vajra Sankalpa' (firm determination) gets herculean projects performed.

The researcher describes how Baba helps his devotees in solving their life problems, and in their spiritual transformation and salvation. He has revealed how his organization is organized.

This sociological study is a must for all those who wish to know most authentic and detailed information on Sri Sathya Sai Avatar and His works. Rao's book' God And His Gospel' (1995) provides a brilliant sociological account of Baba's way of life and his activities and contributions for the welfare of the mankind.

10. Reddy, A. Adivi (1995)

Reddy's book '*Uniqueness of Swami and His Teachings*' is a masterpiece work on the uniqueness of Sai Baba's divine reality, his global mission, teachings and contributions.

This review of sociological writings reveals that while Sri Sathya Sai Baba's divine personality and his teachings and mission have been studied sociologically by some scholars, only Sai Baba's mystic phenomenon needs to be studied further by sociologists. The impact of Baba's charismatic personality on his devotees, the organization and functioning of Baba's mission, devotee's changing behavior patterns, social service activities, Baba's influence of politicians in India and abroad, sociological implications of Baba's miracles, Sri Sathya Sai's utopia and how his devotees are trying to make it a practical reality through devotion and dedicated, united and voluntary efforts are some of the important topics on which sociological studies need to conducted by future researchers.

References

1. Baba, Sri Sathya Sai, 'Spcial Life & Atmic Sadhna: A Message' *Sanathana Sarathi*, April 1994, pp. 40-43

2. Maz Weber Quoted in Freund, Jaulain, *The Sociology of Max Weber.* London; Panguin, 1968, p.195.

3. Robinson. Duane, 'Building a World Communiity' in Sai Baba and His Message: A Challenge to Behavioural Sciences, (eds) S.P. Ruhela & Duane Robinson. New Delhi: Vikas Publishing House, 1976, pp. 138-148.

4. Robinson, Duane, 'Building the Sai Community', Ibid, pp. 145-160.

5. Robinson, D., 'Sri Sathya Sai Era: Glimpses of a Spiritual Revolution' in *Golden Age.* Brindavan, Kadugodi: Sri Sathya Central Trust, 1980, pp. 5-11.

6. Ruhela, 'Educational Reconstruction in the Sai Age' in *Sai Baba and His Message*, Op. Cit, pp.171-194.

7. Goel, B.S. *Psycho-analysis and Meditation. Kurukshetra*: Third Eye Fundation, 1986.

8. Ibid.

9. Ibid.

10. Saran, A.K., 'The Crisis of Modem Man' in *A Value Orientation to Our System of Education, (*ed) V. K. Gokak. New Delhi: M. Gulab Singh & Sons, 1973, 288.

11. Ruhela, S.P. 'The Sai Baba Movement' in *The Sai Baba Movement* (ed) S.P. Ruhela. New Delhi. Arnold Heinemann, 1985.Ruhela, S. P. 'Baba; A Challenging Sociological Phenomenon' in *Golden Age*, Op Cit., 1990, pp. 89-94.

12. Ruhela, 'The Educational Theory of Sri Sathya Sai Baba', *University News*, Sept. 7, 1992, pp. 4-10.

13. Ruhela, S.P., *Sri Sathya Sai Baba and the Future of Manking*. New Delhi: Sai Age Publications, 1991.

14. Rastogi, R. P., 'Reconstruction of Social System' in *Human Values and Education*, (ed) S.P. Ruhela. New Delhi: Sterling Publishers, 1985, pp. 179-2.13.

15. Rastogi. R.P., 'Moral Regeneration of the Somali People' in *The Preferred Future Development in Somalia,* (eds) M.F. Aidid & S.P. Ruhela. New Delhi: Vikas Publishing House, 1993, pp. 106-111.

16. Babb, Lawrence A., 'Sathya Sai Baba's Miracles' in *Religion In India*, (ed) T. N. Madan. New Delhi: Oxford University Press, 1994, pp. 277-292.

17. Babb, Lawrence A., 'The Puzzle of Religious Modernity' in *India: 2000: The Next Fifteen Years* (ed) James R. Roach. New Delhi: Allied Publishers, 1986, p[p.57-78].

(i) Book: *Redeemptive Encounters*: Three Modern Styled in the Hindu Tradition (Part 3). Berkley & Los Angeles: University of California Press, 1986.

(ii) Paper: 'Sathya Sai Baba's Saintly Play' in *Saints and Virtues*. Berkeley and Los Angeles: University of Califormnia Press, 1987.

18. Bhardwaja, Krishna, *Social Change in India*. Jaipur: Arihant Publishing House, 1995.

19. Kasturi, N. *Sathyam Sivam Sundaram*, (Vols. I - IV), *p Cit*

20. Kasturi, N., *Eswaramma: The Chosen Mother*, *Op cit.*

21. Kasturi, N" *The Loving God, Op. Cit.*

22. Kasturi, No. 'The Interview He Grants' in *Garland of Golden Rose*. Prasanthi Nilayam,: Sri Sathya Sai Trust, 1975, pp. 50-53.

23. Rasgotra, M..K., 'Baba: The Hope of Mankind' *Ibid.*

24. Rasgotra, M.K., 'An Avatar's Reality: His Powers and His Mission, in *Golden Age* Op. *Cit,* 1980, pp. 51-56.

25. Rasgotra, M.K., *Convocation Address at the VIII* Convocation of Sri Sathya Sai Institute of Higher Learning', *Sanatana Sarathi*, 1989, pp. 321-322.

26. Rasgotra, M.K., 'Sri Sathya Sai Mission for the Right World Order', in *Sai Vandana*(ed.) S.N. Saraf. Prasanthi Nilayam: Sri Sathya Sai Institute of Higher Learning, 1990, pp. 99-102.

27. Venugopal, 'Synthesis between Spirituality and Materialism' Blitz, Oct. 16, 1976.

28. Rao, M.N. Sri Sathya Sai Baba: A Story of God as Man, *Op. Cit.*

29. Rao, M. N., *God and His Gospel.* Prasanthi Nilayami Sri Sathya Sai Towers and Hotels Pvt. Ltd., 1995.

30. Raddy, A. Adivi, *Uniqueness of Swami and His Teachings.* Prasanthi Nilayami Sathya Sai Books & Publications Trust, 1995.

Chapter - 10

CONTRIBUTIONS OF PSYCHOLOGISTS AND PSYCHOTHERAUPISTS

"Change your vision, and the world will appear accordingly.
Let the eyes be charged with the Divine, it will see all as God.
It is foolish to try to reshape the world; shape yourself as the
embodiment of Peace, Love and Reverence. Then you will see
all as Love and Compassion and Humility."

- Sri Sathya Sai Baba

Sri Sathya Sai Baba is striving to transform the entire mankind by his divine charisma, love, advice and emphasis on *Namasmaran* (Chanting the name of God), Sadhana (Meditation) and Seva (Social service). He is trying to improve the psychology of the modern man which is haunted by all kinds of fears, alienation, anomie (norm-less-ness) and disquiet and abnormalities.

A number of scholars having their background in Psychology, Psychotherapy and Psychiatry have been attracted towards Baba and they have written on him with their disciplinary perspectives. The contributions of Dr Desiraj Dhairyam, Dr Samuel Sadweiss, Dr. B.S. Goel, Dr Erlundur Haraldsson, Dr Karlis Osis and Dr Allen S. Levy deserve mention in this review of writings on Sri Sathya Sai Baba.

1. Desiraj Dhairyam (1976,1994)

Dr. Desiraj Dhairyam, a Roman Catholic and a leading psychotherapist of Madras, published his article 'The Divine Psychotherapist" in the early 1970s. He noted as under:

"Where the human psychotherapist helps the individual
slowly and laboriously over many years with principles and

methods which are themselves subject to much controversy, Bhagavan Shri Sathya Sai Baba helps hundreds every day by seeing them for a few seconds and bestowing on them his divine compassionand understanding and help with the utmost casualness, simplicity, immediacy. Prasanthi Nilayam, the abode of his divine presence, is a divine psychotherapeutic centre. People come from far and near, many from the sophisticated Western countries, to spend days and weeks in that *ashram*.

Bhagavan's darshan is a unique event in this land which has had the traditional belief in darshan for so many centuries. Each individual experiences a personal dialogue with Bhagavan where he is able to communicate with Bhagavan his problems, his conflicts, and his aspirations and where, in turn, he receives enlightenment, solace, support, and solution to his conflict.

> ...His (Bhagavan's) love touches each one, whatever he is, and however he is. But his touch brings to each an awareness of his own spiritual status and a glimpse of his goal. One feels glad that one is accepted inspite of one's faults and failings; one's complacence is shaken; one's pride is pricked; one is stirred as never before, to strive for enlightenment."

In his article 'Baba—The Divine Healer' (1994)1, Dhairyam recalls at he first met Baba in 1960 and became his devotee after certain isis in his life between 1964 and 1968. He has given his experiences under:

> "Bhagavan sees physical illness in the context of *Karma*, rebirth and ultimate spiritual salvation."
> "...Certain persons He cures of their physical illness. Certain others He does not. The physical cure is, it seems to me, always the minor aspect of His cure. He touches the heart and the soul of that person. When the person is not 'physically cured' still a cure has taken place....Bhagavan is extremely reticent about His cures and non-cures.
> ...What are the unique attributes of Bhagavan, the divine healer of the world. His healing is anologous to layers in a pyramidal structure,. The foundation layer is the healing of the physical,

economic and other environmental ills of the person. On that foundation is affected the mind and emotional healing. The Apex layer is the spiritual healing. He has come to motivate people to transcend caste, creed and race in their religious life. ...Bhagavan's message is hard for Indians and non-Indians. But the path is made easy by the divine presence of Baba. Therein He is a divine healer....Bhagavan's healing is beyond time and place and space. Cures have been reported in America, in various places in India while Bhagavan is miles away. All that He requires is faith."

2. Samuel Sandweiss (1976)

Dr Samuel Sandweiss, an American Psychiatrist and then Assistant Professor of Clinical Paychology in the University of California, came to Sai Baba in 1972 and he was so much impressed by Baba that he wrote his famous book 'Sai Baba: The Holy Man...and the Psychiatrists' (1975)'. He infact began finding fault with his own scientific knowledge and training. He stated, "In Sai Baba's presence I learned that the deepest and most profound experience of love grows out of devotional attitude towards the divine — a principle which is completely absent from modern psychiatry." No longer does Sandweiss trust the rational mind's ability to analyze and solve problems. From psychiatry he has changed to a new curative system which he calls 'Sai-chiatry.'4

Prof V.K. Gokak in his Foreword to the book has written, "Dr Sandweiss's own experiences with Baba are not only interesting but fairly typical. He is first rendered unsettled and 'unmade' and then remade in the light of spirit. The "monkey-mind" crumbles gradually and gives up its struggle and is replaced by a genuine sensitivity and receptivity. Allowing his scepticism to fly as high and as long as it can, he still realises that, if there is any honesty in doubt, it has to admit and accept the existence of a soul and a transcendental reality—a new spiritual dimension to the universe. He also grasps the truth about the role of the Avatar in human affairs. In short, Dr Sandweiss undergoes a profound transformation. He becomes a different person, gaining as he does a new spiritual dimension."5

In his article 'Sai Baba's Challenge to Modern Psychiatry' (1976)'- Sandweiss has made these valuable observations:

"I first met Sathya Sai Baba three years ago. I went to India as a Western psychiatrist to study the psychology of religion first hand and left with a deep sense of mystery about a being I could not comprehend. Sai Baba represented a deeply felt challenge to both my personal and professional life. He challenged my basic values and beliefs, the way I viewed and made sense out of reality, the very center of my existence. And as a psychiatrist with a belief system which in great measure reflected modern psychiatric thought, I saw that Sai Baba represented a deeply imposing challenge to my profession.

What is it that should produce such a reaction in me? The first tnd most obvious challenge was to my sense of reality, psychiatrist or iot. The extraordinary miracles and powers that Sai Baba demonstrates s absolutely contrary to the vision of reality that many of us hold. For nany Western scientists who believe the only phenomena worthwhile investigating are those that can be perceived through the senses or measured and evaluated with instruments, witnessing His reality, a dimension beyond the senses, in absolutely foreign territory. How hard it is to believe that he can materialize objects from thin air, that in fact vibhuti is materializing from a picture of Sai Baba in a home of a devotee in California or Mexico 12,000 miles away from him. How hard it is to believe that he is capable of remarkable clairvoyant, telepathic and healing powers that include documented cases of miraculous cures of almost all diseases imaginable including having brought back a devotee from the dead. That he is able to transform himself into other forms and transport himself great distances instantaneously, that he has been seen in two or more places at once and in fact is believed to be omnipresent, omniscient and omnipotent absolutely defies the vision of reality that most modern scientists have.

Sai Baba represents a basic challenge to world consciousness in general, to the darkness that has dulled our awareness of the higher life. This lowering of consciousness is evident in the world community in general and certainly also present in the field of psychiatry. It is common place these days to find a lack of belief and faith, in a divine dimensions, conscious and loving, with which we can develop a personal and intimate relationship. Most of us are totally unable to see what the saints and sages throughout the ages have taught; that all creation is a grand miracle manifestation of divine will, and that God is present in all names and forms. In fact being labelled an agnostic or an atheist in this dark age is in some distorted way a status symbol, supposedly reflecting a clear modern vision of reality. Perhaps it is just because of this darkness,

174

this narrowing of consciousness that Sai Baba has come at this time to boldly demonstrate to the world community the reality of the spiritual dimension and give us the faith to direct ourselves towards higher goals... Swami creates some objects the same way he created the universe.

This divine truth that Sai Baba demonstrates so boldly, that all creation is based on the will of the spiritual dimension, that our truest identity is an incorporal state of pure bliss and love, will indeed be difficult for the field of psychiatry in general to accept. For even though this behavioral science has brought an element of peace and happiness to untold numbers of lives, one of its glaring weaknesses and short comings is the lack of awareness of a spiritual dimension and the integration of spiritual principles into its body of knowledge. In fact most psychiatric theory and practice reflects a vision of reality which leaves out almost completely the possibility that our true identity may lie beyond space and time and that we may actually be, at our very center, pure bliss and love. I know of no concept in modern psychiatry likened to that of the Atma and most psychiatrists indeed identify self with body, emotions and mind, considered by Sai Baba as elements of the small self. Because so many psychiatrists do not believe in a higher self or a dimension of consciousness beyond duality the position is frequently taken that "God is manufactured by man; belief in the higher self is a defense against emotion." And as so many psychiatrists basically don't believe in the spiritual dimension beyond the senses there is therefore an over-emphasis and over-focus on senses and emotions, elements of the small self which rise in importance to such a degree as to be the focuse of worship. This position is an absolutely dangerous one. It is well known in the field of spirituality that being attached to feeling leads one deeper into the world of duality and into suffering. Yet psychiatrists generally misinterpret such spiritual practices and detachment from emotions, self-control, discipline, morality and surrendering oneself to God as generally being repressive and in fact a pathological denial of one's basic identity in emotions.

Here is where Sai Baba's presence can be a challenge to and bring light into the field of psychiatry. This confusion about the place of spirituality, this distortion and misunderstanding of spiritual attitudes and truths must become clarified in the field of psychiatry.

This danger is expressed in modern day psychiatry in a number of ways. Firstly, it is expressed in the lives of many psychiatrists' themseleves. It is known, for instance, that there is a high rate of suicides among psychiatrists and it is not infrequent to see many of the same problems in this population as in the general population. They include marital difficulties and divorces and cultivation of a lot of sometimes faddish unusual and in fact sometimes bizarre ideas and theories. A great proportion of psychiatrists openly profess to be agnostics and atheists and believe that religious beliefs have been one of the primary forces leading to repression-emotional illness. Psychiatry must grow to a deeper sense of responsibility in this area and help establish a clearly defined moral code and proper mode of conduct that is essential for society and the human being to survive. The moral and spiritual concepts of directing our lives with discipline and sense of responsibility and the importance of surrendering our selfish wants and desires in order to attain higher goals for ourselves and for the welfare of others must be voiced clearly and loudly by the field of psychiatry.

Another central challenge that Baba represents to Western Behavioral Science is a challenge to an egotistical attitude that many of us have developed of actually believing that we can understand human nature and cure people ourselves. It is a challenge to the distorted belief that the small self is the doer with the identification of self with mind. My attraction in spiritual writings to such concepts as Atma (the real self: one's divinity: imperishable, immutable, infinite, eternal) and moksha (a merging of the wave with the ocean from which it appears to differ; liberation from delusion, release from the circle of birth and death; the attainment of eternal joy) was simply too great to allow me to be bound by the limited conceptions of self adhered to in modern psychiatry.

A comparison of the psycho-analytic process of free-association with the practices of meditation originated in the East points out in a concrete way the differences between East and West in attitudes and approaches towards mind and self. The aim of both of these processes is towards realizing our deepest inner nature, and a central element in each is becoming aware of being an observer and witness-but for different reasons. In free-association one becomes the observer as a means to an end in order to watch thoughts and emotions as they bubble up into awareness. The assumption is that these thoughts and feelings are valuable because they eventually lead to underlying conflicts which when found can be resolved; therefore one is directed to attend to and follow them. Meditation, on the other hand, simply is aware of one's self as witness may be an end in itself. The experience of being centered or focused in full awareness in the 'here and now' may lead us into deeper experience of our true nature. Meditation is supposed to take us beyond the mind to the point where we can watch passing thoughts and feelings without being seduced into attending to and following them.

If the mind is to be used at all it is to be directed by the will of the observer to create an inner spiritual experience, such as that which evokes a sense of awe of creation, or an all encompassing sense of love and peace. This can be done by mentally repeating the name of God and trying to visualize light, or any number of techniques. These experiences tend to tame the mind, encouraging the experience of divinity believed to lie at the center of our identity. By staying in touch with one's self as witness and with an aspect of the divine, one may eventually reach the place where witness and witnessed, the 'I' and the 'that' merge and become one. By contrast if one is free—associating on an analyst's couch and drops into a place of great peace and quiet, this may be interpreted as resistance to the flow of material, and the individual is encouraged back into following his thoughts and feelings.

Baba has said, "The scientist looks outside and is always saying "What is this?" (that which can be perceived by the senses; existing in the world of emotion or grasped by the mind). But the saint is always looking inside and his question is, "What is that?" (that which is beyond the senses, beyond emotions, beyond the grasp of the mind).

This identification of self with mind, I felt, led to an egotistical attitude about the place of the therapist and his ability to fully understand human nature and cure people. Baba's presence absolutely challenges this position. He teaches about humility, social service as an act of worship to God, the central importance of devotion in our lives and awareness that all healing comes about through God, is a challenge to the sense of importance that many behavioral scientists have mistaken by acquired. For just being in Sai Baba's presence and witnessing a reality that is beyond anything our low level of consciousness can comprehend and grasp is enough to humble one into awareness of how much we do not know and to develop a sense of awe and mystery toward creation and a devotion toward God, to recognize that God is infact the doer.

Then there is a mentality developing in America in general and also in the field of psychiatry which is looking toward quick methods and instant cure-alls the fantasy that one can develop an overnight utopia by practicing a certain mystic technique or magic method. And even though when I see so many new theories and practices being originated daily in psychiatry with wild claims heatedly supporting absolutely contrary and differing theories and practices we continue to keep on hoping for the magic cure and grasping for impossibilities.

It is indeed refreshing to witness Sai Baba's challenge to this absurd situation. He does not promise that the way will be quick and easy and without pain. Rather he teaches what we all know somewhere deep down in our souls to be true, that we must develop patience, perseverence and steadiness. "The slow and the steady win the race." It is indeed refreshing and encouraging that Sai Baba teaches an age old truth — right living, duty and discipline, a moral system that has been taught throughout the ages by saints and sages and that is indeed timeless. This characteristic of the teachings itself reflects its truth as the teachings are always the same. And even though we may be attracted to the promises of over-night cures, the flashy style and influential rhetoric from lesser personalities we will somehow realize Sai Baba's teachings of the age old and universal message of love, responsibility, discipline, social service and surrender to God represents truth.

I feel that Sai Baba's basic challenge to the Western Behavioral scientist is the same as his challenge to everyone everywhere. It is a challenge to the darkness. He is here to bring light into our lives. His mission is to turn the Behavioral Scientists like the world community in general into spiritual aspirants who recognize the reality of God and whose work reflects awareness of the spiritual dimension and reflects man's deepest yearning to realize God. Psychiatrists must become aware that the ultimate goal in psychiatry is actually the same as that of religion: to find the God or Atma within, the experience of love. On reflecting my own yearning that psychiatry awaken to Sai Baba reality I would prefer calling psychiatry "Sai-chiatry," the Sai-chiatry of love, the Sai-chiatry of Atma consciousness."

In his next book 'Spirit and The Mind' (1985), Sandweises showed through his experience with Sri Sathya Sai Baba "that abstract concepts about consciousness, dua:i..;, love and the primacy of the spirit have meanings even to those hardcore behavioural scientists who believes that the final solution of suffering will be found in brain chemistry and psychopharmabiology. For them there may be no sense of a connection between biology on the one hand and morality, devotion and higher levels of consciousness on the other. But if Baba's apparent materializations of matter from "will"— which he calls expressions of love — are found to be real, then we are seeing concrete evidence that matter is a function of consciousness, and not vice-versa. If higher level of consciousness are fundamental to biology, then one day we may ultimately rely on the achievement of these states of consciousness for the treatment of all earthly ills."

On the basis of his experiences he has described how spiritual insight relates to a psychiatrist's personal growth, his way of conceptualizing psychological problems, his therapeutic approaches and, ultimately his capacity as a therapist.'

3. Dr B.S. Goel (1985)

Dr B.S. Goel (later famous as Siddheswar Baba of Bhagaan village in Haryana) had the background of history and psychiatry. His famous book Third Eye and Kundalini: An Experiential Account of Journey From Dust to Divinity (1985)' is a wonderful account of his experiences of the awakening of his Kundalini due to Baba's blessings and indirect guidance. He has described the main principles of spiritual therapy, the secret behind the concept of God and various spiritual practices, and how human barriers can be transcended by Guru's help.

4. and 5. Dr Erlendur Haraldsson and Dr Karlis Osis

Dr Haraldsson was Professor of Psychology and Dr Osis was his colleague in the Department of Psychology, University of Iceland, Iceland. They both visited Sai Baba many times and wrote their experiences with Baba in a number of publications. They both got a number of chances to witness Sai Baba's miracles in interviews with Baba. They got interested in discovering the mystery of Baba's miracles. Haraldsson undertook an extensive study of Baba's 'miracles and found them genuine' as he has concluded in his book 'Miracles are My Visiting Cards: (1987)". He has not contributed anything substantial by way of his psychological research in the Sai Baba's phenomenon, but his contribution in trying to understand Baba's miracles is substantial and well received.

In his paper 'Sathya Sai Baba and the Sceptics (1990)"', he gave these interesting experiences.

"People's beliefs and approaches to life vary as much as their physical appearances. No one is exactly the same. So is the crowd that flocks to Puttaparthi. I was one of it in 1973 along with a colleague and fellow-scientist Dr Karlis Osis. We approached Sathya Sai Baba as open-minded skeptics. We were researchers and wanted to experiment with nothing less then those rare gifts of producing miracles that Sai Baba possessed. The differences of his approach and our's soon became evident when we became fortunate enough to meet Swami in person.

We wanted tests and demonstrations of his miracles. He wanted to engage us in discussions on the spiritual life. "Daily life and the spiritual life should be interwoven like a double rudraksha", he remarked. Neither of us knew at that time what a rudraksha is, and our interpreter could not make the meaning clear to us. We stubbornly insisted that Swami explain what he meant. When verbal communication failed he waved his hand and it was there, a beautiful double rudraksha. It was only later when I met Dr Sathyanarayan Rao, the Director of the Botanical Survey of India in Calcutta that I realized the rarity of the object I had seen so wondrously appear in Swami's hand. This leading botanical institution of India had-in spite of many efforts-never in its history been able to procure a double rudraksha for its large collection of different species and kind of rudrakshas, which is probably the largest in the world. Sai Baba made a double rudraksha appear on the spur of the moment just to explain the meaning of a word which we insisted to know.

We soon realized that we were not dealing with any ordinary individual. We were quickly forced to consider seriously the possibility that the miraculous and the spiritual was as interwoven in Sai Baba as He wanted daily life and the spiritual life to be interwoven in us.

My colleague Dr Osis remarked in our discussion, after our first two meetings with Sai Baba, "So far, we have in our research only observed sparks of paranormal gifts. In Swami we may have a full flame."

We, therefore, persisted in our efforts and made another journey to India, again trying to convince our amiable Swami of the importance of scientific research of the seemingly endless flow of phenomena that deeply puzzled us, the experts in this field.

We argued for the scientific approach and Swami for the importance of spirituality and the truths of universal religion. Again we wanted to experiment with his gifts. On one occasion when he had argued long for our approach as we sat on the floor several feet away from him, he said to my colleague: "Look at your ring." A few moments earlier I had seen on Dr Osis' finger the beautiful golden ring with a picture of Swami, which he had presented to Dr Osis during our first visit.

Now, as both of us looked at the ring on my colleague's finger, we saw that the stone with Swami's picture on it, had suddenly disappeared from the ring, although the frame and the notches which had held the stone firmly for a year were unbent and fully intact. Sathya Sai Baba had not touched us in this interview and the ring had been on Dr Osis' finger all the time.

We were greatly astonished. Swami remarked with a smile: "This was my experiment."

We never found a satisfactory explanation for this disappearance of a solid object. Also, Douglas Henning, the leading American magician, could not offer us any explanation. We questioned what we had observed but now we were forced to become more sceptical of some of the basic assumptions of physical science.

One of the many qualities in Sai Baba that I have learned greatly to admire, is his steadfast service to his country. Unlike most Indian Swamis he has chosen not to go abroad but to remain with his people and work for their physical and spiritual well being and moral renewal.

In spite of this, he has become an inspiration and example to vast numbers of people who can be found in even the furthermost corners of the world. What can be more beautiful than to be bestower of gifts to the hearts of men.?"

Prof. Erlendur Haraldsson studied Sai Baba's miracles extensively and published his research findings in his book Miracles are My Visiting Cards. The following excerpt of his pioneering research was published in Sunday Chronicle" of 18 July, 1993.

"What cvidencs do we have for and against the genuineness or para-normality of the extraordinary phenomena widely reported about Sai Baba? Since these phenomena are of various kinds, it seems appropriate to consider each of the major types separately.

The alleged appearance of objects (or "materializations") is the most prominent and perplexing aspect of Sai Baba's repertoire, though he frequently refers to those productions as small items or "mere trivialities". Let us begin our assessment by weighing the evidence for the various alternative hypotheses that might explain this phenomenon.

First, a little can be added to our earlier discussion of hypnosis as an explanation, namely that Baba hypnotizes people not to see from where he actually takes the objects that he produces. This explanation assumes that all people are readily hypnotized.

Next is the question of whether Sai Baba has accomplices. During the forty years of Sai Baba's active life as a religious leader and performer of apparent miracles, he has had many close attendants and associates. Over the years their turnover has been considerable, for various reasons. At the present time, Baba has no attendant who was with him in the 1940s or 1950s. Sai Baba has accomplices to help him in a sleight of hand production of objects, he must have had a considerable number of them over these forty years. Besides, he usually has no close associate or attendant with him when he gives audiences or interviews to individuals or groups, the occasion during which he produces most of the objects. If Sai Baba was using sleight of hand, he would need not only accomplices to bring the objects to him and perhaps help him prepare his performances, but also jewellers and goldsmiths to supply the objects, as well as people to transport them to him. Baba's production of these objects is on such a large scale that a few jewellers would probably be needed to fulfil his requirements for jewellery supplies alone.

If accomplices are involved, be they devotees or jewellers, they would be in a position to exert tremendous pressure on Sai Baba, since his movement, at least a million members strong in India and abroad, might suffer a severe blow if one of these accomplices revealed his secret. Some of those who were once very close to Baba later left him and turned their backs on him; it seems unlikely that they would not reveal their involvement in a fraud of such proportions if there were one. Krishna, for example, was disillusioned with Baba and is severely critical of him; yet he freely admits that he was never aware of anything to arouse his suspicion about the physical phenomena and that he has no normal explanation for them.

There are rumors in India that jewellers supply Sai Baba with the jewellery. Three men, all sympathizers or devotees of Baba, but none of them close to him, have expressed the view to me that jewellers in Bangalore, perhaps also in Anantapur and Mangalore, may supply him with his gifts. If this were true, they pointed out, the jewelers would for financial reasons be unwilling to reveal their involvement. According to their theory, the pieces would be stored in a safe place, and Baba would then apport them from that place to wherever he is at the moment when he needs a particular piece. None of these men adhered to the sleight of hand hypothesis. They were unable to give or point to any evidence to support their view, their views seem therefore to be founded on hearsay that I have been unable to confirm.

...When most people first see Baba produce an object, they believe that he does it by sleight of hand; they think he must take the object out of his sleeves, his bushy hair, or some other place, without their being aware of it. Magicians do their tricks in this way, usually skillfully enough to baffle their audiences.

Does he take the objects out of his hair? I have taken a few hours of films and videotapes of Sai Baba during darshan, when he often produces vibuti. In these films he rarely touched or reached his hair. On other occasions, during darshan as well as in interviews, I also noted that he seldom reached for his hair.

Sai Baba's clothing is unusual and not generally worn in India: a one piece robe that fans to his ankles, has a slit up to the middle of th. calf on both sides, and has sleeves that reach his wrists. Two loose golden buttons close the top at the neck, but no other buttons or openings can be seen. He has several such robes, all of the same design. They are made of thin synthetic material and apparently, have no pockets or folds. Underneath, I have been told by his former attendants, he wears only briefs or a dhoti. The climate is hot in India, people wear thin simple clothes, and so does Sai Baba.

A tailor in Whitefield makes Sai Baba' probes, usually several at a time, since Baba frequently gives them away to devotees after he has worn them for some time. I have visited the tailor and seen the robes he was sewing. I have also seen some that Baba has given to devotees. None of them had pockets or folds or potential hiding places. One may ask whether these pieces are just for show and differ from the ones that he actually wears, but we have no evidence to support such a conjecture. In his younger days his devotees would often bring him new robes or clothes which he would put on. Apparently he produced objects just as easily wearing those robes as when he was wearing his own.

I never had the opportunity to examine clothing that Sai Baba actually had on, but some people I have met have done so.... They found that it contained no pockets or hiding places.

Baba's robes are thin, like the material in men's shirts, and sunlight shines through them easily. Neither when the sun does not shine through the window in Baba's interview room nor out in the open have I, even at close range, been able to see any shadows that might indicate the presence of a hidden object. When Baba is outside and the wind blows, the robe may cling to his body; but on such occasions neither I nor anyone I have spoken to has seen any protrusion indicating a hidden object.

For sceptical observers Baba sometimes pushes his sleeves high up his arms when producing objects. Also, I have sat quite close to him and been able to see up into his rather wide button-less sleeves, and I have never observed anything suspicious.

In brief, I have found no evidence that his clothing contains pockets or any magicians' paraphernalia that could be used as hiding places for objects and that would probably be necessary to exercise sleight of hand.

I have made eight trips to India during which I have interviewed in depth dozens of people, spoken more casually to many more people, and listened to and checked up on numerous rumours; but I have never found any solid evidence to support the sleight-of-hand hypothesis.

Since Baba's colleges were founded in Whitefield and Puttaparthri, Baba is mostly attended by students. A few of them have left him, usually after losing faith in his claim to be an avatar. When that happens they also tend to lose faith in the genuineness of the phenomena; for the two seem for many to be two sides of the same coin. Some of these apostate students (such as Satish Kumar, whom I met in Hyderabad in the summer of 1983) believe that Baba makes pellets of solid vibhuti in his bathroom by wetting it slightly and then letting it dry; these pellets he then supposedly keeps between his fingers: when he gives darshan outside, they conjecture, he has three, four or five of those pellets and crushes them between his fingers as the need arises. It should be added that none of these students claim to have witnessed Baba make any of the presumed pellets. This may explain some of the vibhuti phenomenon. For those instances when Baba produces large amounts, such as when he produced on demand many handfuls during his visit to the Roerichs, the students have no plausible explanation.

The evidence offered by these students seems slight. To me it seems that they have made conjectures based on a psychological need to explain away the miracles after they lost faith in Baba's godliness. Be that as it may, these observations, weak as they are, should keep up our vigilance as long as Sai Baba has not given any experimental evidence of the para-normality of his physical productions.,..

I am not alone in not being able to find evidence of fraud in Sai Baba. His Indian critics, such as Dr Narasimhaiah and the Miracle Committee have also not come across anything that can be clearly interpreted as evidence of fraud. And they certainly have not lacked the will to seek and find such evidence.

On the other hand, we also have no direct, experimental evidence that the physical phenomena are genuine. Only a carefully conducted investigation with a thorough examination of Sai Baba's body and other necessary controls could produce such evidence. A large amount of indirect evidence might be compelling, but it may never provide the same certainty as a carefully conducted experiment, especially if the experiment were successfully repeated by several qualified experimenters. Sai Baba has unfortunately and regrettably refused so far to allow such an investigation.

It is, however, not only the lack of evidence of fraud that keeps the question open. Some years ago Dr Osis discussed our observations with Dough Henning. Henning said that he could, with advance preparation, duplicate all the phenomena he saw on the film. But when Dr Osis described the incident in which the enamel stone with Sai Baba's picture disappeared from Dr Osis' ring, Henning commented that this was beyond the skills of magicians. He stated further that if Sai Baba produces objects on demand, then he is performing feats that no magician can duplicate.

After all the interviews and inquiries, what evidence do we have that Baba does actually produce objects on demand? It seems not to be uncommon for Baba to produce objects in response to a specific situation, but one can perhaps argue that the situation was in some way foreseen or staged by him. Such might have been the case when he produced a double rudraksha for me, though it did not look that way to Dr Osis or myself When Baba and the interpreter could not explain the meaning of a double rudraksha, he produced one on the spot.

...There are also some instances when Baba produced something and distributed apparently all of it to a group of people; however, when someone arriving later, or accidently left out, asked for a share, Baba then produced more immediately. Dr Osis and I observed one such incident in the interview with the Vice-President of India, and another in the interview with the Roerichs; Baba produced a good deal of hot, oily Indian sweet and gave it to everyone present. Mrs Roerich happened to be in the kitchen at that time. When back, she brought it to Baba's attention and asked for the sweet, which he immediately produced, enough not only for her but also for several people to have a second helping.

Even Krishna, who is highly critical of Baba, reports some such incidents. Once when they were travelling, he asked Baba for an apple. Baba walked up to a nearby tamarind tree and picked from it an apple. Krishna also reported that he was fond of the Indian sweet kova, which was not available in Puttaparthi, and that sometimes he would ask Baba for this sweet. Baba would always produce it for him. The Raja of Venkatagiri reports being present when Baba told some devotees to ask for any kind of fruit they wanted. They got what they asked for, not from Baba's hand, but from a nearby tamarind tree, Mrs Radhakrishna and her daughter Vijaya Hemchand report even more startling incidents, such as when Baba put leaves into their hands and asked them to think of something they wanted (such as chocolate, fruit, or small statues). When they opened their fists, they found that they had wished for on their palms.

It seems therefore that Baba has indeed produced objects on demand. It adds some strength to the evidence that there are two or more witnesses to some of these incidents. One may argue that some of these claims are exaggerations, are based on faulty memory or even are lies. The frequency of such claims reduces the value of such interpretations, though they in principle can never be absolutely ruled out.

There are other aspects of Baba's productions that may be difficult or impossible for a magician to produce, especially in India where sophisticated gadgetry would be impossible to obtain in a remote Indian village. Frequently he is said to have produced hot foods, sometimes steaming hot, even after he has been out of his quarters for an hour or longer.... For example, Amarendra Kumar stated that some of the foods that Baba produced were "as if fresh from the oven, and sometimes too damned hot-too hot, in fact—as if you had just taken them out of the frying pan." Many more people have reported to me witnessing such phenomena. Most of these incidents occurred on the banks of the Chitravati River, where Baba was said to have taken some hot food out of the sand. If a trick was involved; a heater must have been placed with the foods in the sand before Sai Baba and his group arrived. That would have been difficult in the 1940s and 1950s, and have involved considerable preparation. Frequently it has been reported to me that he has produced hot food when he was travelling and the party stopped on the wayside for refreshment.

Baba also produces liquids, such as oils and medicine, in his hands and gives it to someone or rubs it on the person. A moment later, however, his hands seem dry, even though he has not touched anything to dry his hands or fingers. On one occasion, I personally observed an incident of this kind at close range.

Finally, Sai Baba is reported to produce objects never or rarely seen or unknown in nature. First-hand observations of three such cases have been reported to me; but none of the objects concerned have been preserved, a loss that greatly reduces the value of these reports. One example is typical of the three:

Leelamma, a botanist in Guindy outside Madras, who has known Baba since the 1940s, related to me in an interview in November 1977 that Sai Baba once told her to pick an apple from a tamarind tree in Puttaparthi. She found the apple on the tree and with Baba's permission cut off the part of the branch on which both the apple and tamarind leaves were attached. She preserved this specimen for some time in formaldehyde in the college at which she teaches. Eventually the apple was somehow detached from the branch. Later people would not believe that the two pieces had been joined and she finally threw the specimen away.

What then is our conclusion about the physical phenomena? For lack of experimental evidence it can only be somewhat tentative, though the testimony is extensive and consistent over four decades. Whether some of the physical productions, in some periods of Baba's life, may have been produced by sleight of hand, we cannot, of course, ascertain. What we can, however, squarely state is that in spite of a long-lasting and painstaking effort, we found no direct evidence of fraud."

Journalist Ch Susheel Rao interviewed Prof Haraldsson in 1993. The following interview was published in The Sunday Chronicle (July 18, 1993).

'I'm Disappointed with Baba'

Astonishing paranormal phenomena have always aroused the curiosity of psychical researchers. To dispassionately unravel these mysteries calls for a conscientious approach. Erlendur Haraldsson, professor of psychology at the University of Iceland, author of 'Miracles Are My Visiting Cards,' had all the patience that was necessary for 10 years to understand the Sai mystic. "I am quite disappointed. If only Sai Baba had accepted for laboratory investigation, it would have been a great contribution to science revealing the secret behind paranormal incidents, if indeed they occur," he says. Haraldsson has also authored 'Of This World or Another' in Icelandic. It was about the parapsychic experiences of the Icelanders. Another book of his is 'Insurgence in Khurdistan' published in German and Icelandic languages. He co-authored 'At the Hour of Death' with Dr Osis.

Along with Dr Richard Wiseman, psychologist, University of Hertfordshire, United Kingdom, Haraldsson is now in the country on a trip sponsored by the British Society for Psychical Research to conduct controlled experiments with a few swamis.

In an exclusive interview with Sunday Chronicle during his visit to the city in 1993 Haraldsson reveals what efforts went into the writing of his latest book 'Miracles Are My Visiting Cards.' Excerpts:

How many time did you personally meet Sai Baba and witness his reported miracles before writing the book?

At least 10-15 times in sessions ranging between 15 and 30 minutes. This was over a period of 10 years when a colleague, Dr Osis and I met him in 1973 at Puttaparthi.

Were you convinced of his miracles?

He surprised us by materialising a double rudraksha, which I later got confirmed was made of 22-carat gold, out of nowhere and gave it to me (Haraldsson now wears it around his neck). He also gave my friend Dr Osis a gold ring. Once he even made the embedded stone in the ring vanish right in front of our eyes. These things, it is said even magicians can do if they prepare themselves.... But the vanishing of the stone in the ring was something a well-known magician in the United States, Doug Hanning, could not explain. There were many other incidents too but we were not totally convinced as the Baba was refusing to cooperate in a laboratory investigation.

Why do you think he did not allow a scientific and controlled investigation?

We were scientists and not devotees of Sai Baba. Several times I tried to convince him that he would be doing a great favour to science if he agreed for investigations but he was firm about not heeding our request. When I saw that he would never cooperate, I went ahead with the publication of the book as it was not worth waiting. But if I were Sai Baba, I would have accepted the proposal of a controlled investigation. Sai Baba considers him self to be a spiritual person and says miracles are irrelevant.

Do you believe that parapsyhic events are possible?

It cannot be said for sure that they are scientifically impossible. In fact there are a few experiments which suggest that these things can occur, but a clear picture has not emerged so far. I have investigated psychic phenomena for a long time and science accepts only things for which there is evidence.

Having talked to his devotees, ex-devotees and even spending long sessions with him personally, what overall impression do you gather about the Baba?

I am not the religious type to be interested in Sai Baba. He interested me only because of the paranormal incidents that are related to him. I have much respect for him but I was not attracted to him. I had a liking for him because he was a delightful person. He is charming and gentle but what use is it to me? I was adopting a scientific approach to find out the cause of the para- psychic events

What impact do you think your book on Sai Baba would have on the Indian people?

When I met Sai Baba last, to my surprise, he told me he had read the book. This was published only in the United States, United Kingdom, Germany, Italy, Japan and Spain. He seemed to be happy but had some complaints about some parts of the book where I had quoted some exdevotees. He felt they were not fair to him in their criticism. I don't really know what impact the book would have once it is out in India by October.

You must have received some feedback from the countries where the book was published before....

Some devotees liked it and some did not. I tried to be objective all the time.

Are you frustrated because you could not unravel the "truth" behind the miracles?

I am disappointed because the Baba did not cooperate the way I wanted him to. I'm just waiting to see the video tape based on which Deccan Chronicle, I learnt, had published a story exposing the Baba.

This could be clinching evidence. (Haraldsson said he was "convinced" after seeing the tape later).12

Dr Karlis Osis (1980)

Dr. Karlis Osis, an internationally Known parapsycholistst, in his brief article 'Parapsychology and Sathya Sai Baba' (1980)" reported that he and Dr Haraldsson contacted a large number of Sai devotees and discovered that they had experience Baba's miracles, seen him in dreams, and they knew that Baba cured people. They were convinced of Baba's omniscience.

Thus we find that these contributors have contributed more in the field of psychiatry or psychotherapy rather than in psychology while studying Sri Sathya Sai Baba.

References

1. Dhairyam, D., 'The Divine Psychotherapist' in Sai Baba and His Message, (eds) S.P. Ruhela & D. Robinon. New Delhi: Vikas Publishing House, 1976, pp. 67-75.
2. Dhairyman, D., 'Baba-The Divine Healer', Sanathana Sarathi, 1994.
3. Sandweiss, Samuel, *Sai Baba - Holy Man... and the Psychiatrist.* San Diago, California: Brithday Publishing Co., 1975.
4. Sud, K.N., Review of Sandweiss' above book in *The Hindustan Times,* Jan. 2, 1977.
5. Gokak, V.K., 'Foreward', Samuel, Op Cit.
6. Sandweiss, Samuel H., 'Sai Baba's Challenge to Modem Psychiatry', in Ruhela & Robinson, Op Cit., pp. 76-87.

7   Sandweiss, Samuel, *Spirit and The Mind*. Prasanthi Nilayam: Sri Sathya Sai Books & Publications Trust, 1985.

6. Goel, B.S., *Third Eye and Kundalini*: An Experiential Account of Journey From Dust to Divinity. Kurushetra: Third Eye Foundation of India, 1985.

7. Haraldsson, Erlendur, *Miracles are My Visiting Cards*: An Investigative Report on the Psychic Phenomena Associated With Sathya Sai Baba. London: Century Hutichinson Ltd., 1987.

8. Haraldsson, Erlendur, 'Sathya Sai Baba and the Skeptics' in *Sathya Sai-The Eternal Charioteer*, Hyderabad: Sri Prasanthi Society, 1990, pp 62-63.

9. Sunday Chroncle (Hyderabad), July 18, 1993.

10. Rao, Ch Susheel, Interview with Erlendur Haraldsson-'I'm disappointed with Baba', Ibid.

11. Osis, Karlis, 'Parapsychology and Sathya Sai Baba' in *Golden Age*. Prasathi Nilayam: Sri Sathya Sai Books & Publications, 1980, pp. 257-258.

...Bhagavan's *darshan* is a unique event in this land which has had the traditional belief in darshan for so many centuries. Each individual experiences a personal dialogue with Bhagavan where he is able to communicate with Bhagavan his problems, his conflicts, and his aspirations and where, in turn, he receives enlightenment, solace, support, and solution to his conflict.

...His (Bhagavan's) love touches each one, whatever he is, and however he is. But his touch brings to each an awareness of his own spiritual status and a glimpse of his goal. One feels glad that one is accepted inspite of one's faults and failings; one's complacence is shaken; one's pride is pricked; one is stirred as never before, to strive for enlightenment."

In his article *'Baba—The Divine Healer'* (1994)1, Dhairyam recalls at he first met Baba in 1960 and became his devotee after certain isis in his life between 1964 and 1968. He has given his experiences under:

"Bhagavan sees physical illness in the context of *Karma*, rebirth and ultimate spiritual salvation."

"...Certain persons He cures of their physical illness. Certain others He does not. The physical cure is, it seems to me, always the minor aspect of His cure. He touches the heart and the soul of that person. When the person is not 'physically cured' still a cure has taken place....Bhagavan is extremely reticent about His cures and non-cures.

...What are the unique attributes of Bhagavan, the divine healer of the world. His healing is anologous to layers in a pyramidal structure,. The foundation layer is the healing of the physical, economic and other environmental ills of the person. On that foundation is affected the mind and emotional healing. The Apex layer is the spiritual healing. He has come to motivate people to transcend caste, creed and race in their religious life.

...Bhagavan's message is hard for Indians and non-Indians. But the path is made easy by the divine presence of Baba. Therein He is a divine healer.... Bhagavan's healing is beyond time and place and space. Cures have been reported in America, in various places in India while Bhagavan is miles away. All that He requires is faith."

5. Samuel Sandweiss (1976)

Dr Samuel Sandweiss, an American Psychiatrist and then Assistant Professor of Clinical Paychology in the University of California, came to Sai Baba in 1972 and he was so much impressed by Baba that he wrote his famous book 'Sai Baba: The Holy Man...and the Psychiatrists' (1975)'. He infact began finding fault with his own scientific knowledge and training. He stated, "In Sai Baba's presence I learned that the deepest and most profound experience of love grows out of devotional attitude towards the divine — a principle which is completely absent from modern psychiatry." No longer does Sandweiss trust the rational mind's ability to analyze and solve problems. From psychiatry he has changed to a new curative system which he calls 'Sai-chiatry.'4

Prof V.K. Gokak in his Foreword to the book has written, "Dr Sandweiss's own experiences with Baba are not only interesting but fairly typical. He is first rendered unsettled and 'unmade' and then remade in the light of spirit. The "monkey-mind" crumbles gradually and gives up its struggle and is replaced by a genuine sensitivity and receptivity. Allowing his scepticism to fly as high and as long as it can, he still realises that, if there is any honesty in doubt, it has to admit and accept the existence of a soul and a transcendental reality—a new spiritual dimension to the universe. He also grasps the truth about the role of the Avatar in human affairs. In short, Dr Sandweiss undergoes a profound transformation. He becomes a different person, gaining as he does a new spiritual dimension."5

In his article 'Sai Baba's Challenge to Modern Psychiatry' (1976)'- Sandweiss has made these valuable observations:

"I first met Sathya Sai Baba three years ago. I went to India as a Western psychiatrist to study the psychology of religion first hand and left with a deep sense of mystery about a being I could not comprehend. Sai Baba represented a deeply felt challenge to both my personal and professional life. He challenged my basic values and beliefs, the way I viewed and made sense out of reality, the very center of my existence. And as a psychiatrist with a belief system which in great measure reflected modern psychiatric thought, I saw that Sai Baba represented a deeply imposing challenge to my profession.

What is it that should produce such a reaction in me? The first tnd most obvious challenge was to my sense of reality, psychiatrist or iot. The extraordinary miracles and powers that Sai Baba demonstrates s absolutely contrary to the vision of reality that many of us hold. For nany Western scientists who believe the only phenomena worthwhile investigating are those that can be perceived through the senses or measured and evaluated with instruments, witnessing His reality, a dimension beyond the senses, in absolutely foreign territory. How hard it is to believe that he can materialize objects from thin air, that in fact vibhuti is materializing from a picture of Sai Baba in a home of a devotee in California or Mexico 12,000 miles away from him. How hard it is to believe that he is capable of remarkable clairvoyant, telepathic and healing powers that include documented cases of miraculous cures of almost all diseases imaginable including having brought back a devotee from the dead. That he is able to transform himself into other forms and transport himself great distances instantaneously, that he has been seen in two or more places at once and in fact is believed to be omnipresent, omniscient and omnipotent absolutely defies the vision of reality that most modern scientists have.

Sai Baba represents a basic challenge to world consciousness in general, to the darkness that has dulled our awareness of the higher life. This lowering of consciousness is evident in the world community in general and certainly also present in the field of psychiatry. It is common place these days to find a lack of belief and faith, in a divine dimensions, conscious and loving, with which we can develop a personal and intimate relationship. Most of us are totally unable to see what the saints and sages throughout the ages have taught; that all creation is a grand miracle manifestation of divine will, and that God is present in all names and forms. In fact being labelled an agnostic or an atheist in this dark age is in some distorted way a status symbol, supposedly reflecting a clear modern vision of reality. Perhaps it is just because of this darkness, this narrowing of consciousness that Sai Baba has come at this time to boldly demonstrate to the world community the reality of the spiritual dimension and give us the faith to direct ourselves towards higher goals... Swami creates some objects the same way he created the universe.

This divine truth that Sai Baba demonstrates so boldly, that all creation is based on the will of the spiritual dimension, that our truest identity is an incorporal state of pure bliss and love, will indeed be difficult for the field of psychiatry in general to accept. For even though this behavioral science has brought an element of peace and happiness to untold numbers of lives, one of its glaring weaknesses and short comings is the lack of awareness of a spiritual dimension and the integration of spiritual principles into its body of knowledge. In fact most psychiatric theory and practice reflects a vision of reality which leaves out almost completely the possibility that our true identity may lie beyond space and time and that we may actually be, at our very center, pure bliss and love. I know of no concept in modern psychiatry likened to that of the Atma and most psychiatrists indeed identify self with body, emotions and mind, considered by Sai Baba as elements of the small self. Because so many psychiatrists do not believe in a higher self or a dimension of consciousness beyond duality the position is frequently taken that "God is manufactured by man; belief in the higher self is a defense against emotion." And as so many psychiatrists basically don't believe in the spiritual dimension beyond the senses there is therefore an over-emphasis and over-focus on senses and emotions, elements of the small self which rise in importance to such a degree as to be the focuse of worship. This position is an absolutely dangerous one. It is well known in the field of spirituality that being attached to feeling leads one deeper into the world of duality and into suffering. Yet psychiatrists generally misinterpret such spiritual practices and detachment from emotions, self-control, discipline, morality and surrendering oneself to God as generally being repressive and in fact a pathological denial of one's basic identity in emotions.

Here is where Sai Baba's presence can be a challenge to and bring light into the field of psychiatry. This confusion about the place of spirituality, this distortion and misunderstanding of spiritual attitudes and truths must become clarified in the field of psychiatry.

This danger is expressed in modern day psychiatry in a number of ways. Firstly, it is expressed in the lives of many psychiatrists' themselves. It is known, for instance, that there is a high rate of suicides among psychiatrists and it is not infrequent to see many of the same problems in this population as in the general population. They include marital difficulties and divorces and cultivation of a lot of sometimes faddish unusual and in fact sometimes bizarre ideas and theories. A great proportion of psychiatrists openly profess to be agnostics and atheists and believe that religious beliefs have been one of the primary forces leading to repression-emotional illness. Psychiatry must grow to a deeper sense of responsibility in this area and help establish a clearly defined moral code and proper mode of conduct that is essential for society and the human being to survive. The moral and spiritual concepts of directing our lives with discipline and sense of responsibility and the importance of surrendering our selfish wants and desires in order to attain higher goals for ourselves and for the welfare of others must be voiced clearly and loudly by the field of psychiatry.

Another central challenge that Baba represents to Western Behavioral Science is a challenge to an egotistical attitude that many of us have developed of actually believing that we can understand human nature and cure people ourselves. It is a challenge to the distorted belief that the small self is the doer with the identification of self with mind. My attraction in spiritual writings to such concepts as Atma (the real self: one's divinity: imperishable, immutable, infinite, eternal) and moksha (a merging of the wave with the ocean from which it appears to differ; liberation from delusion, release from the circle of birth and death; the attainment of eternal joy) was simply too great to allow me to be bound by the limited conceptions of self adhered to in modern psychiatry.

A comparison of the psycho-analytic process of free-association with the practices of meditation originated in the East points out in a concrete way the differences between East and West in attitudes and approaches towards mind and self. The aim of both of these processes is towards realizing our deepest inner nature, and a central element in each is becoming aware of being an observer and witness-but for different reasons. In free-association one becomes the observer as a means to an end in order to watch thoughts and emotions as they bubble up into awareness. The assumption is that these thoughts and feelings are valuable because they eventually lead to underlying conflicts which when found can be resolved; therefore one is directed to attend to and follow them. Meditation, on the other hand, simply is aware of one's self as witness may be an end in itself. The experience of being centered or focused in full awareness in the 'here and now' may lead us into deeper experience of our true nature. Meditation is supposed to take us beyond the mind to the point where we can watch passing thoughts and feelings without being seduced into attending to and following them.

If the mind is to be used at all it is to be directed by the will of the observer to create an inner spiritual experience, such as that which evokes a sense of awe of creation, or an all encompassing sense of love and peace. This can be done by mentally repeating the name of God and trying to visualize light, or any number of techniques. These experiences tend to tame the mind, encouraging the experience of divinity believed to lie at the center of our identity. By staying in touch with one's self as witness and with an aspect of the divine, one may eventually reach the place where witness and witnessed, the 'I' and the 'that' merge and become one. By contrast if one is free—associating on an analyst's couch and drops into a place of great peace and quiet, this may be interpreted as resistance to the flow of material, and the individual is encouraged back into following his thoughts and feelings.

Baba has said, "The scientist looks outside and is always saying "What is this?" (that which can be perceived by the senses; existing in the world of emotion or grasped by the mind). But the saint is always looking inside and his question is, "What is that?" (that which is beyond the senses, beyond emotions, beyond the grasp of the mind).

This identification of self with mind, I felt, led to an egotistical attitude about the place of the therapist and his ability to fully understand human nature and cure people. Baba's presence absolutely challenges this position. He teaches about humility, social service as an act of worship to God, the central importance of devotion in our lives and awareness that all healing comes about through God, is a challenge to the sense of importance that many behavioral scientists have mistaken by acquired. For just being in Sai Baba's presence and witnessing a reality that is beyond anything our low level of consciousness can comprehend and grasp is enough to humble one into awareness of how much we do not know and to develop a sense of awe and mystery toward creation and a devotion toward God, to recognize that God is infact the doer.

Then there is a mentality developing in America in general and also in the field of psychiatry which is looking toward quick methods and instant cure-alls the fantasy that one can develop an overnight utopia by practicing a certain mystic technique or magic method. And even though when I see so many new theories and practices being originated daily in psychiatry with wild claims heatedly supporting absolutely contrary and differing theories and practices we continue to keep on hoping for the magic cure and grasping for impossibilities. It is indeed refreshing to witness Sai Baba's challenge to this absurd situation. He does not promise that the way will be quick and easy and without pain.

Rather he teaches what we all know somewhere deep down in our souls to be true, that we must develop patience, perseverence and steadiness. "The slow and the steady win the race." It is indeed refreshing and encouraging that Sai Baba teaches an age old truth — right living, duty and discipline, a moral system that has been taught throughout the ages by saints and sages and that is indeed timeless. This characteristic of the teachings itself reflects its truth as the teachings are always the same. And even though we may be attracted to the promises of over-night cures, the flashy style and influential rhetoric from lesser personalities we will somehow realize Sai Baba's teachings of the age old and universal message of love, responsibility, discipline, social service and surrender to God represents truth.

I feel that Sai Baba's basic challenge to the Western Behavioral scientist is the same as his challenge to everyone everywhere. It is a challenge to the darkness. He is here to bring light into our lives. His mission is to turn the Behavioral Scientists like the world community in general into spiritual aspirants who recognize the reality of God and whose work reflects awareness of the spiritual dimension and reflects man's deepest yearning to realize God. Psychiatrists must become aware that the ultimate goal in psychiatry is actually the same as that of religion: to find the God or Atma within, the experience of love. On reflecting my own yearning that psychiatry awaken to Sai Baba reality I would prefer calling psychiatry "Sai-chiatry," the Sai-chiatry of love, the Sai-chiatry of Atma consciousness."

In his next book 'Spirit and The Mind' (1985), Sandweises showed through his experience with Sri Sathya Sai Baba "that abstract concepts about consciousness, dua:i..;, love and the primacy of the spirit have meanings even to those hardcore behavioural scientists who believes that the final solution of suffering will be found in brain chemistry and psychopharmabiology. For them there may be no sense of a connection between biology on the one hand and morality, devotion and higher levels of consciousness on the other. But if Baba's apparent materializations of matter from "will"— which he calls expressions of love — are found to be real, then we are seeing concrete evidence that matter is a function of consciousness, and not vice-versa. If higher level of consciousness are fundamental to biology, then one day we may ultimately rely on the achievement of these states of consciousness for the treatment of all earthly ills."

On the basis of his experiences he has described how spiritual insight relates to a psychiatrist's personal growth, his way of conceptualizing psychological problems, his therapeutic approaches and, ultimately his capacity as a therapist.'

6. Dr B.S. Goel (1985)

Dr B.S. Goel (later famous as Siddheswar Baba of Bhagaan village in Haryana) had the background of history and psychiatry. His famous book Third Eye and Kundalini: An Experiential Account of Journey From Dust to Divinity (1985)' is a wonderful account of his experiences of the awakening of his Kundalini due to Baba's blessings and indirect guidance. He has described the main principles of spiritual therapy, the secret behind the concept of God and various spiritual practices, and how human barriers can be transcended by Guru's help.

7. and 5. Dr Erlendur Haraldsson and Dr Karlis Osis

Dr Haraldsson was Professor of Psychology and Dr Osis was his colleague in the Department of Psychology, University of Iceland, Iceland. They both visited Sai Baba many times and wrote their experiences with Baba in a number of publications. They both got a number of chances to witness Sai Baba's miracles in interviews with Baba. They got interested in discovering the mystery of Baba's miracles. Haraldsson undertook an extensive study of Baba's 'miracles and found them genuine' as he has concluded in his book 'Miracles are My Visiting Cards: (1987)". He has not contributed anything substantial by way of his psychological research in the Sai Baba's phenomenon, but his contribution in trying to understand Baba's miracles is substantial and well received.

In his paper 'Sathya Sai Baba and the Sceptics (1990)"', he gave these interesting experiences.

"People's beliefs and approaches to life vary as much as their physical appearances. No one is exactly the same. So is the crowd that flocks to Puttaparthi. I was one of it in 1973 along with a colleague and fellow-scientist Dr Karlis Osis. We approached Sathya Sai Baba as open-minded skeptics. We were researchers and wanted to experiment with nothing less then those rare gifts of producing miracles that Sai Baba possessed. The differences of his approach and our's soon became evident when we became fortunate enough to meet Swami in person.

We wanted tests and demonstrations of his miracles. He wanted to engage us in discussions on the spiritual life. "Daily life and the spiritual life should be interwoven like a double rudraksha", he remarked. Neither of us knew at that time what a rudraksha is, and our interpreter could not make the meaning clear to us. We stubbornly insisted that Swami explain what he meant. When verbal communication failed he waved his hand and it was there, a beautiful double rudraksha. It was only later when I met Dr Sathyanarayan Rao, the Director of the Botanical Survey of India in Calcutta that I realized the rarity of the object I had seen so wondrously appear in Swami's hand. This leading botanical institution of India had-in spite of many efforts-never in its history been able to procure a double rudraksha for its large collection of different species and kind of rudrakshas, which is probably the largest in the world. Sai Baba made a double rudraksha appear on the spur of the moment just to explain the meaning of a word which we insisted to know.

We soon realized that we were not dealing with any ordinary individual. We were quickly forced to consider seriously the possibility that the miraculous and the spiritual was as interwoven in Sai Baba as He wanted daily life and the spiritual life to be interwoven in us.

My colleague Dr Osis remarked in our discussion, after our first two meetings with Sai Baba, "So far, we have in our research only observed sparks of paranormal gifts. In Swami we may have a full flame."

We, therefore, persisted in our efforts and made another journey to India, again trying to convince our amiable Swami of the importance of scientific research of the seemingly endless flow of phenomena that deeply puzzled us, the experts in this field.

We argued for the scientific approach and Swami for the importance of spirituality and the truths of universal religion. Again we wanted to experiment with his gifts. On one occasion when he had argued long for our approach as we sat on the floor several feet away from him, he said to my colleague: "Look at your ring." A few moments earlier I had seen on Dr Osis' finger the beautiful golden ring with a picture of Swami, which he had presented to Dr Osis during our first visit.

Now, as both of us looked at the ring on my colleague's finger, we saw that the stone with Swami's picture on it, had suddenly disappeared from the ring, although the frame and the notches which had held the stone firmly for a year were unbent and fully intact. Sathya Sai Baba had not touched us in this interview and the ring had been on Dr Osis' finger all the time. We were greatly astonished. Swami remarked with a smile: "This was my experiment."

We never found a satisfactory explanation for this disappearance of a solid object. Also, Douglas Henning, the leading American magician, could not offer us any explanation. We questioned what we had observed but now we were forced to become more sceptical of some of the basic assumptions of physical science.

One of the many qualities in Sai Baba that I have learned greatly to admire, is his steadfast service to his country. Unlike most Indian Swamis he has chosen not to go abroad but to remain with his people and work for their physical and spiritual well being and moral renewal.

In spite of this, he has become an inspiration and example to vast numbers of people who can be found in even the furthermost corners of the world. What can be more beautiful than to be bestower of gifts to the hearts of men.?"

Prof. Erlendur Haraldasson studied Sai Baba's miracles extensively and published his research findings in his book Miracles are My Visiting Cards. The following excerpt of his pioneering research was published in Sunday Chronicle" of 18 July, 1993.

"What cvidencs do we have for and against the genuineness or para-normality of the extraordinary phenomena widely reported about Sai Baba? Since these phenomena are of various kinds, it seems appropriate to consider each of the major types separately.

The alleged appearance of objects (or "materializations") is the most prominent and perplexing aspect of Sai Baba's repertoire, though he frequently refers to those productions as small items or "mere trivialities". Let us begin our assessment by weighing the evidence for the various alternative hypotheses that might explain this phenomenon.

First, a little can be added to our earlier discussion of hypnosis as an explanation, namely that Baba hypnotizes people not to see from where he actually takes the objects that he produces. This explanation assumes that all people are readily hypnotized.

Next is the question of whether Sai Baba has accomplices. During the forty years of Sai Baba's active life as a religious leader and performer of apparent miracles, he has had many close attendants and associates. Over the years their turnover has been considerable, for various reasons. At the present time, Baba has no attendant who was with him in the 1940s or 1950s. Sai Baba has accomplices to help him in a sleight of hand production of objects; he must have had a considerable number of them over these forty years. Besides, he usually has no close associate or attendant with him when he gives audiences or interviews to individuals or groups, the occasion during which he produces most of the objects. If Sai Baba was using sleight of hand, he would need not only accomplices to bring the objects to him and perhaps help him prepare his performances, but also jewellers and goldsmiths to supply the objects, as well as people to transport them to him. Baba's production of these objects is on such a large scale that a few jewellers would probably be needed to fulfil his requirements for jewellery supplies alone.

If accomplices are involved, be they devotees or jewellers, they would be in a position to exert tremendous pressure on Sai Baba, since his movement, at least a million members strong in India and abroad, might suffer a severe blow if one of these accomplices revealed his secret. Some of those who were once very close to Baba later left him and turned their backs on him; it seems unlikely that they would not reveal their involvement in a fraud of such proportions if there were one. Krishna, for example, was disillusioned with Baba and is severely critical of him; yet he freely admits that he was never aware of anything to arouse his suspicion about the physical phenomena and that he has no normal explanation for them.

There are rumors in India that jewellers supply Sai Baba with the jewellery. Three men, all sympathizers or devotees of Baba, but none of them close to him, have expressed the view to me that jewellers in Bangalore, perhaps also in Anantapur and Mangalore, may supply him with his gifts. If this were true, they pointed out, the jewelers would for financial reasons be unwilling to reveal their involvement. According to their theory, the pieces would be stored in a safe place, and Baba would then apport them from that place to wherever he is at the moment when he needs a particular piece. None of these men adhered to the sleight of hand hypothesis. They were unable to give or point to any evidence to support their view, their views seem therefore to be founded on hearsay that I have been unable to confirm.

...When most people first see Baba produce an object, they believe that he does it by sleight of hand; they think he must take the object out of his sleeves, his bushy hair, or some other place, without their being aware of it. Magicians do their tricks in this way, usually skillfully enough to baffle their audiences.

Does he take the objects out of his hair? I have taken a few hours of films and videotapes of Sai Baba during darshan, when he often produces vibuti. In these films he rarely touched or reached his hair. On other occasions, during darshan as well as in interviews, I also noted that he seldom reached for his hair.

Sai Baba's clothing is unusual and not generally worn in India: a one piece robe that fans to his ankles has a slit up to the middle of th. calf on both sides, and has sleeves that reach his wrists. Two loose golden buttons close the top at the neck, but no other buttons or openings can be seen. He has several such robes, all of the same design. They are made of thin synthetic material and apparently, have no pockets or folds. Underneath, I have been told by his former attendants, he wears only briefs or a dhoti. The climate is hot in India, people wear thin simple clothes, and so does Sai Baba.

A tailor in Whitefield makes Sai Baba' probes, usually several at a time, since Baba frequently gives them away to devotees after he has worn them for some time. I have visited the tailor and seen the robes he was sewing. I have also seen some that Baba has given to devotees. None of them had pockets or folds or potential hiding places. One may ask whether these pieces are just for show and differ from the ones that he actually wears, but we have no evidence to support such a conjecture. In his younger days his devotees would often bring him new robes or clothes which he would put on. Apparently he produced objects just as easily wearing those robes as when he was wearing his own.

I never had the opportunity to examine clothing that Sai Baba actually had on, but some people I have met have done so.... They found that it contained no pockets or hiding places.

Baba's robes are thin, like the material in men's shirts, and sunlight shines through them easily. Neither when the sun does not shine through the window in Baba's interview room nor out in the open have I, even at close range, been able to see any shadows that might indicate the presence of a hidden object. When Baba is outside and the wind blows, the robe may cling to his body; but on such occasions neither I nor anyone I have spoken to has seen any protrusion indicating a hidden object.

For sceptical observers Baba sometimes pushes his sleeves high up his arms when producing objects. Also, I have sat quite close to him and been able to see up into his rather wide button-less sleeves, and I have never observed anything suspicious.

In brief, I have found no evidence that his clothing contains pockets or any magicians' paraphernalia that could be used as hiding places for objects and that would probably be necessary to exercise sleight of hand.

I have made eight trips to India during which I have interviewed in depth dozens of people, spoken more casually to many more people, and listened to and checked up on numerous rumours; but I have never found any solid evidence to support the sleight-of-hand hypothesis.

Since Baba's colleges were founded in Whitefield and Puttaparthri, Baba is mostly attended by students. A few of them have left him, usually after losing faith in his claim to be an avatar. When that happens they also tend to lose faith in the genuineness of the phenomena; for the two seem for many to be two sides of the same coin. Some of these apostate students (such as Satish Kumar, whom I met in Hyderabad in the summer of 1983) believe that Baba makes pellets of solid vibhuti in his bathroom by wetting it slightly and then letting it dry; these pellets he then supposedly keeps between his fingers: when he gives darshan outside, they conjecture, he has three, four or five of those pellets and crushes them between his fingers as the need arises. It should be added that none of these students claim to have witnessed Baba make any of the presumed pellets. This may explain some of the vibhuti phenomenon. For those instances when Baba produces large amounts, such as when he produced on demand many handfuls during his visit to the Roerichs, the students have no plausible explanation.

The evidence offered by these students seems slight. To me it seems that they have made conjectures based on a psychological need to explain away the miracles after they lost faith in Baba's godliness. Be that as it may, these observations, weak as they are, should keep up our vigilance as long as Sai Baba has not given any experimental evidence of the para-normality of his physical productions.,..

I am not alone in not being able to find evidence of fraud in Sai Baba. His Indian critics, such as Dr Narasimhaiah and the Miracle Committee have also not come across anything that can be clearly interpreted as evidence of fraud. And they certainly have not lacked the will to seek and find such evidence.

On the other hand, we also have no direct, experimental evidence that the physical phenomena are genuine. Only a carefully conducted investigation with a thorough examination of Sai Baba's body and other necessary controls could produce such evidence. A large amount of indirect evidence might be compelling, but it may never provide the same certainty as a carefully conducted experiment, especially if the experiment were successfully repeated by several qualified experimenters. Sai Baba has unfortunately and regrettably refused so far to allow such an investigation.

It is, however, not only the lack of evidence of fraud that keeps the question open. Some years ago Dr Osis discussed our observations with Dough Henning. Henning said that he could, with advance preparation, duplicate all the phenomena he saw on the film. But when Dr Osis described the incident in which the enamel stone with Sai Baba's picture disappeared from Dr Osis' ring, Henning commented that this was beyond the skills of magicians. He stated further that if Sai Baba produces objects on demand, then he is performing feats that no magician can duplicate.

After all the interviews and inquiries, what evidence do we have that Baba does actually produce objects on demand? It seems not to be uncommon for Baba to produce objects in response to a specific situation, but one can perhaps argue that the situation was in some way foreseen or staged by him. Such might have been the case when he produced a double rudraksha for me, though it did not look that way to Dr Osis or myself When Baba and the interpreter could not explain the meaning of a double rudraksha, he produced one on the spot.

...There are also some instances when Baba produced something and distributed apparently all of it to a group of people; however, when someone arriving later, or accidently left out, asked for a share, Baba then produced more immediately. Dr Osis and I observed one such incident in the interview with the Vice-President of India, and another in the interview with the Roerichs; Baba produced a good deal of hot, oily Indian sweet and gave it to everyone present. Mrs Roerich happened to be in the kitchen at that time. When back, she brought it to Baba's attention and asked for the sweet, which he immediately produced, enough not only for her but also for several people to have a second helping.

Even Krishna, who is highly critical of Baba, reports some such incidents. Once when they were travelling, he asked Baba for an apple. Baba walked up to a nearby tamarind tree and picked from it an apple. Krishna also reported that he was fond of the Indian sweet kova, which was not available in Puttaparthi, and that sometimes he would ask Baba for this sweet. Baba would always produce it for him. The Raja of Venkatagiri reports being present when Baba told some devotees to ask for any kind of fruit they wanted. They got what they asked for, not from Baba's hand, but from a nearby tamarind tree, Mrs Radhakrishna and her daughter Vijaya Hemchand report even more startling incidents, such as when Baba put leaves into their hands and asked them to think of something they wanted (such as chocolate, fruit, or small statues). When they opened their fists, they found that they had wished for on their palms.

It seems therefore that Baba has indeed produced objects on demand. It adds some strength to the evidence that there are two or more witnesses to some of these incidents. One may argue that some of these claims are exaggerations, are based on faulty memory or even are lies. The frequency of such claims reduces the value of such interpretations, though they in principle can never be absolutely ruled out.

There are other aspects of Baba's productions that may be difficult or impossible for a magician to produce, especially in India where sophisticated gadgetry would be impossible to obtain in a remote Indian village. Frequently he is said to have produced hot foods, sometimes steaming hot, even after he has been out of his quarters for an hour or longer.... For example, Amarendra Kumar stated that some of the foods that Baba produced were "as if fresh from the oven, and sometimes too damned hot-too hot, in fact—as if you had just taken them out of the frying pan." Many more people have reported to me witnessing such phenomena. Most of these incidents occurred on the banks of the Chitravati River, where Baba was said to have taken some hot food out of the sand. If a trick was involved; a heater must have been placed with the foods in the sand before Sai Baba and his group arrived. That would have been difficult in the 1940s and 1950s, and have involved considerable preparation. Frequently it has been reported to me that he has produced hot food when he was travelling and the party stopped on the wayside for refreshment.

Baba also produces liquids, such as oils and medicine, in his hands and gives it to someone or rubs it on the person. A moment later, however, his hands seem dry, even though he has not touched anything to dry his hands or fingers. On one occasion, I personally observed an incident of this kind at close range.

Finally, Sai Baba is reported to produce objects never or rarely seen or unknown in nature. First-hand observations of three such cases have been reported to me; but none of the objects concerned have been preserved, a loss that greatly reduces the value of these reports. One example is typical of the three:

Leelamma, a botanist in Guindy outside Madras, who has known Baba since the 1940s, related to me in an interview in November 1977 that Sai Baba once told her to pick an apple from a tamarind tree in Puttaparthi. She found the apple on the tree and with Baba's permission cut off the part of the branch on which both the apple and tamarind leaves were attached. She preserved this specimen for some time in formaldehyde in the college at which she teaches. Eventually the apple was somehow detached from the branch. Later people would not believe that the two pieces had been joined and she finally threw the specimen away.

What then is our conclusion about the physical phenomena? For lack of experimental evidence it can only be somewhat tentative, though the testimony is extensive and consistent over four decades. Whether some of the physical productions, in some periods of Baba's life, may have been produced by sleight of hand, we cannot, of course, ascertain. What we can, however, squarely state is that in spite of a long-lasting and painstaking effort, we found no direct evidence of fraud."

Journalist Ch Susheel Rao interviewed Prof Haraldsson in 1993. The following interview was published in The Sunday Chronicle (July 18, 1993).

'I'm Disappointed with Baba'

Astonishing paranormal phenomena have always aroused the curiosity of psychical researchers. To dispassionately unravel these mysteries calls for a conscientious approach. Erlendur Haraldsson, professor of psychology at the University of Iceland, author of 'Miracles Are My Visiting Cards,' had all the patience that was necessary for 10 years to understand the Sai mystic. "I am quite disappointed. If only Sai Baba had accepted for laboratory investigation, it would have been a great contribution to science revealing the secret behind paranormal incidents, if indeed they occur," he says. Haraldsson has also authored 'Of This World or Another' in Icelandic. It was about the parapsychic experiences of the Icelanders. Another book of his is 'Insurgence in Khurdistan' published in German and Icelandic languages. He co-authored 'At the Hour of Death' with Dr Osis.

Along with Dr Richard Wiseman, psychologist, University of Hertfordshire, United Kingdom, Haraldsson is now in the country on a trip sponsored by the British Society for Psychical Research to conduct controlled experiments with a few swamis.

In an exclusive interview with Sunday Chronicle during his visit to the city in 1993 Haraldsson reveals what efforts went into the writing of his latest book 'Miracles Are My Visiting Cards.' Excerpts:

How many time did you personally meet Sai Baba and witness his reported miracles before writing the book?

At least 10-15 times in sessions ranging between 15 and 30 minutes. This was over a period of 10 years when a colleague, Dr Osis and I met him in 1973 at Puttaparthi.

Were you convinced of his miracles?

He surprised us by materialising a double rudraksha, which I later got confirmed was made of 22-carat gold, out of nowhere and gave it to me (Haraldsson now wears it around his neck). He also gave my friend Dr Osis a gold ring. Once he even made the embedded stone in the ring vanish right in front of our eyes. These things, it is said even magicians can do if they prepare themselves.... But the vanishing of the stone in the ring was something a

205

well-known magician in the United States, Doug Hanning, could not explain. There were many other incidents too but we were not totally convinced as the Baba was refusing to cooperate in a laboratory investigation.

Why do you think he did not allow a scientific and controlled investigation?

We were scientists and not devotees of Sai Baba. Several times I tried to convince him that he would be doing a great favour to science if he agreed for investigations but he was firm about not heeding our request. When I saw that he would never cooperate, I went ahead with the publication of the book as it was not worth waiting. But if I were Sai Baba, I would have accepted the proposal of a controlled investigation. Sai Baba considers him self to be a spiritual person and says miracles are irrelevant.

Do you believe that parapsyhic events are possible?

It cannot be said for sure that they are scientifically impossible. In fact there are a few experiments which suggest that these things can occur, but a clear picture has not emerged so far. I have investigated psychic phenomena for a long time and science accepts only things for which there is evidence.

Having talked to his devotees, ex-devotees and even spending long sessions with him personally, what overall impression do you gather about the Baba?

I am not the religious type to be interested in Sai Baba. He interested me only because of the paranormal incidents that are related to him. I have much respect for him but I was not attracted to him. I had a liking for him because he was a delightful person. He is charming and gentle but what use is it to me? I was adopting a scientific approach to find out the cause of the para- psychic events

What impact do you think your book on Sai Baba would have on the Indian people?

When I met Sai Baba last, to my surprise, he told me he had read the book. This was published only in the United States, United Kingdom, Germany, Italy, Japan and Spain. He seemed to be happy but had some complaints about some parts of the book where I had quoted some exdevotees. He felt they were not fair to him in their criticism. I don't really know what impact the book would have once it is out in India by October.

You must have received some feedback from the countries where the book was published before....

Some devotees liked it and some did not. I tried to be objective all the time.

Are you frustrated because you could not unravel the "truth" behind the miracles?

I am disappointed because the Baba did not cooperate the way I wanted him to. I'm just waiting to see the video tape based on which Deccan Chronicle, I learnt, had published a story exposing the Baba.

This could be clinching evidence. (Haraldsson said he was "convinced" after seeing the tape later).12

Dr Karlis Osis (1980)

Dr. Karlis Osis, an internationally Known parapsycholistst, in his brief article 'Parapsychology and Sathya Sai Baba' (1980)" reported that he and Dr Haraldsson contacted a large number of Sai devotees and discovered that they had experience Baba's miracles, seen him in dreams, and they knew that Baba cured people. They were convinced of Baba's omniscience.

Thus we find that these contributors have contributed more in the field of psychiatry or psychotherapy rather than in psychology while studying Sri Sathya Sai Baba.

References

7. Dhairyam, D., 'The Divine Psychotherapist' in Sai Baba and His Message, (eds) S.P. Ruhela & D. Robinon. New Delhi: Vikas Publishing House, 1976, pp. 67-75.

8. Dhairyman, D., 'Baba-The Divine Healer', Sanathana Sarathi, 1994.

9. Sandweiss, Samuel, *Sai Baba - Holy Man... and the Psychiatrist.* San Diago, California: Brithday Publishing Co., 1975.

10. Sud, K.N., Review of Sandweiss' above book in *The Hindustan Times,* Jan. 2, 1977.

11. Gokak, V.K., 'Foreward', Samuel, Op Cit.

12. Sandweiss, Samuel H., 'Sai Baba's Challenge to Modem Psychiatry', in Ruhela & Robinson, Op Cit., pp. 76-87.
    7 Sandweiss, Samuel, *Spirit and The Mind.* Prasanthi Nilayam: Sri Sathya Sai Books & Publications Trust, 1985.

12. Goel, B.S., *Third Eye and Kundalini*: An Experiential Account of Journey From Dust to Divinity. Kurushetra: Third Eye Foundation of India, 1985.

13. Haraldsson, Erlendur, *Miracles are My Visiting Cards*: An Investigative Report on the Psychic Phenomena Associated With Sathya Sai Baba. London: Century Hutichinson Ltd., 1987.

14. Haraldsson, Erlendur, 'Sathya Sai Baba and the Skeptics' in *Sathya Sai-The Eternal Charioteer*, Hyderabad: Sri Prasanthi Society, 1990, pp 62-63.

15. Sunday Chroncle (Hyderabad), July 18, 1993.

16. Rao, Ch Susheel, Interview with Erlendur Haraldsson-'I'm disappointed with Baba', Ibid.

17. Osis, Karlis, 'Parapsychology and Sathya Sai Baba' in *Golden Age*. Prasathi Nilayam: Sri Sathya Sai Books & Publications, 1980, pp. 257-258.

Chapter - 11

CONTRIBUTIONS OF EDUCATIONISTS

One of the major contributions of Sri Sathya Sai Baba to the world is his unique system of education known as 'Sai System of education.' In realization of the fact that education throughout the world in general, and in India in particular, is full of several basic defects and all sorts of anachronism, Sri Sathya Sai Baba has presented before the world during the last three decades a unique model of 'Integrated Education.' In his innumerable public discourses and his benediction addresses delivered at the annual convocations of the 'Sri Sathya Sai Institute of Higher Learning' and in the annual summer courses on 'Indian Culture and Spirituality' for university students and teachers, Baba has been repeatedly and vigorously emphasizing that human values, morality and spirituality must be made the essential base of the education of children and youth.

"Education should be effulgence;" "it should be for life, not for living", "... it must confer humility", "it must develop proper values", "it must promote love for the motherland", "it must be character- building in nature"— with such pious ideals Sri Sathya Sai Baba has been endeavouring to spiritualize modern education in India and abroad. He is not against modern education in physical sciences and technology, social sciences and humanities, but he is insistent on amalgamating it with the real education of spirit, morality and concern for the welfare of society.

According to Sri Sathya Sai Baba:

> "It is indeed deplorable that the education of the spirit has been totally neglected, while attention is devoted to the training of skills and for gleaning and garnering information.
> ...My *Sankalpa* (determination) is to provide to the youth with an education, which, while cultivating their intellegence, will also purify their impulses and emotions and equip them with

the physical and mental disciplines needed for drawing upon the springs of calmness and joy that lie in their own hearts. Their higher nature will have to be fostered and encouraged to blossom, by means of study, prayer and Sadhana, contact with the sages, saints and spiritual heroes and heroines of their land and place them on the path of self-confidence, self-sacrifice and self- knowledge"

Baba has initiated a multipronged programme to impart such 2ducation. He has established institutions of formal education-schools, colleges and university. He has established non-formal educational institution of 'Bal Vikas' classes to be run by purely voluntary dedicated Sai devotees to enrich children in their localities in spiritual and cultural contents. He has also established the non-formal institution of 'Study Circle' for Sai devotees to be organized by the respective Sai Samities (units) of his organization throughout the world, whereby the devotees may be socialized and enlightened in the knowledge of spirituality, religion and morality through mutual discussion in primary groups in the neighbourhoods. Besides these, 'EHV' (Education in Human Values) is a unique global movement launched by Sri Sathya Sai Baba. Various kinds of activities like production of books for children, lesson plans, resource books for teachers, re-orientation courses for Bal Vikas Gurus, teachers and Sai devotees, and lectures, seminars, exhibitions, etc; are organized by Sai Samities throughout the world. Baba thus functions not only as the formal Chancellor of Sri Sathya Sai Institute of Higher Learning at Prasanthi Nilayam, but, as a matter of fact, he is the "Chancellor to the spiritual university of the world", as Prof S. Sampat aptly said in his comments as moderator of the panel discussion on "Sai Education and the New World Order" at Brindavan (Kadugodi, Bangalore) campus of Baba's university on 29 May. 1992.

Baba has launched a very comprehensive and matchless programme of education at the global level in order to correct and spiritually and morally elevate mankind. He is imparting moral and spiritual education not only to millions of grown-up devotees but also to children and adolescents in countless homes, schools and colleges throughout the world... Bhagavan's peerless educational vision and innovative functional programme needs to be brought to the notice of all parents, teachers, educationists, social and political leaders throughout the world so that in each and every country genuine efforts could be made to improve the quality of life and character of the people and to make our planet mother earth a really happy, loving and ideal place to live."2 This is how an eminent educationist Dr. Selvie Das, Former Vice-Chancellor of Mysore University and presently Member, Union Public Service Commission, New Delhi, has assessed Sai Baba's contributions to the cause of education.

The spiritual and educational ideas of Sri Sathya Sai Baba have attracted and inspired a number of educationists, educational administrators, social and physical scientists who are Sai devotees. They have contributed to the better understanding and publicity of the Sai system of education through their articles, papers, books and contributions to seminars and re-orientation courses for teachers and Sai devotees throughout the world.

A brief review of their contributions is presented below: 1. Prof V.K. Gokak (1973, 1979)

The first Vice-Chancellor of Sri Sathya Sai Institute of Higher Learning, Dr V.K. Gokak, was the first onje to collect, understand, compile and then give a concrete, systematic and practical shape to the various invaluable ideas of Sri Sathya Sai Baba on spirituality, morality, society and global re-awakenig through the instrumentality of education. He edited the book 'A Value Orientation to Our System of Education' (1973)1 wherein were compiled Baba's addresses, and papers of different speakers and proceedings of the first Summer Course on Indian Culture and Spirituality, organised by Baba at Brindavan (Bangalore) in 1972.

Gokak published the following papers relating to the theme of Sai System of Education:

(i)   Ideals of Sai Education (1974)[4]
(ii)   Baba's Views on Education' (1974)[5]
(iii)   The Underlying Principles of Bhagavan's Philosophy of Education (1975)[6]
(iv)   Moral, Religious and Spiritual Education (1975)[7]
(v)   The Sathya Sai Theory of Education (1979)[8]
(vi)   Manifestation of Divinity (1983)[9]

All these learned articles of Prof. Gokak are significant, but his last paper is the most comprehensive and important one among them.. In it he has emphasized that Sri Sathya Sai Baba's stress on the five universal values of *Sathya, Dharma, Shanti, Prema* and *Ahimsa* certainly should be, and could be, provided for the integrated system of education to produce 'Integral Man' (as conceived by Aurobindo) or 'Manav who is on his way to becoming Madhav' (as conceived by Sri Sathya Sai Baba—the *Avatar* of the Age).

Gokak presented a comparative analysis of the Sathya Sai experiments in education in India and experiments done at the International Institute of Integral Human Science in Montreal (Canada) under the inspiration of Dr Rossner, Founder-President and Prof (Mrs) Marilyn Zwaig Rossner, Co-Founder of the Institute. Gokak revealed that Sri Sathya Sai Baba's aim was to produce a new man through a judicious blending of spiritual, moral and modern contents of education.[10]

Gokak pointed out his formulations in such concrete terms:

"These five pillars of Baba's philosophy (Sathya, *Dharma, Shanti, Prema* and *Ahimsa)* yield the five ideals of higher education- knowledge, skill, balalnce, insight or Vision and Identity) sense of or Oneness. Knowledge as its own end is one of the aims of liberal education. The capacity to think has to be roused and applied to life-situations...The idea of general or great issues in education, should no doubt, be emphasized. The engineering student should have, some poetry or music and the student of literature some science as living experience and not as a load on memory...The next aspect of education (Dharma) consists in imparting certain skills which will enable one to earn a decent living... Balance is the key to integrated personality. Vision is the fourth factor. A human being is but purblind soul-sight. Non-violence is the counterpart of a feeling of identity with every sentient and non-sentient thing in creation....It is Baba's view that each student should be guided on the path of self-confidence, self-satisfaction, self-sacrifce and self-realization."

2. Prof. R.G Kulkarni (1975)

In his brief article' Sai Enshrined in Villages' (1975).12 Prof R.G. Kulkarni of Sri Sathya Sai College, Brindavan, Kadugodi, mentioned that Baba exhorted his college students to recognize "the signs of the times and share the joy of the Sai march into the villages". He observed that "The villages are quickly blooming at the touch of Baba's lotus feet. Tiny tots who were nuisances at home, in the field, on the streets, and in the schools have become sprightly rays of sunshine, showering smiles on all the faces they fall upon. They come out of Bal Vikas classes to tell their parents, brothers and sisters, wonderful tales of gods and heroes, to croon soft sweet songs and to run on family errands with alacrity and joy..."

3. Prof. N. Kasturi (1975)

In his brief article 'Lok Vikas' (1975)13 Kashri mentioned Baba's love towards children as evidenced by his Bal Vikas movement.

4. Anima Mukerjee and

5. Dr J Hemalata (1976)

Anima Mukerjee and Hemalata, then Principal and Vice-Principal of Sri Sathya Sai College for Women at Anantapur, in their article "The Sai Programme of Higher Education (1976)14 decribed the ideals of Sai education and the academic and moral excellence achieved by their college girls under the guidance and supervision of Baba.

6. Dr S. Bhagavantam (1979)

In his article 'Sri Sathya Sai Colleges: A New Way of Life for the Youth (1979)15, Dr. S. Bhagavantam, a renowned scientist and Baba's then close devotee, revealed that in Sai colleges "...dignity of labour is not only talked of but practised. The report between the teachers and the taught is such that the trend is to approach the ideal of our ancient Gurukul system. Simple living is not preached but practised. Distinctions are played down to such a low key that a visitor is unable to distinguish between the children of affluent and highly placed parents from those of the poorer ones...there is not a skill or branch of learning in which the students of these colleges do not acquire a high proficiency...Colleges are run separately for boys and girls...I have doubt that if educationists with an open mind come to live and watch the subtle forces that are at work in Sathya Sai colleges and hostels, they will find a healthy revolution taking place providing the much needed opportunities for a new way of life for the youth of this country in particular and of the world at large".

7. V. Balu (1980)

In his book 'The Glory of Puttaparthi' (1980),16 journalist V. Balu wrote a beautiful chapter 'Sai Baba on Teachers and Education' on the basis of his observation and interviews with Dr S. Bhagavantam, Prof. V.K. Gokak.

Vice-Chancellor and Principal Narendra of Sri Sathya Sai College of Arts, Science and Commerce, Whitefied (Kadugodi), A.V. Belasham, Telugu Pandit from an elementrary school in the Medak district of Andhra Pradesh. He revealed that in February 1980 Sri Sathya Sai Study Circle was formed to bring together all teachers and educationists interested in serving humanity through education. Balu's conclusions about Baba's system of education is — "In short, Sai Education helps to bring to the surface the perfection and goodness innate in human beings and train them to do their worldly duties with discipline and devotion, in a selfless manner."

8. Prof. Shanta Diwakar (1986)

In her review article 'Fifteen Years of Bal Vikas Programme', Shanta Diwakar mentioned the aims of Bal Vikas Programme and its beginning and fifteen years programme till 1983 which year is celebrated as Bal Vikas Year. She revealed that "It all started with 'My Children' to'Our Children".

It was mostly mothers who started informally Bal Vikas Education through devotional group singing, teaching, strotas and Japa, telling stories from the epics and puranas. The simple beginning gradually became a strong all India movement when Baba addressed the teachers as 'Gurus'...Baba declared that he would himself take up the task of training the Gurus since none was qualified to perform the task with the right perspective... Bal Vikas programme has expanded from simple informal Sunday home classes to regular structured non-formal education classes, which comprise six to seven years of continuous education supplementing school education. Student camps and rallies form an important part of the Bal Vikas programme...Eswaramma Day celebrations form an integral part of Bal Vikas programme.

This is an important article which highlights the history of this movement which Baba has launched for his love for humanity. She has also written a valuable article on 'Bal Vikas Movement'published in 'The Sai Baba Movement' edited by Ruhela in 1986.

9. Jay a Gopinath (1983)

In her article 'Bal Vikas Education as a Base for Acadcmic Excellence in Colleges',19 Jaya Gopinath, a teacher in Sri Sathya Sai

Institute of Higher Learning, Anantapur Campus, pointed out that "The alround training and learning imparted to children at Bal Vikas makes the child confident, skillful and ready to imbibe and absorb what is good and beneficial... Bal Vikas discovers the idea, and in the mind and at college level it can be cut and its many faceted brillance brought out. The discovery is important."

10. K. Mani (1983)

In her article 'Education in Human Values' (1983)20, K. Mani mentioned that value-oriented education as propagated by Baba aimed at character, building and personality development, and there were three approaches— Direct approach, Indirect or Incidental approach, and Integrated approach - to provide it. She noted that till 1983 there were 33 centres of training all over India working under the guidance of Bhagavan Sri Sathya Sai Bal Vikas Education Trust, Prasanthi Nilayam, and the Trust had then 200 centrally trained and 400 locally trained resource personnel to conduct the orientation course in Human Values in different states.

11. Villy Nanji (1983)

Miss Villy Nanji (now Mrs V. Doctor), who had assisted T.R. Kulkarni of the Department of Applied Psychology of the University of Bombay, in the conduct of the research study 'Psychological Evaluation of Sri Sathya Sai Bal Vikas Centres Bombay' in 1975, came out with a number of suggestions to help the *Bal Vikas* grow both in quantity and quality in her article 'Looking Back: Looking Forward' (1983).21 Her suggestions were: long range planning; examination system should be changed - internal assessment through continuous periodic tests, quiz sessions, grading the written work and creative work of the child, his overall participation in the Bal Vikas and his change in habits and personality development could be recorded; thinking about the teaching techniques to motivate the children to learn should be done; students should be given initiative to conduct bhajans, story telling should be creatively done and parents should be regularly involved.

12. Prof. S.P. Ruhela (1974,1983,1986,1992)

In June 1974, Dr S.P. Ruhela delivered two written lectures on the theme 'Education in the Sai Age India.'22 in the Summer Course on 'India Culture and

Spirituality' organized under the guidance of Sri Sathya Sai Baba at Brindavan (Bangalore). As a sociologist of education, he presented the findings of his theoretical research identifying several fundamental differences in the views of Sri Sathya Sai Baba and modern sociology and social psychology about the real nature of man and society, and pointed out that due to the faulty conception, the sociological and socio-psychological foundations of education were wrong and dysfunctional, and Baba's invaluable concepts of the child, teacher, aims of education, curriculum, teaching and learning, examination, and administrative control could indeed help in the reconstruction of education in India.

In 1983, he published his paper 'Education in Human Values: A Synoptic View'23 in which he mentioned the present societal context, using Baba's analysis of the contemporary crisis of values, in which education in human values became essential. He analysed the nature and kinds of values, the various models of value education being imparted in the institutions of Sikhs, Jains, Christians, Arya Samajists, Rama Krishna Mission, Chinmayanand Mission, Sai Mission, etc, and identified the various strategies and methods of value inculcation.

In 1986, he brought out an edited work *'Human Values and Education'*[24] on the occasion of Baba's 60th Birthday. Twenty learned papers by distinguished educationists, philosophers and social scientists highlighting the various dimensions of education in human values—both theoretical and applicational were invited for this pioneering volume on value education. The contributors included eminent educationists like Prof. P.N Mathur, Prof. N.K. Dutt, Prof. P.P. Sharma, Prof Zeba Bashiruddin, Prof. S.N. Saraf, Prof R.N. Safaya, Prof V.R. Taneja, Prof P.N. Rastogi, Prof Kireet Joshi, Prof L.K. Oad, Dr R. Agnihotri, Prof P.S. Verma, Dr B.N. Sharma, Dr Majid Ali, and Ruhela. This interdisciplinary volume, "a rare book of its kind", as the reviewer Gregory Naik assessed it, aptly met the felt need of the educationists, *Bal Vikas Gurus* and enlightened citizens throughout the world.

In May 1992, *Ruhela prepared an analytical research paper 'The* Educational Theory of Sri Sathya Sai Baba'25 especially for the summer course on Indian Culture and Spirituality at Brindavan; however, it could not be presented there as he was not given any time for it. It was then published in the University News (21 Sept. 1992). In this contribution, he highlighted eleven predominant elements of Sai Philosophy and eleven predominant elements of Sai Sociology, and thus brought out the philosophical and sociological foundations of Sai system of education. He analysed that "... Baba's educational philosophy does not belong to Idealism per se or to 'Transcendental Idealism' alone; it is infact a broad integral or integrated philosophy of education which is a judicious and functional blending of these four powerful philosophies: (1) Idealism, (2) Pragmatism, (3) Reconstructionism, and (4) Futurism or anticipatory socialization of the unknown future. Idealism reigns supreme in Baba's theory of Education, while the other three philosophies also find their due place, of course, to a lesser degree. He evidenced this by recalling Baba's pertinent statements to this effect and by showing evidences from the curricula of studies of Baba's university.

In 1994, he brought an edited book[26] under the same title, compiling nine papers of scholars and Baba's most pertinent discourses and benedictory addresses related to the themes of spirituality, society and education. The contributions of Prof. V.K. Gokak,[27] Prof. S. Sampat[27]. Prof. Shanta A. Diwaka,[29] Miss Judith Berry[30], T. Meyer[31] and those of the author were presented in this volume with Dr Selvie Das' Preface. This book has now been republished under the title 'Sri System of Education and World Crisis (1995)[32]

13. Dr. S.N. Saraf: (1986,1993)

In his paper 'Education in Human Values',[33] Saraf, the second Vice-Chancellor of Baba's university, briefly mentioned the "two most significant contributions made by Sri Sathya Sai Organization in the field of 'Education in Human Values';

(i)   The Programme 'Education in Human Values' is so designed that it falls within the framework of the Indian Constitution, without violating its secular character..."

(ii) ... The evolution of an integrated system of five basic human values of truth, righteous conduct, peace, love and non-violence which are integrated and linked with five domains, namely, physical, intellectual, emotional, psychic and spiritual which define the human system in toto."

In conclusion, Saraf said:

"In conclusion systematic implementation of the programme 'Education in Human Values', in line with the accepted secular norms of equal respect for all religions, unity of faiths, emotional, social and national integration, Indian-ness based on recognised pedagogical techniques and psychological principles evolved and refined by Sri Sathya Sai Organization over the years, after considerable experimentation, is yielding rich dividents. Many State Governments and Corporations in India and various countries abroad have gone ahead with its implementation seeking, in the initial stages, assistance of expertise of Sri Sathya Sai Education in Human Values Trust, the torch bearers of this movement'"

In 1993, Saraf brought out a volume 'Bhagavan Sri Sathya Sai Baba: The Eternal Educator'[35] in which he compiled Baba's benediction addresses at his University's convocations and the comments of visitors to his university.

14. Prof. S. Sampat (1992,1994)

Prof Sampat, the third Vice-Chancellor of Baba's university, published a brilliant paper on Baba's university, entitled 'Sri Sathya Sai Institute of Higher Learning - An Experiment in Integral Education - Placing Human Values at the Fore-Front. "In The Hindu (1992) which was also published in Ruhela's The *Educational Theory of Sri Sathya Sai Baba*[36] (1994). In this paper, he presented the profile of the aims, objectives, curricular transactions and daily life of Baba's university and concluded in these words:

"Sri Sathya Sai Institute of Higher Learning is endowed with the power of a Lighted Lamp which can light other lamps to illumine the paths to be traversed by teachers and learners alike everywhere. The conversion of this potential to reality could be the prayer of all those who have at heart the well-being of the Nation and, indeed, of humanity as a whole."

In a chapter on 'Integrated Education', in his book (1994) Sampat mentioned the need of Baba's spiritual ideals in technical education.

15. Prof. K. Hanumanthappa (1993)

Prof Hanumanthappa, the fourth Vice-Chancellor of Baba's university, published an article on "Challenges and Responses of Higher Education in India': Relevance of Sri Sathya Sai system of Education' in the *University News* (8 Nov, 1993). In this paper, he critically analysed the educational scenario of the country, challenges of the future, and quoting form Baba and observations of the visiting committee of UGC, and the then President of India R. Venkataraman, stated that Baba's university and Sri Sathya Sai System of Education stand for excellence, and are, therefore, extremely relevant.

16. V. Vithal Babu (1994)

V. Vithal Babu, Editor,'*Economy & Trade*', New Delhi, and an ardent Sai devotee in his paper 'Value Education for World Peace'-9 published by him, highlighted Baba's mission on EHV (Education in Human Values), and the role Sri Sathya Sai Institute of Higher Learning, Bal Vikas, Planetorium, Eternal Heritage Museum and Super Hospitality at Prasanthi Nilayam are playing. He pointed out that "The Sai Movement on Human Values and his Mission on Education in Human Values have been eulogised both nationally and internationally". Sai Mission on Education in Human Values has aroused "new awakening" on the primacy and relevance of value education in the present crisis- ridden world. UK for instance has officially accepted the Programme, Mauritius being the late having initiated the teaching of human values in its schools. Educators overseas have been adapting the Programme to suit their own cultures. USA, for example, has tailored the programme appropriate to its own American culture and to its own State and Federal Statutes concerned with education. So too U.K., also a good many Latin American countries"

17. Rao, M. N. (1995)

Rao has contributed a valuable chapter on 'Horizons of Global Education 'in his recent book '*God And His Gospel*' (1995).[40]

Seminars and Re-orientation Courses for Teachers and *Bal Vikas Gurus*

A number of inspired Sai devotees have been lecturing in and contributing their articles on a variety of themes of Sai system of education and human values preached by Baba, in seminars, orientation courses for teachers, Bal

Vikas Gurus and Sai devotees and writing their experiences in various Sai journals, newsletters, etc. in India and foreign countries like USA, UK, Australia, Far East, Africa, etc. Some of the prominent contributors as such are Prof Rohidkar. Prof. Shanta Diwakar, Mr. and Mrs. Victor Kanu, Jamsai, Antony Craxi, Dare Ogunkolati, Kishin Khubchandani, Paul Dhall, T. Meyer, Judith Berry, A. Druker, Hislop, V. Srinivas, Indulal Shah, Kirit Patel, Bejoy K. Mishra, Vinod Lai, Goldstein etc.

Some of the most interesting reports of seminars and reorientation courses and publications on EHV programme, which the researcher has come across, are as under:

(i)   Sathya Sai Education in Human Values: Manual for Africa[40] (Dare Ogunkolati and Kishin Khubchandani, Central Coordinators for Region V-Africa) (Year of Publication not mentioned);

(ii)   Divinity and Love: The Essence of Human Values Programmed (Pal Dhall, Sathya Sai Organization of Australia and Papua, New Gunea);

(iii)   L'Alba di una Nuova Era (In Italian)[42] (Craxi, Antonio and Sylvia; Moderna: Liberia Internazionale Sathya Sai, 1982);

(iv)   Proceedings of Sri Sathya Sai African Conference on Education in Human and Community Services held at Accra, Aug. 1986.[43]

Research Studies

Although the Sai system of education has been in operation for the last 25 years or so, there is a virtual lack of research in it. Only 6 research studies out of which are Ph. D. studies, have so far come to our notice:

1. Kulkarni, T.R. (1975)

Dr Kulkarni conducted a 'Psychological Evaluation of Sri Sathya Sai Bal Vikas Centres. Bombay: A scientific investigation of}piritual training centres[44] and published its interim report in 1975. Twenty Bal Vikas children of Bombay were taken up for study and they were studied with the help of IQ Tests, two scales for Parent Evaluation, Upbringing Scale, Youth Adjustment Analyser Inventory, The Allport- Vernon Lindzey Study of Values, and Moral Development Scale. The study showed that "the Bal Vikas Centres have succeeded to a considerable extent in achieving their objectives. "It was found that the children receiving the Bal Vikas training manifest positive signs ofimproved personality, better developedcultural values, a respectfulattitude towards parents, a more enlightened outlook on life—in short a gain which if retained, and developed in the succeeding stages of the programme, should result into full flowering of the hidden cultural and spiritual potentiality of man."

2. Sambhi, Punam (1978)

Miss Punam Sambhi conducted a research study 'A Critical Evaluation of Bal Vikas Programme in Simla' for her Master's Degree in Education in the School of Education, Himachal Pradesh University, Simla when the present author was Professor, Head and Dean of Education there. Based on a randomly selected sample of 50 children who attended Bal Vikas classes regularly and a sample of 50 students forming the Control Group who were regular students of formal institutions, this study revealed significant differences between both these groups.

"The Mean of the Experimental Group was remarkably high in all the areas of C.R.P.B.I., moral judgement and self-concept. The researcher's hypothesis "Moral Judgement, Self-Concept and Behaviour towards the parents of those students who attended the Bal Vikas Programmes, was better than those who did not attend it "was proved." She concluded that the Bal Vikas Programme is really helpful in inculcating the moral values in children. The review of this study was published in 1983.

3. Ramachandran, S. (1988)

Ramachandran conducted his doctoral research on 'A Critical Study of the Development of Human Values Among Secondary School Pupils'[45] (Waltair: Andhra University). In his study he has found that the awareness of human values as stressed by Sai Baba greatly helped the school students.

[46]. Punam Sambi[47] (1989) Madhu Kampani[48] (1990) and R. T. Nanda [49] (1996) have conducted Ph. D. studies in different topics relating to Value Education—the most significant aspect of Sai System of Education. All these studies are yet unpublished. Nanda has studied the various contemporary approaches to value education in India including the Sai Approach theoretically-as well empirically, and has found that the Sai approach to value

education is indeed very enlightened, functional and worthy of universal irhplemenation.

We find a virtual lack of research studies in the field of Sai education. It is hightime that a number of researches are conducted in this field on topics such as the measure of success achieved by the educational institutions launched by Sri Sathya Sai Baba, their administrative ethos, academic functionality, their curricular and co- curricular activities, innovations, and their impact on the students and the society at large.

REFERENCES

1. Sri Sathya Sai Baba quoted in *'Sai Avatar': Souveni*r. Delhi: Sri Satya Sai Seva Organization, Oct. 20, 1990.
2. Dr. Selvi Das' Foreword to: Ruhela, S.P. (Ed.), *The Educational Theory of Sri Sathya Sai Baba*. Faridabad: Sai Age Publications, 1994, p. xi.
3. Gokak, V.K. (Ed.), *A Value Orintation to Our System of Education*. New Delhi: Gulab Singh and Sons, 1973.
4. Gokak, V.K., *Ideals of Sai Education*. Prasanthi Nilayam, 1974.
5. Gokak, V.K. 'Baba's Views of Education' in *Bhagavan Sri Sathya Sai Baba: The Man and the Avatar. New Delhi*: Abhinav Prakashan, 1975, pp. 115-145.
6. Gokak, V.K., 'The Underlying Principles of Bhagavan's Philosophy of Education' in *Garland of Golden Rose*. Prasanthi Nilayam: Sathya Sai Central Trust, 1975, pp. 21-25.
7. Gokak, V.K., 'Moral, Religious and Spiritual Eduation' in *Sai Baba and His Message* (eds) Ruhela, S.P. & Robison, D. New Delhi: Vikas Publishing House, 1976, pp. 195-202.
8. Gokak, V.K., 'The Sathya Sai Theory of Eduation' in *Golden Age*. Prasanthi Nilayam: Sri Sathya Sai Books and Publications Trust, 1980, pp. 181-206.
9. Gokak, V.K., 'Manifestation of Divinity' in *Blossoming Human Excellence*. 1983.
10. Gokak, V.K., 'The Sathya Sai Theory of Education' *Op Cit.*
11. *Ibid.*
12. Kulkarni, R.G., 'Sai Enshrined in villages' in *Garland of Golden Rose, Op Cit*, pp. 77-79.

13. Kasturi, N., 'Lok Vikas' in *Blossoming Human Excellence, Op Cit.*

14. Mukerjee, Anima and Hemalata, J., 'The Sai programme of Higher Education' in Ruhela & Robinson, *Op Cit*, pp. 203-211.

15. Bhagavantam, S., 'Sri Sathya Sai Colleges: A New Way of Life For the Youth', in *Golden Age*, Brindavan; Kadugodi: Kindomof Sathya Sai, 1979.

16. Balu, V., The Glory of Puttaparthi. Delhi: Motilal Banarasi Das, 1980, pp. 115-136.

17. Diwakar, Shanta, 'Fifteen Years of Bal Vikas' in *Blossoming Human Excellence*, Op Cit.

18. Diwakar, Shanta,'Sri Sathya Sai Bal Vikas Movement' in *The Sai Baba Movement*, (ed) Ruhela, S.P. New Delhi: Arnold Heinemann, 1986.

19. Gopinath, Jaya, 'Baba Vikas Education as a Base for Academic Excellence in Colleges' in *Blossoming Human Excellence, Op Cit.*

20. Mani., K. 'Education in Human Values' Ibid.

21. Nanji, Villy, 'Looking Back: Looking Forward', *Ibid.*

22. Ruhela, S.P., 'Education in Human Values: A Synoptic View', *University News*, July 13, 1987.

23. Ruhela, S.P. 'Educational Recostruction in the Sai Age India' in *Sai Baba and His Message*, Op Cit., pp. 171-194.

24. Ruhela, S.P. (Ed.), *Human Values and Education*. New Delhi: Sterling Publishers, 1986.

25. Ruhela, S.P., 'The Educaitonal Theory of Sri Sathya Sai Baba', *University News*, Sept. 21, 1992, pp. 4-10.

26. Ruhela, S.P. (Ed.), The Educational Theory of Sri Sathya Sai Baba. *Op Cit.,* 1994.

27. Gokak, V.K. 'Moral, Religious and Spiritual Education', Op Cit. (7)

28. Sampat, S. 'Sri Sathya Sai Institute of Higher Learning: An Experiment in Integral Education-Placing Human Values at the Forefront' in *The Educational Theory of Sri Sathya Sai Baba, Op Cit.,* pp. 130.

29. Diwakar, Shanta, 'Sri Sathya Sai Bal Vikas Movement' *Op Cit.*

30. Berry, Judith, 'Sathya Sri Integrated Teaching Techniques for Primary Education' in The Educational Theory of Sri Sathya Sai Baba, *Op Cit*, pp.109-119. (Originally published in *The Sai World Gazettee* (UK), June, 1987).

31. Meyer, T" 'Sai Discipline; Ibid, pp. 87-108. (Originally published in the Sai World Gazette (UK), June 1987.

32. Ruhela, S.P. (Ed.), *Sai System of Education and World* Crisis. New Delhi: M.D. Publications, 11, Darya Ganj, 1995. (Revised edition of The Education Theory of Sri Sathya Sai Baba, Op Cit.)

33. Saraf, S.N., 'Education in human Values' in *Human Values and Education,* (ed.) Ruhela, Op Cit., pp 64-74.

34. Ibid.

35. Saraf, S.N., *Blmgavan Sri Sathya Sai Baba: The Eternal Educator.* Bombay: M.D. Rajan Typographic, 1993.

36. Sampat, *Op Cit.*, 130-142.

37. Sampat, 'Integrated Education-The Sai Vision' in *Technology Stepping into the 21 st Century.* New Delhi: Vikas Publishing House, 1994, pp. 241-246.

38. Hanumanthappa, H., 'Challenges and Responses of Higher Education: Relevance of Sri Sathya System of Education, *University News*, Nov. 8, 1993, pp.4-9.

39. Babu, V. Vithal, *Value Education for World Peace.* New Delhi: Author, B-12, Amar Colony, Lajpat Nagar-IV, 1994.(unpublished paper).

40. Rao, M. N., *God and His Gospel.* Prasanthi Nilayam: Sri Sathya Sai Towers Hotels Pvt. Ltd., 1995, pp. 223-256.

41. *Sathya Sai Education in Human aluVes: Manual for Africa.* Central Coordinators for Region V (Africa), Sathya Sai Organization.

42. Dhall, Pal, *Divinity and Love'. The Essence of Human Values Programme.* Drummpyne, NSW, Australia: Sri Sathya Sai Organization of Australia and Papua New Guinea, 1994. (Minographed).

43. Craxi, Antonio Craxi, Sylvia, L *'Alba di una Nuova Era. (*In Italian). Modena: Liberia Internazionals Sathya Sai, 1982.

44. *Proceedings of Sri Sathya Sai African Conference on Education in Human Values and Community Services Held at Accra,* August, 1986. Prasanthi Nilyam: World Council of Sri Sathya Sai Organizations.

45. Kulkarni, T.R. & Nanji, Villy, *Psychological Evaluation of Sri Sathya Bal Vikas Centres*: A Scientific Investigation ofSpritusl Training Centres: An Intrim Report. Bombay: Sri Sathya Sai Institute of Research, 1975.

46. Sambi, Punam, *A Critical Evaluation of Bal Vikas Programme in Simla.* Simla: School of Education. H.P. University, 1978. (Unpublished M. Ed. Dissertation). Brief Research abstract in: *Blossoming Human Excellence,* Op Cit.

47. Sambhi, Punam, *A Study of the Value Patterns and Some Personality Variables of the Students Studying in Three Institutions - Sri Sathya Higher Secondary School, Missionary School and Central School in Andhra Pradesh.* Simla: Himachal Pradesh University, Unpublished Ph. D. Thesis in Education, 1989.

48. Kampani, Madhu, *Education in Human Values: Concept and Practical Implications.* Prasanthi Nilayam: Sri Sathya Sai Institute of Higher Learning, Uupublished Ph. D. Thesis in Education, 1990.

49. Nanda, R. T., *A Study of Contemporary Approaches to Value Education and Their Effectiveness in Promoting Human Values.* New Delhi: Jamia Millia Islamia, Institute of Advanced Studies in Education, Unpublished Ph. D. Thesis, submitted in 1996.

Chapter - 12

CONTRIBUTIONS OF
MANAGEMENT SCIENTISTS

"Because I have confidence in the power of truth and of thespirit, I believe in the future of mankind."

Albert Schweitzer,
'Out of My Life & Thought, Mentor.'

In this modern world of complex organizations and institutions, the importance of management sciences is being realized seriously. Behavioural scientists from the disciplines of Psychology, Sociology, Social Anthropology, Political Sciences, Economics and Commerce Public Administration, etc, are engaged in making contributions to the emergence of an indisciplinary field of studies called 'Management Science'. It is concerned with theories and practices of providing effective management leadership, getting things done as per targets or goals decided earlier, and providing a functional environment for maximum productivity efficiency.

In the capitalist economy, maximization of economic gains being the predominant concern of the controllers of production units, exploitation of the workers by all sorts of strategies and means has become the universal phenomenon. The principles of colonial administration and capitalist management have modelled the functioning of all modern institutions world-wide. Distrust, hoodwinking, exploitation, coercion and disharmony characterize most of the existing managements in civil administration, industry, business, social services, etc.

Sri Sathya Sai Baba has given to the world a set of spiritual and moral principles which, if implemented earnestly, can change the whole ethos of managements and administrations all over the world and create a positive climate for alround production, growth and social harmony.

Some management scientists have been attracted to Sri Sathya Sai Baba's spiritual and moral ideas and they have tried to discover as to which of these ideas can be meaningfully incorporated in their modern management science. Among such scholars, the names of A.N. Haksar, M.L. Chibber, R.K. Sehgal, Jack Hawlay, K. Venkat Rao and Aime Levy deserve mention. The first three have contributed full books on this subject while the others have published articles showing how Baba's teachings can revolutionize the management science.

A. N. Haksar (1989)

Haksar, an eminent management expert and Sai devotee, carefully observed Sri Sathya Sai Baba's style of role-functioning and concluded in his book 'Sai Baba Manager Divine' (1993)[1] that he is 'Manager Divine'. He discovered in Baba's teachings several valuable points which all managers of institutions and social organizations will find extremely helpful. He has analysed how Sri Sathya Sai organization is ideally organised and managed by Baba and how its functionaries are self-motivated to play their roles in this spiritual and social service organization to the best of their capacities. According to Haksar:

(i) "My own understanding of Baba's teachings and lessons is that, in essence and in the first analysis, as we live and work on this earth, the human factor is of the first and greatest importance;"

(ii) Baba's teachings of selflessness, right conduct, love, truth, dedication, devotion, discipline, unity between thought, word and deed, self-confidence, and treating duty as God are essential qualities for successful managers of all kinds of organizations and institutions;

(iii) Baba explains that a manager is the composite of what each letter in the word stands for;

M - Mind of man;
A - Awareness of atma;
N - Nature of nation;
G - Guidelines for goodness;
E - Enquire into ethos;
R - Rule of laws."

(iv)   Baba has taught us that unity, purity and diversity in humanity should be recognized; that man, society, world are the trinity, and that unity and harmonious effort bring progress in living society constituting the world."

(v)   "Managers in every walk of life everywhere, can develop greater self-confidence to enlarge their capabilites through the Sai way. Baba says "At the bottom of the glass of water of worldly life is the sugar of spirituality. Stir it with the spoon of devotion and discipline and enjoy the sweetness of divinity even as you attend to your daily duties..."

Haksar concludes that Baba's Prasanthi Nilayam Ashram is an ideal school for all practising managers - politicians, bureaucrats, government officials, managers of industry, commerce and voluntary organization, etc.

2. Dr. M.L. Chibber (1990,1994)

Lt. Gen. (Retd) Dr M.L. Chibber, an ardent Sai devotee, has studied Sri Sathya Sai Baba's teachings carefully and tried to discover and show how Baba's teachings can be of great help to all leaders and managers of all kinds of institutions. In his article 'Leadership Training for Sathya Sai Students' (1990)[2] and later on in his book 'Sai Baba's Mahavakya on Leadership' (1994)[3], Chibber has held that Baba's teachings provide a holistic theory and a set of invaluable practical strategies which must be adopted by all modern leaders throughout the world.

Chibber has discovered from Baba's ideas that leadership is a byproduct of spirituality, and unless there is spirituality at the base of role playing as leader, no effective leadership can be provided. Baba's *'Mahavakya'* (Great Gospel), which Chibber has expanded in the form of this book, is as under:

"To Be: is the source of leadership;

To do: is the style of leadership by personal example;

To see and To Tell: are the functions, tools and techniques of leadership."

Baba says, "A leader is one who gives up all possessiveness, strives solely for the well being of society and holds himself forth as an ideal human being." According to Chibber's discovery in Baba's teachings, a leader should be selfless, courageous; he should have will power and initiative, knowledge of self and job, capability of dealing with people, vision and love that is more than a mother's love. *'Sathyam Vad, Dharmam Char'* (Speak the truth and follow the righteousness) should be the guiding principle for him.

In his review of Chibber's book, Prof. S Sampat has said 'The book aims at carrying the message of hope, love and compassion to millions of potential leaders in various echelons of activity."

Sri Sathya Sai Baba has written the 'Foreword' as well 'Afterword' to this book. Baba has emphasized that one should have knowledge of self, one's work and social environment, character, dedication to the welfare of all and the reputation of the country, discipline, spirit of sacrifice and unity in thought, word and deed.

3. Prof R.K. Sehgal (1990)

In his paper 'Bhagavan Baba — The Master Communicator' (1990)[4], Prof. Sehgal, a professor in Baba's University Faculty of Business Management, has mentioned that Baba's teachings provide the right kind of perspectives for really effective communication. Baba's emphasis is as under:

i) Real communication is from 'Heart To Heart through the language of Love.

ii) Have freedom of heart and not freedom of mind

iii) Every sound will resound and every image will cause a reflection. Therefore, whatever we communicate to another person is nothing but a reflection of what is in our heart. The most important person with whom you can communicate is you.

iv) Congruency between thought, word and deed is not only a must for effective communication but also a necessary precondition for our behaviour and conduct as a human being.

v) Truth is purity, and purity is divinity.

Sehgal observes "It is very exciting to feel and observe Bhagavan's non-verbal behaviour—body movements, facial expressions, eye behaviour, personal appearance, clothing, para language, touch, taste, smell. At times when he looks at us, love can be seen flowing in an unending stream from his eyes. Other times, He gives us such a hard look that one does not know where to hide."

Sehgal concludes by holding that "Bhagavan is the Master Communicator". All communicators should learn from Bhagavan.

4. Dr. Jack Hawley (1993)

Dr Hawley in his *book 'Reawakening the Spirit in Work: THE POWER OF DHARMIC MANAGEMENT: Living And Working With Integrity'* (1993)[5] has mentioned his discovery that "when you search for the soul of any idea you have to enter into your own soul." The book is about human spirit, respect, and dignity, living gracefully and living a full life of action — things emphasized by Baba and deeply valued by the author.

In his article 'Bhagavan's Concept of *Dharmic* Management'[6] published in *Sanathana Sarathi*, August, 1994, Hawly has mentioned:

(i)   Bhagavan had directed him to write the above-mentioned book on 'Dharmic Management' and so he was motivated to research into Baba's educational philosophy ∧nd apply it to business management;

(ii)   Swami (Baba) tells us that the powerful demons devouring us are - ego, greed, desire, deceit and fear. We must enlist the aid of the power that is mightier than these demons; we have to turn towards spirit, following Bhagavan's teachings always turn Godward.

(iii)   The following prescriptions for character building suggested by Baba impressed the management specialist Dr Hawley:

    (a)   Be in the world, not of the world,

    (b)   Listen to the inner truth,

    (c)   Dharmic Credo: We must cultivate and nurture a silent garden of soul; we must let the God guide our every act,

    (d)   Never, ever go so far that it harms others or yourself,

    (e)   Limit your desires,

    (f)   Continuously pay attention to our own purification;

    (g)   Make integrity the integral element of the leadership of Organizational Character. This can be done as under:

    (h)   The leader has to model personal integrity and then has to demand it;

    (i)   The leader must be crystal clear about his own and the organizational values;

    (j)   The leader of character takes as the primary task of leadership nothing less than conferring Dharma —bestowing goodness on a human system.

5. Dr K. Venkata Rao (1993)

In his article 'Human Values In Management' (1993)7, Rao, a member of the Faculty of Business Management of Baba's University, mentions that Baba has emphasized the need for teaching human values to MBA students through a variety of courses, such as Indian Ethos and Values, Self-development, The Great Indian Leaders, Group Dynamics etc.

Rao mentions that Baba has emphasized the following crucial points in regard to management:

(i)   Indian managers should not blindly initiate the western practices, but should keep in mind the Indian milieu and national ethos.

(ii)   Human values based on the five cardinal principles of truth, right conduct, peace, love and non-violence must be the basis of management practices in India.

(iii)   Swami dispelled the notion that truthfulness in business will result in loss. "Running a business honestly must be regarded as a form of social service and spiritual sadhana." False advertisements must be scrupulously avoided, workers' problems must be promptly attended to and problems solved satisfactorily.

(iv)   The managers should not get-upset or ruffled when they have to face a difficult situation. They should remain calm, and observe peace (shanti). In all situations they should practise shanti by conducting themselves with utmost obedience and humility towards their superiors, with friendly feelings towards their equals, and with a spirit of compassion towards their subordinates.

(v)   Swami has observed that love {prema) is the most powerful weapon that can be used to find solutions to problems.

Rao has observed that in the different organizations of Baba, people work with a higher degree of self-motivation and spirit of dedication that is something unique.

6. Aime Levy (1995)

In his article 'Values Human in Management'8 published in the *Sanathana Sarathi* (April 1995), the British management expert Aime Levy has reported that initiative to introduce Human Values in Management started in 1994 with Swami's blessings, "to explore ways to introduce the five great values of Love, Peace, Right Action, Truth and Non-violence into the British Workplace."

Two working parties were set up to tackle the broad issues from two directions:

The *Top-To-Bottom Group* was to concentrate on the issues as seen from a management perspective.

The *Boltom-To-Top Group* was to concentrate on the issues from the individual worker's perspective.

The *TTB (Top-To-Bottom)* working party was made up of about 12 core members who had a range of management and systems experience. It met once a month and reported to the wider group every three months.

In the initial meetings individual members of the group set out their viewpoints on the issues involved, how and in what order they should be tackled.

As this progressed, two major factors emerged: it was found these the most fruitful work merged when the discussions were allowed to follow a non-preset direction which seemed to flow intuitively. The second which emerged by that the outputs from the meetings seemed less concerned how the group members felt others should implement human values in management and more with the real benefits which the members, as individuals were gaining; "we were growing in understanding and were more able to implement what we had learned in our workplace. In other words, we found that the direction of the working party had moved from its original remit to set out how managers should introduce our suggested way of operating to a situation where we were being led to improving our own approach to how we worked and to introducing HVM in our own work places and practices. We felt, as a group, that the more we were willing to give up control of our outcomes and to leave it to Swami to operate through us the more productive our work became."

The author recalls, "Swami has always told us that if we wish to effect change then we must start with changing ourselves." "We are not living, we are being lived."

These writings by management researchers reveal to us that Baba's spiritual ideas are being appreciated and implemented in teaching and management.

Satya Pal Ruhela

Refrences

1. Haksar, Ajit, *Sai Baba Manager Divine*. New Dewli: Author, 1989 (Year of Publications not mentioned).
2. Chibber, M.L., 'Leadership Training for Sathya Sai Students', in *Sai Vandana* (ed) Saraf, S.N. Prasanthi Nilayam: Sri Sathya Sai Institute of Higher Learning, 1990, pp. 10-13.
3. Chibber, M.L.,*Sai Baba Mahavakya on Leadership*. New Delhi: M & M Publishers, 1994.
4. Sehgal, 'Bhagavan Baba-The Master ommunicators' in Sai Vandana, Op Cit, pp. 189-191.
5. Hawley, Jack, *MANAGEMENT: Living And Working With Intergrity Reawakeing the Spirit in Work: THE POWER OF DHARMIC*. San Francisco: Berret Koehler, 1993. (Published in India: New Delhi: Tata Me Graw-Hill).
   'Preface' published in *FACETS* (London), Winter 1993, p. 10.
6. Hawley, Jack, 'Bhagavan's Concept of Dharmic Management,' *Santhana Sarathi*. April 1994, pp. 109-112.
6. Levy, Aime, 'Human Values in Manageemnt', *Sanathana Sarathi*, April 1995, pp. 110-112.

234

Chapter -13

CONTRIBUTIONS OF PHYSICAL SCIENTISTS

"Science and spirituality are like the two legs that enable man to progress towards his goal."

- Sri Sathya Sai Baba

"Science", said Thomas H. Huxley, "is simply common sense at its best, that is, rigidly accurate in observation, and merciless to fallacy in logic."[1] The basic principles of science are cause-effect relationship, empiricism, objectivity, rigorousness and logic. It is generally seen that almost all scientists disbelieve in religion, spirituality, mysticism, God and all ideas and practices related to them. They think that there is no God but only nature, and that they can understand the secrets of nature by their scientific theories, concepts, methods and tools."

However, there have been and are still some scientists like Newton, Einstein, Bhagvantam etc, who believe in God, spirituality and religious and mystic phenomena and concepts.

Sri Sathya Sai Baba, the contemporary divine Incarnation, has in a number of his discourses and conversations with scientists and other enlightened people often commented adversely on the anti-God attitudes and ignorance of the physical scientists and the harms that modern science is doing to the mankind through its destructive, poisonous and inhuman inventions.

Some of the significant statements of Baba on science are as under:

(1) "Science seeks to know all about creation, but the Veda reveals the knowledge about the Creator. All the natural sciences are concerned with knowledge about created things. But there is a Creator who is the same in all of them. In the quest of understanding objects in Creation, man is forgetting the Creator."[2]

(2) "Scientists are tending to realise the basic unity of the energy that fill the universe. Vedantha describes that Unity is Brahama (the Supreme all-pervading Absolute Consciousness). The terms used are different, but in substance they are saying that the same thing; namely, that the One subsumes the Many".[3](*Sanathana Sarathi*, March, 1995)

(3) Many describe science today as a powerful acquisition, but science holds before man a great opportunity, that is all. It cannot be as great a power as it is imagined to be. If it is devoid of character it brings disaster."[4]

(*Sathya Sai Speaks*, Vol. XI, Ch.22)

Most scientists have been and are sceptical or critical of Baba; they do not believe in his supernatural miracles. Some of them have been demanding that Baba should submit himself before them and let them test his miracles in their laboratories. In 1976, Dr Narasimhaiah, Vice-Chancellor of Bangalore University, had made such a demand and this had created a lot of controversy in the country.[5]

However, some scientists have faith in Baba's divinity and in their writings they have mentioned how Baba has influenced them. Let us briefly review their contributions as such.

1. Dr.S. Bhagavantam (1970s)

Dr Bhagavantam was Director of Indian Institute of Management, Bangalore, and Scientific Adviser to the Ministry of Defence, Government of India, before coming to live with and serve Baba in the first half of the 1970's. He witnessed a number of miracles of Sri Sathya Sai Baba in his house and in Baba's Ashram. Baba cured his son through a miraculous operation, give him miraculously created Gita from the riverbed sand of Chitravati river flowing near Baba's village, and did many other miracles in his presence, which convinced him of Baba's divine powers as Avatar.

In his articles he gave his experiences with Baba which are of interest to all scientists as well as public in general.

(i)   In his article 'The Inexplicable Sai Baba' (1975),[6] Bhagavantam mentioned about Baba:

"He does many things which seem humanly impossible. In short, when in a direct confrontation with him, one quickly finds that one has no words to describe what one is going through. Being in his presence is something which can only be experienced by each for himself.... While advising on diverse matters, he gives the unmistakable impression of being the embodiment of wisdom. To say that these and many other facets of his daily routine are inexplicable by any human standards, is to put the matter in a very mild manner. He is a phenomenon. He transcends laws of science as we now understand them and he is untouched by human passions and human desires. He is divine,"

(ii) In his article "Lord of Miracles' (1975),[7] Bhagavantam gave his personal experience of Baba: This whole article has already been published in this book as Chapter 6(i)

The reader may see that one. In his paper 'Sri Sathya Sai Baba - An Incarnation of Divinity in the Contemporary Era"[9] in *Golden Age* (1980), Bhagavanam wrote:

B. "Many people ask the question, "Can you explain the divinity you claim to experience in Sri Sathya Sai Baba in scientific terms?" Can any one explain the joy caused by a beautiful painting in terms of the chemicals which constitute the paints used by the artist? It would make no sense. A thing of beauty is a joy for ever. *Sat, Chit* and *Anand* perceived in a human form are the Divine aspects of the Eternal in Him.... The name and form of Baba are the Tatashta Lakshanas of the manifested Avatar, an incarnation of Sathya Sai of the contemporary times. For this reason, the age in which we are living may truly and justifiable be called the *"Golden Age."* A number of scientists like M.V.N Murthy[10],[11] S.V. Pappu[12]. Kiran Paul[13], Sudarshan[14], Rupak Changkakoti[15], Dr. A.V. Laksminarasimha[16]. D.V.K. Nagendra Rao[17] S.G. Subba Rao[18], Pitala Krishna[19], Dr. S.K. Bose[20], M. Nageswara Rao[21]. Sampat[22] etc, have been impressed with Baba's miraculous creations and his divine personality as *Avatar.* In their writings they have described their experiences as such.

The Infinite Golden Aura of Sri Sathya Sai Baba

Dr. R.N. Shukla, Director (Retd.) National Chemical Laboratory, Pune, is the Chairman of a number of organizations in areas connected with Human Energy Research, Aura research, Astro Physics and Complementary Medicine Research.

Once, a few decades ago, several internationally acclaimed Indian Scientists, associated with ISRO (Indian Space Research Organization), wished to meet Baba after a conference at Bangalore. I had the good fortune to accompany them to Puttaparthi. Next day in the morning, a special meeting was arranged for the five of us, scientists, in Baba's sitting room. Baba spoke to us elaborating on ancient space-science and research in the culture of India, Bharatiya Samskruti. He mentioned about the contributions made by Maharshi Vishwamitra, Rishi Bharadwaja and others. He also spoke about the guru Gurukul traditions of ancient India, citing the famous *Rishi-Gurukula* of Sandipani, *Mahamuni* Agastya and others, along with the specialty discipline of each. As we were leaving, Baba blessed the scientists by gifting each of the astrally procured and materialized diamond pearl rings and emerald pendants and so on. Everybody got overvehlmed by Baba's gifts and the depth of his discoursed on ancient scientific developments.

Dr. V. G. Bhide, one of the scientists, was blessed with an emerald ring. All of a sudden he approached Baba, with his emerald ring in his palm and prayed thus, "Baba you have blessed me by this ring, created astrally, for which, I am very happy and convinced. But Baba, for my curiosity, can you kindly make this ring disappear now?" Baba just gave a broad smile and said, "Dr. Bhide, I have personally done nothing at all! But as your meeting with me is over now, we must disperse!" We all came out of the hall somewhat unhappily. But suddenly I got a thought and I turned to Dr. Bhide and asked him to open his palm containing the emerald ring. There was no trace of the ring! It had vanished! This was a practical lesson taught to us scientists not to suspect and question those realized beings that have taken human form and descended amongst us purely to shower their grace and love on all mankind.

Baba's Aura

In July 1991, I had a chance to go to Bangalore. My wife was anxious for Baba's blessing. I was also invited to deliver some lectures at the University in Prasanthi Nilayam. We decided to go by the Kurla express from Mumbai, get down at Dharmavaram from where Prasanthi Nilayam is about 80 kms away.

But both of us slept through and missed getting down at Dharmavaram. We woke up only when the train reached Bangalore. We were a bit perturbed at this. However, to our great happiness, our co-passengers in the train tore us that Baba was at Bangalore and we could see him the next day morning at Whitefield. What a blessing!

Next day, we had Baba's Darshan and Pada-sparshan. The *Vibhuti* he gave us had the cheerful fragrance of the night queen flowers (*Ra-trani*). But this was during the day! Both of us were totally awestruck by this experience. I was tried requested to give a talk before devotees, in the College Auditorium, along with two others. Baba told each of using talk on particular topic for 40 minutes. Baba said. "Dr. Shukla, you talk on Cosmic Energy, Dr. Philips on terrestnge Chemistry and Dr. Chu on the Baba biography, a back written by Dr. Chu. General discussions will follow in the end". I insisted on being permitted to study and reached Baba's Aura which he allowed after some initial reluctance. Aura is the human Bio-energy picture of normal electromagnetic current voltage measurement done through social meters. Presently, Aura detection has done PIP Camera (Poly Phase Contrast Photography).

Using an accurate multimeter, I read 5 volts and 8ampere as voltage and electric current readings, as Baba's Aura. This was recorded thrice and the readings were the same Baba then laughed and asked me whether I was satisfied with the readings, and asked me to take the readings again. I took another set of readings. The multimeter hands initially refused to move, but suddenly clicked the record infinity voltage and amperes reading! Baba could increase his own internal energy and convent his human bio-energy into small tiny nano-gold particles that emerged out of his skin as Shining lustrous golden Aura as measured later by our PIP Camera. This recording was done not just by us but also by the Japanese. German and Dutch scientists present in our group. We were allstartled! But Baba told us jokingly that we should merge in Baba, and become B.A.B.A – double graduates of Baba Spiritual University – Being, Awareness, Bliss, *Atma*!

(Courtsy: *DIVINE GRACE: SATHYA SAI BABA*, IndiaToday Impact Presentation, Spcial Volume, 2012)

This scientific testimony reveals how physical scientists have been ben humbled before the divine powers ofSri Sathya Sai Baba.

References

1. Huxley quoted in *The Great Quotations,* New York: Washington Square Press Inc., 1959, p. 855.
2. Sri Sathya Sai Baba quoted in: Kamla Arora, A *Philosophical Study of Sri Sathya Sai Baba in the Context of Religico-Philosophical Milieu.* Delhi: University of Delhi, Department of Philosophy, 1989. (Unpublished Ph.D. Thesis in Philosophy).
3. *Sanathana Sararathi,* March, 1995.
4. *Sri Sathya Sai Speaks,* Prasanthi Nilayam: Sri Sathy Sal Books and Publications Trust, (Vol. XI, Ch. 12).
5. Dr. Narasimaiah's three letters of June 2 and 16 and July 5, 1976 were published in *Sunday* (Weekly, Calcutta) Sept. 5, 1976.
6. Bhagavatam, S., 'The Inexplicable Sai Baba' in *Galand of Golden Rose* PrasanthiNilayam, Sri Sathua Sai Central Trust, 1995, pp. 16-18.
7. Bhagavantams, 'The Lord of Miacles' in *Sai Baba and His Message. (eds)* S.P.Ruhela and D. Robinson. New Delhi: Vikas Publishing House. 1976,
8. Bhagavatam, S, 'Sai Baba: the Inexplicable and Inscrutable' *Blitz Weekly,* Sept. 4, 1976, pp. 12-14.
9. Bhagavatam, 'Baba: An Incarnation of Divinity in the Contemporary Era' *Gulden Age.* Prasanthi Nilayam: Sri Sathya Sai Books and Publications Trust 1980, pp 227 229.
10. Murthy M.V.N., "Science-Pathways to God Realizations" in *Sai Baba and His Message, Op Cit,* pp. 123-127.
11. Murthy, M.V.N., *The Greatest Adventure-From Sai to Sai. P*arasanthi Nilayam: Sri Sathya Sai Books and Publications Trust, 1983.
12. Pappu, 'Sciences-Symphony of Sai Love and Science' in *Golden Age.* Brindavan Kingdom of Sathya Sai, 1989, pp. 174-198.
13. Patel, Kiran B., 'The Bright Tomorrow', *Ibid,* pp. 179-180.
14. Sudarshan, 'My Life with Light' *Ibid,* 184-196.
15. Changk;.koti, Rupak, 'The Divine Sculptor', *Ibid,* pp. 202-203.
16. Lakhaniinarasimhiah, A.V.'Sai- The Immanent Brahaman' *Ibid,* pp. 200-201.
17. Rao, D. V.K. Nagendra, 'The First Cause', *Ibid* pp 208-210.
18. Rao, Subba, 'Mind-boggling Miracles of Sathya Sai Baba', *Sathya Sai, The Avatar of Love.* Hyderabad: Sri Prasanthi Society, 1992, pp. 74-80.

19. Krishna, Pitala, 'Swami's Omnipresence-An Experience in USA', Ibid, pp. 142-144.

20. Bose. S.K., 'My Sai Sivam' in *Sathya Sai-The Eternal Charioteer.* Hyderabad; Sri Prasanthi Society, 1990, pp. 49-51.

21. Rao, M Nageswara 'Yet To Make Many Visits', *Ibid* pp. 164-165

22. Sampat, S., *Technology Stepping Into 21st Century.* New Delhi: Vikas Publishing House, 1994, pp. 241-246. (Chapter on; 'Integrated Education - Sai Vision' Also see Sampat's excellent 'Foreword' to A. Adivi Reddy's book *'Unqueneness of Swami'.* Ruhela, R,N.,'The Infinate Golden Aura of Sai Baba', in *Divine Grace,* India Today Impact Pesentation, 2012, pp.79-79.

Chapter - 14

CONTRIBUTIONS OF MEDICAL SCIENTISTS

"What are the unique attributes of Bhagvan Sri Sathya Sai Baba? His healing is analogous to layers in a pyramidical structure. The foundation layer is the healing of the physical, economic and other environmental ills of the person...The apex layer is the spiritual healing. "

-- Dr. Desiraj Dhairyaml

I

In the ancient prayer to Sri Sathya Sai Baba by sung Maharishi Vishwamitra, discovered in *Vishwamitra Naadi*, it is mentioned that Sri Sathya Sai is 'Dhanvantari-amsa', that is. He is, having the attributes or qualities of Dhanvantari, the ancient divine physician. In the ancient *Suknadi*, it was mentioned that he would cure people of their ailments by his divine powers and will also start hospitals for the welfare of the suffering mankind. These predictions have remarkably come true.

Sathya Sai Baba has during the last six decades been removing all kinds of health problems and diseases of his devotees by his miraculaus creations of Vibhuti, medicines, Sivalingas, etc. He has done some miraculous operations materialising the tools of operation, cotton, linen, medicines etc. He has miraculuously cured cancer and so many diseases of his devotees just by saying 'Cancer cancelled' or the like.

In private interviews granted to devotees he has often been giving valuable advice about health, food and disease prevention. In recent years in some of his discourses he has publicly given his divine guidance in matters of health and medicine.

We have corne across four of his discourses, especially on the themes of health, food and diseases. On 31 May, 1992 he delivered a discourse on 'Food' to the participants of the Summer Course at Brindavan, which the present researcher also was privileged to hear, and the other three are his discourses as under:

i)   'Food, *The heart and The Mind'2.,.Sanathana* Sarathi, Feb. 94, pp. 36-40);

ii) 'Disease and Divinity',*Sanathana Sarathi*, March 94, pp.66- 69).

iii) Health, Diet and Divinity'4, Sanathana Sarathi, July 1995, pp. 169-74)

As a result of the content analysis of these four valuable discourses, we may present the following as Baba's most important ideas and suggestions on diet, health and disease:

1. The subtlest form of food becomes mind; the subtle form of water becomes Prana. That is how the body becomes.

2. Non-vegetarian food should not be eaten at all. In his discourse on 'The Avatar and the Devotees' on his 69 birthday on 23 Nov. 1994, Baba categorically declared as under:
    'Today let it be anyone, whether one deems himself a devotee or not, he should give up meat eating. Why? Meat eating promotes only animal qualities....How sinful is it to feed on animals, which are sustained by the same five elements as human beings! This leads to demonic tendencies, besides commiting sin of inflating cruelty on animals. Hence those who genuinely seek to become devotees of God have to give up non-vegetarian food. Calling themselves Sai devotees or devotees of Rama and Krishna, they fatten on chickens. How can they be deemed Sai devotees? How can God accept such a person as a devotee? Therefore, whether they are devotees in India or abroad, they should give up from this instant meat-eating."

3. Liquor and smoking also must be given up by all people. Instead of wholesome drink, it is wrong to drink intoxicant. It makes a man forget his true nature. Alcoholic drink is utterly obnoxious. It degrades the addict. It makes him forget hmself.
    "Today cigarette smoking is the cause of many diseases hkr asthama, eosonaphilia and heart ailments....It ruins all in health and shortens one's life-span. Therefore, those who aspire to be the true devotees of God have to give up meat, liquor and smoking.

4. One should not take excessive roots. Vegetables that grow on branches of plants like lady finger above ground are better than root vegetables. Diabetic patients should not take sugar and roots. Heart patienls must avoid 'Hurry, Worry and Curry (thick fatty vegetable soups) as these three cause heart aiments.

5. Speaking at the Valedictory function of the National Symposium on Fluorosis on 30 January, 1994, Baba said:
    "Flourosis causes pain in the joints and affects the bones at finback etc. The affected persons suffer from severe pain in joints. Some germs such as bacteria also enter the system and cause a lot of damage to the human body. Viruses also cause diseases. Polluted food also accounts for the spread of these disease carrying germs. Meat, fish, black and red salt, black coffee and tea also cause spread of flourosis and aggravate it further. To the extent passible, you should change your food habits. Chewing betel leaves also causes tooth decay. Certain drugs sold in the market also aggravate this disease. There are some kinds of antidotes that can be consumed with food to prevent flourosis. You should take sour things like lime, orange and tamrind in greater quantity. You can also take more of tomatoes, potatos and vegetables with Vitamin C. You should also take more of carrots to build the bones; besides these, consuming of green leaves which contain a lot of calcium will also help in keeping off flourosis."

6. Speaking at the Second International Symposium on Cardio-vascular Diseases held in the Sathya Sai Institute Auditorium, on 21 Jan, 1994, Baba emphasised the need to observe the principle of moderation in food habits, work and sleep. The food consumed should be proper, pure and wholesome. Excessive fat consumption causes harm to the physical as well as mental health. Vegetarian food should contain liberal doses of Vitamin C and Vitamin E. Man should learn the art of controling his passions and emotions, which cause stress and strain. Worry, Hurry and Curry (fatty foods) are the root cause of cardiac ailments. Smoking also causes heart problems. Through dieting alone; birds and beasts get their health alright. But man lives on tablets, pills and injections, after venturing into forbidden realm, so far as eating

and drinking are concerned. Drink large quantities of water, boiled and cooled, not during meals, but sometime before and after.

7. Contentment is the best tonic; why inflict on yourself the disease of greed and consume tonics to get strength, and to hanker further? Use the body as a boat to cross the ocean of life.

8. The food one eats should be satvic, it must be earned in righteous manner or honestly; food must be taken in moderation; food must be first offered to God as *Naivaidya*; after *Brahmarpan* one should eat; the food offered to the God should be from the core of your heart; food must be pure; stale food should not be taken. Pakodas etc. must be avoided.

9. There is a close relationship between food, head and God. Thus we see that Baba emphasizes pure, satvic food and simple habits.

III
Contributions of Medical Scientists

Although there might be many medical scientists who are devotees of Sri Sathya Sai Baba, we find that only three of them have written till 1995. Let us briefly review their contributions:

1. Dr. Eruch B. Fanibunda (1976)

Dr. Fanibunda was Hon. Consultant Oral Surgeon, Tata Department of Plastic Surgery, J.J. Group of Government Hospitals Bombay. In 1976 he brought out a beautiful book *'Vision of Divine'*5 In this book, he presented the religion, spiritual teachings and miracles of Baba with very thrilling photographs of Baba taken by him. He has not written anything on food, health and medicine in this book. His main contribution lies on his exposition of Baba's divinity.

2. Dr. Naresh Bhatia (1994)

Dr. Naresh Bhatia, a Blood Bank Officer in the Sri Sathya Sai Institute of Higher Medicine at Prasanthi Nilayam, and his wife Poonam, a Dental Surgeon in the same Institute, are great devotees of Baba. Dr. Naresh Bhatia in his book 'The Dreams and Realities Face to Face with God' described the miracles, love and inspiration of Baba received by him and his family, and how the *Vibhuti* created by Baba has saved the life of some of his patients. He has also described how Baba showed him the glimpses of *Vishnulok* (Abode of Vishnu), and the house of future Prema Sai Incarnation. Bhatia has written the book more as a devotee rather than as a medical scientist, and has not mentioned Baba's ideas on medical matters.

3. Dr Charanjit Ghovi (1995)

Dr (Mrs.) Charanjit Ghovi, who holds high qualifications in Allopathy, Homoeopathy and Ayurveda, is a Sai devotee. In her books *Spirituality and Health* (1994)7 and *Bhakthi and Health* (1995) 8 she has revealed how Baba's advice on spirituality, *Bhakti* and Health are invaluable for maintaning proper physical and mental health. In these books, we learn how the chanting of Om, Gayatri and other mantras contribute to the recovery of helth.

4. Gerald T. Satvic (1995)

This Sai devotee from Holland has in his 400 page book *Know Thyself, the Gateway to Physical, Mental and Spritiual Health, Sathya Sai Baba Messages in his Own Words* and in a reccnt book '*Satvic Food and Health*' (1995)9 compiled the advices of Baba on Satvic (Pure) vegetarian food. The latter book published in India is an invaluable book which must be read and l'ollowed by all people-whether they are Sai devotees or not.

In a recent very important publication '*Divine Grace:Sri Sathya Sai Baba*' (2012), the

cotributions of a numbr of medical spcilaists from India and abroad have been published which reveal they have been very much impressed with Sai Baba's excellent medical servicss. A lot of information on the unique medical services jmay be available on line and also from Capter 5 this book which should open an eye opener and a unique inspirartion to coiuntless philanthrophists and religious and spiritual organizations all over the world.

Thus Sri Sathya Sai Baba's mission has been to educate and cure the mankind and he was full of supreme knowledge in all matters, it is desirable that more medical specialist cientists working in Baba's hospitality and outsiders should write their, obsrvations and experiments and enligten andj inspire moié and more people throughout the world.

Chapter - 15

EPILOGUE

"If Swami did not possess such (divine) power, is it conceivable that people would come seeking Swami's grace from distant countries like Argentina and Australia."

- Sri Sathya Sai Baba quoted in
Sanathana Sarathi, March 1992, p. 49)

This humble self-inspired Sai.devotee like the legendary tribal boy Eklavya of the Mahabhart times, being a social scientist and educationist, has on his own -, out of hIs labour of love and devotion. to Sri Sathya Sau Baba In the last four decades -. has, despite his very difficult finanancual and health conditions and lack of due moral and social support from any body all these sevearsl years silently attempted to review almost all the significant contributions of intellectuals and researchers from different disciplines of knowledge on the multifaceted divine life and contributions of the the great incarnaition of liBhagavan Sri Sathya Sai Baba..It has been his ardent wish and firm determjination to leave behind the mosdt vvakluable legacy of hundreds of contrtributors for the futureinhabitants of this planet who may wish to know more and more about the great Sri Sathya Sai Avatar.

This comprehensive reseach review of the writings on Sri Sathya Sai Baba and his unique contributionsto mankind as observed, understood and recxordedd by alomost alll the perceptible fdevoteees. intellectuals and researchers in humanities, social sciences and physical sciencesleads me to arruive at the following conclusions:

1. Sri Sathya Sai Baba's claims to his unique status of a great incarnation of God have been duly accepted and acknowledged by all the intellectuals who have studied him.

249

2. Sri Sathya Sai Baba's unique charismatic personality as an *Avatar* has been very carefully observed and described vividly by the various contributors. It is for the first time in the history of human civilization that so many intellectuals anti researchers have studied the divine charisma of an *Avatar* using all sorts of their research approaches, methods and tools of investigations.

3. Sri Sathya Sai Baba's invaluable contributions to the humanity's welfare and moral and spiritual upliftmen! through his inspiring divine discourses, his overall insistence on *Nama Smaran* (chanting of Lord's name), *Manav Seva* (Service to mankind) and *Sathya, Dharma, Shanti, Prema* and *Ahimsa*, and his concrete examplary programmes of providing first class and free facilities of education, free medical facilities and pure drinking water (in Ihe Anantapur and Rayalseema districts of Andhra Pradesh) and Chennai conclusively prove that he was indeed a Superman, a Godman of unparalled compassion, powers, skills and capabilities the humanity has ever known. He was striving to make the great utopia of the *Golden Age* of humanity a practical reality dawn in our life time.

4. Sri Sathya Sai Baba's thrilling miracle(not only during his li\gfe time but occuring even now throughout the world) which defy all laws of physical sciences and are beyond the comprehension of the common man, have been closely observed and carefully studied by a number of contributors. Their overall conclusion is that Baba's miracles are, infact, genuine; they indicate his Godliness, and their overall purpose is to make people happy and turn them towards God by solving their problems of life. Not only the devotees but all philosophers, sociologists, psychologists, educationist,, physical scientists and medical experts who have come forward to study the phenomenon of Sri Sathya Sai Baba, have unequivocally confirmed the genuineness and unique nature and fantastic variety of his miracles, which show that his claims of his omnipresence, omnipotence and omniscience are cent per cent true genuime and true.

5. How Sri Sathya Sai Baba, being the 'Yugavatar' (Avatar of the Age), was slowly, silently and gradually changing, reforming and elevating the minds, spirit, aspirations and world-view of the 20th century inhabitants of this planet and guiding and leading them to enter the *Golden Age* of Humanity, has been fairly well understood and appreciated by the intellectuals and researchers during the last three decades.

6.   The overall realization that emerges after a perusal of this review of so many researches and authentic writings of all the important contributors is that Sri Sathya Sai Baba was not only *Jagat Guru* or Godman, but, infact, he was the 'Brahmanand *Nayak*' — 'The Cosmic Emperor'.

7.   While the range and quality of the writings by devotees and scholars of different disciplines are really very impressive, yet we find that the number of research studies on Baba and his *avataric* works in the fields of philosophy, psychology, sociology, social work, education, physical science and medical science is rather less. There is an urgent need that researchers in these fields from India and abroad should come forward to study the various facets of Sri Sathya Sai Baba's Avatarhood, using their sophisticated research methodologies and tools, so that the mankind may he able to understand his divinity and contributions lully

There are several research organizations and research foundations in India and abroad which can liberally finance and publish all sorts of research on various aspects of human life. They should realize the need to encourage and support as many researcht studies on the Sai phenomenon as possible. Inter-disciplinary studies also ought to be encouraged vigorously. Research guides in various disciplines in the Indian universities should eneourage their post graduate and doctoral students to undertake indepth reseaich studies relating to Sri Sathya Sai Baba and the divine and sociall phenomena associated with him.

8.   It is pinching that no researcher of Telugu language has so far done research on the literary style and richness of Baba's Telugu through which media he invaiably gave al his discourses. It is equally pinching that the scholars ol languages have sofar not conducted any research study to reveal the creativity and richness of the prose and poetry of Sri Sathya Sai Baba. Reseaich studies in comparative philosophy, religion and also in comparative sociology are needed to bring out the importance ol Sri Sathya Sai Baba and the ideas and practices associated with him in comparison to other great Gurus, Masters, and agents of change, innovators and benefactors of mankind. The intellectuals and researchers all over the world should realize their role commitment as intellectuals and come forward to study this great divine phenomenon with a deep sense of urgency and in all

earnestness. Their contributions can greatly enrich human civilization and help the mankind in its march to progress and development.

This Divine reservoir of all wisdom, knowledge, blessings and has been with us till recently and so there is still the rare and great chance for all inquisitive intellectuals, researchers and seekers of spirituality contribute futher.

GLOSSARY

Agni	Fire.
Ahamkar, Ahamkaram	Vanity, Pride, vanity.
Anand.Anandam	Joy, pleasure, ecstasy.
Amar	immortal
Amrit, Amrita, Amritha	Nectar, Elixir, Honey
Anandswaroopalara	Embodiment of joy
Antahkarna	Conscience
Anatma	Non-Soul
*Antaryam*i	God, Inner dweller in one's Heart
Anratha	Injustice, alsehood.
Anugraha	Grace
Arpana	Offering
Artha	Wealth, Meaning
Ardhnariswar	Half man-half woman God
Asanthi,	Disquiet, lack of peace
Atma	Soul.
Atmabhasha	Language of the Soul.
Atmjyoti	Splendor of Soul.
Atma Ram	Lord of the soul, God.
Athithi	Gueust, a guest who coime s without prior intimation
Avatar	Incarnation of God.
Avedana	Yearning, application
Bal.Balak	Child
Bal Vikas	Informal child education, a favorite program of Sri Sathya Sai Baba
Bhakta, Bhaktha	Devotee, follower.

Bhakti, Bhakthi	Devotion.
Bhakti	*Yoga* Path of devotion
Bhavsagar	Woridly life as turbulent sea
Brahmchari	unmarried, celibate
Buddhi	Intelligence.
Chit, Chith	Consciousness.
Chaitanya	Supreme Consciousness,
Dan, daan	Charity.
Danav	devil, ghost
Danavta	devilishness, ghostly
Darshan	Having the holy sight of a god or *saint* or important person
Daya	Kindness, mercy.
Deen	Poor
Deenpalank	One who helps the poor
Deeksha	Moral religious instruction.
Dev, Deva	God.
Dhairyam	Courage
Dharma	Religion, duty
Dharma-rakshana	Saving or upholding the religion
Dharmasthapana	Establshing righhteonous
Japam	Meditation, recitation of name
Dhyan, Dhyanam	Meditation, concentration
Drasti	Vision
Dukha	Misery, pain
Gotra	lineage
Guna	Quality
Gyan	Knowledge
Gyan	*Yoga Path of knowledge*
Gyanawarroplara	Embordiment of knowledge
Educare	Sai Baba's global Program of alue based education
Icchamaran	One's power to die at will

Iswara	God
Istdevta	One's chosen god
Jagat	World.
Jap	Iincantation, repetition of God's name
Kim kum	*Vermilion*
Poorna	Full, total, complete
Purna	Total, full, complete
Sar	Gist, truth
Samasth	Total, niversal
Sambhashan	Proper speech, dialogue
Sandhya	Evening
Sandhyavandana	Evening prayer/ meditation
Sansthan	Trust
Sarvaantaryami	Omnipresent, omniscient
Sparsh	Touch
Japamala	Garland of beads for prayers
Jivatma	The heart of a living being.
Jnana, Gyan	Knowledge.
Jyoti	Light.
Kaalchakra	Cycle of time, destiny.
Kaalswaroopa	Time as God.
Kalp Vrikha	Wish fulfilling tree
Kama	Pleasure including sexual pleasure,
Karma	Actions,
Karuna	Pity, sympathy, kindness.
Kiran	Ray of light.
Karodh	Anger
Llakhshya	Goal, aim, target
Leeta	*Game, play, sport*
Lokaguru	Universal Teacher.
Madhav	Lord Krishna.
Mahashakti	Great power, Sai Baba
Mahima	Glory, greatness

Manav	Human being
Manavata	Humanity
Manas	Heart, man.
Manophal	Desire of heart.
Manan	Study, introspection, deep thinking.
Marg	Path, way.
Maya	Illusion, nature.
Mithya	False, untrue.
Moha	Attachment.
Moksha	Salvation., klibration
Mukti	Salvation.
Mulaprakriti	Primal nature
Naam, Nama	Name, name of God
Nagar sankirtan	*Singing religious songs in group while walking in a town or village*
Nansmaran	Remembering/ reciting God's name
Nityakarma	Daily action, daily routine
Karma	Action
KarmaYoga	Path *of action*
Karma yogi	Man of action
Nadi	Ancient palm leaf records forcasting the fulture of persons written thousnds of years back
OM	The Divine Sound, name of God; Also called *Pranava*.
Paramatma	The Supreme Soul, God.
Paramhamsa,	The Supreme Soul,
Pralaya	Nemesis, the time when the world will end
Pasu, Pashu	Animal.
Poorva karma	Actions in past life or lives.
Prabhu	God.
Prakriti	Nature
Prashad Divine	Blessed food for distribution to all
Pratyaksha	Present before oneself, direct

Prasanti, Prashanthi	Highest peace.
Prema, Prem	Love.
Premaswaroopa	The embodiment of love.
Purnavatar	Full incarnation God
Purush	God, male
Pursartha	Man's duty in life
Ratna	diamond.jewl, precious stone
Sahja Prema	Genuine love.
Sadhna	Meditation
Sakshtakara	Physical presence
Sambhasah	Speech, conversation
Samskaram	Purification rites, customs
Sanatana	Perennial, ancient
Sankalpa	Determination.
Santosh, Santiosham	Satisfaction, wait, patience
Saraam,	saar Truth.
Sabnyasi	Mendicant, *one who has left the*
worldly	*life*
Shant, Shantam	Quiet, Peace.
Sharnagati	Shelter.
Sankalp	Determination
Shantalaya	Place of peace, an ashram of peace, this name was given in an ancient nadis for Sai Baba's main ashrams which is presently known as Prashanti Nilayam
Shastras	Scriptures
Shakti	Consort of Lord Shiva, Power
Shav	Corpse
Shivam, Sivam,	Goodness, auspicious
Shiv, Shiva	Lord Shiva.
Siddhi	Special power/ divine power
Sidh ksetrs	Field of energy
Shuddh	Pure

Smriti	Memory
Sooksm sharer	Sprit body
Sraddha	Faith, regard respect
Sundaram	Beauty
Swadharma	One's duty
Tap.tapa, tapam	Penance
	Lord of all the three planes, worlds
Tyaga	Sacrifice, austerity.
Upasana	*Worship.*
Updesam	Preaching.
Vedna	Pain, misery
Vajra Sankalp	Firm determination
Vidya	Knowledge
Viswas, Vishwas	Faith, belief.
Viveka	Discrimination.

Annexure

A. (i) **Request To Sri Sathya Sai Central Trust ntrl Trust for Pemission**

BY SPEED POST

23 January,2015

The Secretary,
Sri Sathya Sai Central Trust,
Prasanthi Nilayam -515134 (Andhra Pradesh)

Subject: Request for your kind permission to re-publish my research book on Sri Sathya Sa Baba entitled "**In Search of Sai Divine**"

Respected Sir,
    Om Sai Ram,

1. I am an humble 79 year old (shall be 80 on 2.2,2015) ardent devotee of Sri Sathya Sai Baba since 1974.I have been seeing Bhagavan Sri Sathya Sai Baba's unique spiritual and social revolution and studying His worldwide multifarious humanitarian activities and His worldwide impact since 1974. By His Grace I also have had many experiences in my life which I briefly mention under Para 4. *i*n order to introduce myself to your honour.

2. I request you to kindly send me by e mail your kind permission to re-publish my research-based book "In Search of Sai Divine" (1996), to which I which I have now added my new chapter on "The Contributions of Sri Sathya Sai Baba to Humanity" and I wish to self-publish now and have already paid the swlf publishing charges to the publisher Partridge India Publishing Co..
    My book "IN SERCH OF SAI DIVINE" *A Comprehensive Research Review of Writings and Researches on Sri Sathya Sai Baba Avatar"* This theoretical research study was done by me out of my love and veneration for our Swami and

259

my wish to highlight the various intellectual contributions to understand Him and spread His glory and preserve it for the present and future generations..

This research based book of mine was first published in 1996 by a private publisher - MD Publications, New Delhi-110005.in 1996. It was appreciated by highly educated Sai devotees and intelligentsia and institutions of higher education

. As its Publisher M.D. Publications, has closed down six years back, this important research work of mine has been out of print and unavailable since 2008. Now I have revised and updated it by adding a very brief yet comprehensive chapter (Ch. No.5), highlighting important Swami's spiritual and social revolution/ movement for the uplift of humanity mentioning the reference/sources from where anyone in the world may get information about the unique humanitarian works of our Bhagavan.

3. <u>I am sending by e mail as well by Speed post the manuscript of this newly added br comprehensive Chapter No. 5 for your kind perusal and approval</u>.

If you may kindly like to see the full manuscript of the book. kindly inform me by e mail, I shall send that also to you by e mail or in hard copy form by Speed post as soon as I receive your kind response to this mail. Your honour shall find it in perfect order;there is nothing critical or controversial in the entire manuscript and your honour shall be pleased with it, kindly e mail to me your permission soon which I may forward to the publisher Partridge ndia publishing company(of the Partridge Penguin Random group. of international publishers.

My book being the story of Sri Sathya Sai Baba's life, the publisher has now asked me to obtain the permission of Sri Sathya Sai Baba's *'legal estate* or His *living relatives* and me to forward the same e mail to them soon, otherwise they will not publish this book, for which I have already paid them about Rs.20,000/-, for their ir Self-publishing, package which I had purchased for this book for bout Rs.20,000/- paid in advance in 2013,

I have already purchased some beautiful images of our Bhagavan from the website *saireflecrtions,*org of your Trust and obtained their permission for using these images for this book:*'In Search of Sai Divine'* some months back.

4, I am now 79 years old, unable to walk, speak and helpless to bear any more stress, I as I am ill for the last many years since I suffered a serious attack of paralysis in 2007 but my life was miraculously saved by Sri Sathya Sai Baba,

I have partially recovered in 2012 and am doing spiritual *sadhana* as much I can do at this advanced age, but now iI am unable to walk, talk, travel and bear any more stress. I earnestly wish that this last research- based book on Bhagavan Sri Sathya Sai Baba may be published as early as possible and I may be able to present it to Him.

I have already spent huge amount of time, energy and money (over Rs.40,00/-) in three years in preparing the revised and updated manuscript, paying the self-publishing charges in advance to the publisher, on computerization, correspondence, on buying the images and many publications, and materials etc. So I wish it be published soon, I may not live for long. I wish it to be published definitely while I am alive.

1) As Secretary of Sri Sathya Sai Baba Trust you are requested to give me the permission as it is required by the publisher since the book is about the unique spiritual and social welfare contributions of Sri Sathya Sai Baba; although His Central Trust holds the copy right on the information of such humanitarian projects all such information has been made available by your Trust on line and in *Sanathan Sarathi* freely. I have condensed this information in my newly added chapter No.5: "The Contributions of Sri Sathya Sai Baba to Humanity". I am enclosing this new chapter in the attachment for your kind perusal and approval. Rest of the chapters of my book are the same as were originally there in 1996 edition book.

I fervently request your honour to send me your kind permission to publish this book soon by e mail. If it is not available to me soon, all my earnest efforts to get this book on Swami published will go waste and I shall be deeply frustrated and shocked and regret for not being fortunate enough to contribute to spread the glory of our dear Swami whom I have been worshipping for the last 40 years. Whatever suggestion for modification or addition you may kindly like to give me, I shall gladly incorporate in the manuscript.

About my humble self

- I had the first *darshan* of Sri Sathya Sai Baba in the first week of April 1973 at New Delhi, isited Prasanthi Nilayam on the auspicious occasion of Shiva Ratri in February, 1994, witnessed the great miracle of manifestation of Jyoti Lingam by Swami and was divinely blessed by Him in these words"... *As far as you are concerned you have attained complete salvation and there are no more rebirths for you. Why is that of all the crores of people in the world only you have seen this manifestation of Divinity. It is a piece of good fortune for you*

- conducted a modest social survey of Swami's village Puttaparthi: met Sri Seshama Raju ji and Sri Janki Ramaiyya ji, both sisters of Swami, villagers, Sri N. Kasturi ji and many devotees, and read all available books and thus prepared His Life story in February 1974, It was published in my book' *Sai Baba and His Message: A Challenge to Behavioral Sciences',* released on Swami's 50th Birthday, in 1974 - sent by Elsie Cowen to Swami, was appreciated by Swam in the presence of Sri Kasturi ji who on that very day informed me of Swami's appreciation through his son Dr.M.V.N.Murthy at Prasanthi Nilayam,

- was invited by Bhagavan/.Prof.V.K.Gokak,VC to deliver two lectures on *"Education in the Sai Age India"* in Second Summer Course on 'Indian Culture': In June 1974;those lectures were published in *Sanatnana Sarathi* in 1994.

- was given the first interview by Swami at Whitefield on in June.195, was assured by Swami: *"I will be always with you."* This divine assurance has been found to be fully true since then in 40 years of my life. My life and my Wife's life have been saved many times from accidents and serious illnesses. by Swami.

- was given the first interview by at Whitefield that occasion on 9.6.195, was assured by Swami:" *I will be always with you."* (This divine assurance of Swami has been found to be fully true since then in 40 years of my life. Swami saved my life and my wife's life many times from accidents and severe illnesses during the last 9 years,

- published my first book *'Sai Baba and His Message*: A Challenge to Behavioral Sciences"(: edited by me and Prof.Duane Robinson of USA. articles of Prof Gokak, Prof. N.Kasuri, Prof. S, Bhagvantam and Mrs,Elsie Cowen

263

were published in that book with their permission, Swami appreciated this book very much saying: to Mrs.Robinson *"Good book, yes, very good book"* She *informed me by post.)* had the fortune of getting 4 interviews with Swami- last interviews in 1998.

- prepared a sociological analytical paper on Sri Sathya Sai Baba's spiritual Movement, was, invited to give a seminar on this topic in I.I.T.,Kanpur,

- helped Sri Sathya Sai *Seva Samities* of Kanpur and Jhansi in organizing Seminars on Sai Value Education-- edited the book on *"Human Values and Education*, the papers of Prof.S.Sampat, Director, I.I.T. Kanpur, Prof. S.N.Saraf,VC,,SSSIHL and several dignitaries were included in the book, which was later on blessed by Swami in an interview at Prasanthi Nilayam. in 1980s.

- served as *Sevadal twice* in Prasanthi Nilayam *ashram* with the *Sevadals* of Delhi and Haryana.bywriting many paper and books on Value education, taught value education to teacher trainees in the universities at New Delhi, Himachal Pradesh, Ladunu (Rajasthan). delivered many lectures on Value Education in seminars and refresher courses, guided three doctoral studies on Value Education -all published. In 1990s.

- Eminent devotee Dr.A. Adivi Reddy in his unique book **"Uniqueness of Swami'** published by Sri Sathya Sai Books and Publications Trust) had, written about me as under on page 59 in Paras 3 & 4:

'S.P.Ruhela, a Sociologist and Educationist of international repute, who has made a critical appraisal of the Sai Mission pays glowing tribute to this organization in the following terms:-

"As one who has seen the progress of the Sri Sathya Sai Mission during the last 17years (since1974) and closely watched its activities, functionaries and social philosophy and the dynamics of human relationships involved in the Sai Organization and who has studied most of the writings of Baba and of others on Baba, His messages and His Mission, the author can emphatically conclude that this Mission is the greatest and the best of all Missions throughout the world, in all respects in terms of its social philosophy, its objectivity, its infrastructure, its range of activities, its followers and its impact.'

- My contributions to spread Sri Sathya Sai Baba's glory were mentioned in *"Sai Baba Compendium"* (Samuel Wser.Inc,USA) in1997).by Prof.Briwn Steel of Ausrralia.

- I was awarded *'Maharshi Bhrigu Samman* 'for 'valuable life time contributions in the fields of behavioral Sciences, literature, humanity and social development, extra-ordinary achievements by his innovative and positive thinking and committed services as a thinker, scholar, Researcher, scientist and teacher for national prosperity, by rprashadInstitutef BehaviourAL Sciences, Agra (U.P.) in 2011.

- presented/donated about 1000 books and publications on SriSathya SiBaa, value education, education, sociology, and spirituality to a number of intuitions' like Sri Sathya Sai International Centre, New Delhi, Sri Sathya Sai College for Women, Aanantapur, 7 universities,4, colleges and 2 public libraries.

- Regularly subscribed and read all the issues of *Sanathaana Sarathi*. from1074 to 204

- Authored a number of books on Sri Sathya Sai Baba"-

1985: Swami's 50th Birthday Sai Baba and His Message –A Challenge to Behavioral Sciences

1985: The Sai Baba Movement

1985: Sai Baba on Human Values and Education

1992 *Sri Sathya Sai Baba::Leben Lehre und Werk*: (German Language)

1993; Sri Sathya Sai Baba: His Life and Divine Role

1994 The Sai Trinity994 The Educational Theory of Sri Sathya Sai Baba995:

1998 Sri Sathya Sai As KalkI Avatar6 In Search of Sri Divine

1996 Immortal ⌐Quotations of Bhagavan Sri Sathya Sai Baba

1996 The Emerging Concept of Education in Human Values

1997 Sri Sathya Sa Baba: Understanding His Mystery and Experiencing His Love

1997: World Peace and Sri Sathya Sai Avatar

1998 How to Receive Ssthya Sai Bsba's Grace.

1999 Lord Krishna and His Present Avatar Sri Sathya SaI Baba

With high regards and SAI RAM,

Yours respectfully,
(Satya Pal Ruhela)
23.1.,2014

PS:

Sir, I have tried many times to e mail you but your e mail address <'srisathyasai,org.in >is not accepting any e mail..Kindly let me know the correct or new e mail address of your Central Trust. Thanks,

Om Sai Ram

S.P.Ruhela.

BY SPEED POST

2 Feb.,2015

<u>REMINDER -1:</u>   By e mail & Speed Post on 2.2.2015

To
The Secretary,
Sri Sathya Sai Central Trust
Prasanthi Nilayam -515 134 (Andhra Pradesh)

Respected Sir,

OM SAI RAM.

I have sent *(by Speed Post and e mail through the Editor since your SSS Central Trust e mail address always to my misfortune remains non-working)* my humble urgent request on 23.1,15 to your honour for kindly sending to me by e mail your kind permission to publish my book on our Swami – '<u>IN SEARCH OF SAI DIVINE</u>', but I have t received any reply from you due to which I am feeling very disturbed and pained <u>Kindly realize my urgent genuine request and respond to me soon by airmail,</u>

As a fellow SAI devotee and your Sai brother I am legitimately entitled to treated by you with Love,, Truth and' 'HELP EVER, HURT NEVER'which are the main teachings of our Swami and which all of us are committed to follow in our lives, Your unresponsiveness and apathy are most painful and cruelty to me who is now 80- years old man who loves Swami and His great Mission and Trust just like you. I am unable to understand as to why as to why I am being deprived of your love., sympathy, moral support and help in spreading our Lord's glory and unique contributions. Like your honour I am also l am an humble Sai devotee for 40 years. Swami is watching each one of us. He alone knows each one's sincerity, inner feelings and intentions. I have been spreading HIS DIVINE GLORY since 1974, and I wish to keep on doing so till my last breath.

I feel that your *dharma* as Secretary/ Trustee of SSS Central Trust is to encourage and help ordinary persons like me also fairly and promptly as much as possible, instead of disappointing me by silence or unresponsiveness. I am. not begging any monitory help or relief articles like food, clothes etc., I am only seeking your kind permission to republish my own book and your kind perusal of its contents and formal permission. Which is needed by thee publisher.

Kindly respond favorably by email immediately so that I may complete the Sai mission of my life and I may not have to suffer great financial loss., dejection in my old age and heart btrsk/..

Thanking you, *Om Sai Ram.*

Yours respectfully,
S.P,Ruhela
2. 2.2015.

(B) Respence from Prasanthi Nilayam
Secretary sssct <secretary.sssct@gmail.com>

4 Feb 2015

Dear Prof. Satya Pal Ruhela, Sairam.

We received the letter dated 23rd January 2015, regarding your book titled "In Search of Sai Divine" along with the manuscript.

We appreciate your sincere efforts to spread the glory of our Beloved Bhagavan Sri Sathya Sai Baba at your advanced age.

Kabirdas said that "If I convert this Earth into paper, whole Earth, and ocean into ink, all the woods into pen, and then start writing, the ink will finish, the paper will finish, of all the woods nothing will be left, but even then, much, much and much and much and much will be left to describe about Him." True to above words, many books are being written on Bhagavan Sri Sathya Sai Baba.

Since it is not our practice to authorize all the works on Bhagavan, devotees are at liberty to publish on own, their understanding, experience and appreciation of the Lord.

I will be happy to meet you on your next visit to Puttaparthi and hear about your experiences with and publications on Bhagavan.

All the best.

Regards
G S R C V Prasada Rao

God is our best friend
(Courtesy: Sonya Ki Tomlinson Wirier)

Have the faith that
Swami is with you,
at all times
and all places.

- Sathya Sai Baba -

Printed in the United States
By Bookmasters